Selected
Magazine Articles
of THEODORE DREISER

Also by YOSHINOBU HAKUTANI:

Critical Essays on Richard Wright
Young Dreiser: A Critical Study
American Literary Naturalism: A Reassessment
The World of Japanese Fiction

Selected
Magazine Articles
of
THEODORE
DREISER

Life and Art in the American 1890s

Edited with an Introduction and Notes by
Yoshinobu Hakutani

RUTHERFORD ● MADISON ● TEANECK
FAIRLEIGH DICKINSON UNIVERSITY PRESS
LONDON AND TORONTO: ASSOCIATED UNIVERSITY PRESSES

© 1985 by Associated University Presses, Inc.

Associated University Presses
440 Forsgate Drive
Cranbury, NJ 08512

Associated University Presses
25 Sicilian Avenue
London WC1A 2QH, England

Associated University Presses
2133 Royal Windsor Drive
Unit 1
Mississauga, Ontario
Canada L5J 1K5

Library of Congress Cataloging in Publication Data

Dreiser, Theodore, 1871–1945.
   Selected magazine articles of Theodore Dreiser.

   Includes bibliographical references.
   1. Hakutani, Yoshinobu, 1935–   . II. Title.
PS3507.R55A16   1985   814'.52   82-49316
ISBN 0-8386-3174-6

Printed in the United States of America

To Frank B. Hood

Contents

Preface

The published criticism of Theodore Dreiser's work has dealt almost exclusively with his novels. His nonfictional writings are seldom commented on, partly because his novels are artistically far more important than his other writing, and partly because his nonfictional work is not readily available in modern editions. But scholars have long known that between his resignation from the editorship of *Ev'ry Month* in September 1897 and the publication of his first novel *Sister Carrie* in November 1900 Dreiser wrote more than 120 pieces, mostly articles, that appeared in various magazines. We also know that a few of his articles were reprinted in the early decades of this century. In recent decades only a very few of these articles have been republished, and they have never been collected and published as a unit.

It is time to read this massive body of writing, which casts considerable light not only upon Dreiser the novelist, but more importantly, upon the 1890s, an exciting era in the development of American civilization. As a cultural historian of sorts, and more significantly as a young man who was to become a major American writer of the new century, Dreiser made thoughtful judgments on the status of the arts in America—painting, sculpture, architecture, music, and literature. His interest was diverse, his vision wide, and he could not fail to encompass the entire spectrum in viewing what was happening in the United States at that time. The late nineties, when his free-lance writing was concentrated, was an important turning point in American history. Witness the booming economy—shortly after the worst depression the nation had experienced—the advancement of technology and industry, the dissemination of new ideas in science and philosophy. In response to these changes in the lives of the American people, Dreiser wrote most of his magazine articles on the spectacle of contemporary society. He became sometimes a dispassionate chronicler of technology and agriculture; at other times he dramatized the delights and tribulations of people individually as well as collectively. All in all, the result is a rare, remarkably coherent piece of Americana seen through the eyes of one man. The present collection, therefore, is an attempt to satisfy the needs of both the general reader and the scholarly specialist.

The first three of these free-lance articles—other than those published in the newspapers and *Ev'ry Month* from 1892 to 1897—appeared in the November 1897 issues of the magazines. A great majority of his articles were published during the period from 1898 to 1900, when he often wrote at a rate of an article a week. According to his correspondences with the magazine editors, the articles published in 1901 and 1902 seem to have been written, or at least prepared, during the writing of *Sister Carrie* (1899–1900); they also belong to his free-lance work of the nineties. From all of these articles I have selected fifty-four pieces, about one-half of them, as indicated by asterisks in the complete checklist provided at the end of the book.

The selections in this book are grouped thematically in seven parts and arranged in each section chronologically in order of initial publication. I have included most of Dreiser's essays on literary figures, such as Hawthorne, Howells, Israel Zangwill, and John Burroughs. I have also included most of the nonfiction success stories, based in many cases on Dreiser's interviews with such public figures as Andrew Carnegie, Marshall Field, Thomas Edison, and Theodore Thomas. For the rest of the categories—"Art and Artist," "The World of Music," "The American Landscape," "Science, Technology, and Industry," and "The City"—I have omitted a number of pieces which are either repeated or, in some instances, superseded by other articles dealing with the same topics. Also omitted are miscellaneous writings on various topics which bear little relationship to any of the major themes dealt with in this collection.

The text of this edition is that of the original publication of each item. All items are signed by Dreiser unless indicated otherwise. Place and time of republication are indicated individually in the footnotes for applicable items. Apparently he was not aware that many of his articles first published in *Success* were republished by its editor Orison Swett Marden in three separate collections without reference to Dreiser's authorship: *How They Succeeded: Life Stories of Successful Men Told by Themselves* (Boston: Lothrop, 1901); *Talks with Great Workers* (New York: Thomas Y. Crowell, 1901); and *Little Visits with Great Americans* (New York: The Success Company, 1903). The changes made in the reprinted articles vary from minor stylistic alterations to considerable revisions in content. Republication of Dreiser's articles in these collections was first noted by John F. Huth, Jr. in "Theodore Dreiser, Success Monger," *The Colophon*, new series 3, No. 3 (Summer 1938), 406–

10. In editing the text for the present volume I have emended obvious spelling errors, but retained the prevailing typography regarding spelling, capitalization, hyphenation, and punctuation as it appeared in the original publication.

As for the illustrations selected for this edition, I tried to reproduce many of the photographs and line drawings originally included in the articles. (The original captions accompany the illustrations.) A majority of the illustrations, which are either photographically of poor quality or nonessential for our purposes, are omitted. In some instances, the original illustration is replaced by a similar material found in another source as indicated. Several of the articles reprinted here had no illustrations in the original publication. Mr. Michael R. Cole of the Kent State University Library obtained many of the illustrative material used, and my wife reproduced them. I am grateful for their services.

Acknowledgments

Completing this book would have been impossible without the help I have received from many sources. First, the Kent State University Research Council granted me an academic leave during the spring term, 1972, when I began to collect these articles. I would like to thank the following libraries for their courtesy: the Library of Congress; the Public Libraries of New York, Boston, Chicago, and Cleveland; the academic libraries at Kent State University, Ohio State University, Case Western Reserve University, Oberlin College, and University of Pennsylvania. Dr. Neda Westlake, curator of the Dreiser Collection at the Charles Patterson Van Pelt Library of the University of Pennsylvania, and Dr. William E. Miller, editor of *The Library Chronicle,* have graciously replied to my queries.

I am always indebted to Dreiser scholars, among them Professors Robert H. Elias and Philip L. Gerber in particular. I would also like to name Professor Arthur O. Lewis, Jr., who guided my first study of Dreiser. It is also pleasant to acknowledge my appreciation of the help I have received from my colleagues and students at Kent State University. Dr. Robert D. Bamberg, chairman of the English Department, Dr. David R. Ewbank, Dr. James L. Radomski, and my wife Michiko each read all or part of the manuscript at some stage of its development and made many useful comments and suggestions. I am forever grateful for their care and interest.

The following museums and copyright owners kindly gave me permission to use the original photographs: the Metropolitan Museum of Art (Frederick W. MacMonnies, "Bacchante and Child," and John Quincy Adams Ward, "Henry Ward Beecher"); Art Commission of the City of New York (Frederick W. MacMonnies's statue of Nathan Hale); the Corcoran Gallery of Art (Paul Weyland Bartlett, "The Bear Tamer"); Pennsylvania Academy of Fine Arts (C. C. Curran, "A Breezy Day"); the New-York Historical Society (John Quincy Adams Ward, "Indian Hunter"); Dorothy Norman (Alfred Stieglitz, "Self Portrait, 1910," "The Incoming Boat, Katwyk, 1894," "Two Towers,

13

New York, 1893–94"). Mr. Harold J. Dies, executor of the Dreiser estate, has readily allowed me to use some of the illustrations by C. B. Falls in *The Color of a Great City* (New York: Boni and Liveright, 1923), pp. 14, 88, 132, 144, 278. And the following publishers have given permission to use in modified form my previously published work: *The Library Chronicle* of the University of Pennsylvania for "Theodore Dreiser's Editorial and Free-Lance Writing," 37 (Winter 1971), 70–85; "Dreiser and American Magazines of the 1890's," 43 (Spring 1978), 55–80; and Associated University Presses of Cranbury, NJ, and London, for *Young Dreiser: A Critical Study.*

Introduction

I

In 1897, Dreiser resigned as editor of *Ev'ry Month* and became a free-lance writer. *Ev'ry Month* was primarily an advertiser of highly conventional, sentimental, popular songs. Though there was no disagreement about the editorial policy between its publishers Howley and Haviland, and Dreiser, the editor, he must have felt a wide gulf between much of the editorial material he was urged to print and his hard-won original views of life. According to Dorothy Dudley, one of the few biographers who interviewed Dreiser, "One day it occurred to him that he was wasting his time 'fixing up other fellows' articles.' Why not market his own? He could see that magazine readers were asking for lively stories about real people and things. They would take him nearer to his heart's desire—to write about life as he saw it. Or at least it seemed to him that such articles would in a literal sense be true, while the fiction of the day must be false in every sense."[1]

Most critics who have commented on Dreiser's magazine work in the nineties believed that he was a hack writer.[2] He wrote a great number of pieces, mostly articles, in a short period of time. But this experience was important in Dreiser's development as a writer. The range of his subject matter was diverse: he wrote poems, essays, sketches, and short stories. He recorded interviews with famous writers, painters, musicians, financiers, inventors, and educators; he wrote about the poor and the wretched; he discussed agriculture and mechanics. The dream of success was one of his dominant themes in these essays, but at the same time the problems and fears stemming from America's urban life at the end of the nineteenth century often occupied his mind. Dreiser's optimism can be detected in his oft-repeated affirmations of progress, but hesitancy and doubt are also reflected in many of his writings. Comparing his free-lance work with his newspaper and editorial writings, one cannot help noticing great change in his mode of expression. His syntax became more effective,

15

his diction less repetitive. His prose at the end of this period showed none of the broody style that had been characteristic of his editorials a few years earlier. In short, Dreiser's experience as a magazine writer greatly assisted the future novelist; the scope and depth of his thinking during these years formed an indispensable part of his work as an American realist.

If he had tried to publish these articles a decade earlier, he would have experienced some difficulty. At the beginning of the 1890s the most prestigious magazines were few: *The Century, Harper's, Scribner's,* and *The Atlantic.* Most of the magazines cost thirty-five cents a copy or more, and they catered to the elite. Toward the end of the century, however, all kinds of changes were taking place in American life, which resulted in an increased demand among general readers for new knowledge in art, music, science, technology, and life in general. To respond to this popular cry for reading, a score of new magazines were introduced, including *McClure's, Munsey's, The Ladies' Home Journal,* and *The Saturday Evening Post.* The new magazines were sold at lower prices (in July 1895, *The Cosmopolitan* and *Munsey's* were ten cents a copy) and attracted a wider audience. At the turn of the century the ten-cent magazines accounted for 85 percent of the total magazine circulation in the United States. In the first decade of the twentieth century, twenty such magazines were published and their total circulation was over five and one-half million.[3] Most of Dreiser's free-lance contributions appeared in such popular and low-priced monthlies.

This upsurge of periodical writing was a significant phenomenon of American culture. The rise of realism after the Civil War had been intimately related to the popularity of the elite magazines. Once these magazines were undercut by the lower-cost competition, the editors of the elite magazines began to direct their efforts toward the general reading public. Before the nineties, magazines such as *The Century* and *Harper's* were out of touch with the world of real human interest. In 1895 Hamlin Garland recognized the importance of the New York-based magazines:

New York to-day claims to be, and is, the literary centre of America. Boston artists one by one go to New York. Literary men find their market growing there, and dying out in Boston. They find quicker and warmer appreciation in New York, and the critical atmosphere more hospitable. The present receives a larger share of attention than in Boston. Henceforward New York, and not Boston, is to be the greatest dictator of American literature. New York already assumes to be able to make or break a novelist or playwright. Certainly it is the centre of magazine production; and the magazine is, on the whole, the greatest outlet for distinctive American art.[4]

Garland's point about the magazine having been the vehicle for "distinctive American art" implies that before this time the taste of American readers had been greatly influenced by the widely circulated British magazines. The distinctive American qualities in literature were what the readers looked for and what the writers were eager to supply. Walter Besant, writing in the London *Author*, noted the "great success" of the American periodicals, which he observed were more popular in London than their English rivals.[5] William Archer, a Scottish critic and playwright, also remarked on this literary phenomenon. Praising the American magazines' "extraordinarily vital and stimulating quality," he wrote: "There is nothing quite like them in the literature of the world—no periodicals which combine such width of popular appeal with such seriousness of aim and thoroughness of workmanship."[6]

What made the magazines so vital and thus attractive to their readers? The answer cannot be found in the copious and lively illustrations the magazines included or the fresh cosmopolitan outlook they provided. The elite magazines in the previous decades had also offered variety in subject matter and kept up with major world events. But these older magazines failed to "come down" to the level of the readers and share the excitements and tribulations of their daily living. Comparing such a magazine as *The Century* with the newcomers, George Horace Lorimer, who took over *The Saturday Evening Post* in 1899, realized that the magazine must respond to the public's interest in business and romanticize it. Lorimer argued that the common men in the streets would buy these magazines and that the women would soon follow. A magazine such as *The Century*, Lorimer thought, failed to keep in mind that those who read it worked.[7]

Dreiser appeared on the scene at an opportune time and, as a reporter or an author of fiction, would never fail to keep Lorimer's advice in mind. Although he felt in his later career how helpless and meaningless man's struggle for existence was, Dreiser did not lose his sensitivity to the dream and power that accompanied such struggle. Dreiser's capacity for compassion, so often discussed in connection with his novels, is equally obvious in his early periodical writings. Recalling the material in the magazines and newspapers in the nineties, Dreiser wrote: "The saccharine strength of the sentiment and mush which we could gulp down at that time, and still can and do to this day, is to be beyond belief. And I was one of those who did the gulping; indeed I was one of the worst."[8] Dreiser was deliberately attempting to conform to the journalistic style of the time. Even though he later looked back on his magazine writing with some contempt, that writing clearly reflected the decade's ideas and sentiments—the significance of which Dreiser himself then scarcely noticed. Moreover, his pedestrian prose style was an indication of his lifelong commitment to deal with common problems in the most common way possible.

II

Among Dreiser's magazine articles, by far the largest part—about thirty items—dealt with art and artists. His interest in the visual arts was demonstrated in his own works—*The Financier* (1912), *A Traveler at Forty* (1913), *The "Genius"* (1915), *A Hoosier Holiday* (1916), *Twelve Men* (1918), *The Color of a Great City* (1923), and *A Gallery of Women* (1929). In these works one is struck by Dreiser's intimate and often professional knowledge of the subject. Small wonder that his acquaintance with art was first made while he was a free-lance writer in the late nineties. In the early nineties, however, Dreiser's interest in drama was greater than it was in art. As a struggling newspaper reporter, he was ambitious to become a playwright. In those days, drama criticism occupied a prominent place in the newspaper, and his interest was naturally developed in that direction. Once he had established himself as a magazine editor and contributor, he could not help noticing the readers' attraction to the colorful illustrations that were included in the popular magazines. Also the art of engraving was making a change in the way monthly magazines were presented. The contents of many periodicals, too, reflected a growing sentiment for the aesthetic in general. After the industrial development of the new nation, its citizens looked for their spiritual satisfaction in art. Such men as William Vanderbilt and John Pierpont Morgan were celebrated not only as successful financiers but also as passionate art lovers with huge collections of paintings.

Despite his enthusiasm for the visual arts, Dreiser was by no means an expert in the field. In the beginning, his writings about painting and sculpture betrayed superficiality and showed at best a layman's unabashed wonder at the vague notion of the beautiful. As he cultivated his taste and accumulated experience by visiting studios and making the acquaintance of artists, Dreiser became more confident in his commentary. By late 1897 he was already a member of the Salmagundi, the most prestigious artists' club in New York. Through such affiliations, he was requested by the painter J. Scott Hartley to compile an album of the work of George Inness, Hartley's father-in-law.[9]

In his dealing with artists, Dreiser was always trying to elicit a theory of art to which he was congenial. Initially, he was anxious to resolve the artist's dilemma of reconciling poetry with that newly born child of the times—realism. In "Art Work of Irving R. Wiles," he made a sweeping indictment of realism: "A painter who must needs take a striking situation from every-day life and paint in all details as they would probably be found in real life, is, in a way, photographic and not artistic."[10] Dreiser agreed with Wiles' "art for art's sake" doctrines; realizing that each of the painter's works was based on "a prosaic enough reality" (*Metropolitan*, 7:359), Dreiser concluded that the artist's sense of beauty came not from reality itself but from his imagination. This concept was also expressed in another article published at the same time. After venturing an analogy with the "idealist" school of Watts and Rossetti, Dreiser pondered how both the ideal and the real could coexist in the work of Benjamin Eggleston, a portrait painter from Minnesota well-known around the turn of the century. "Perhaps it would be better to say," Dreiser wrote, "that he has the gift of imparting to subjects realistically treated the poetry of his own nature, thus lifting them far above the level of 'faithful transcripts' of nature and life."[11]

Many of his articles about artists during this period were also concerned with what was to become a major theme in his own work: the relationship of man to nature. Dreiser was convinced earlier in his career that the artist's obligation was to portray man in his natural state. This duty, of course, clashed with convention as his novels show. In commenting on artists, Dreiser praised and respected those who shunned convention. Homer C. Davenport, a well-known caricaturist of the time, was like Dreiser a product of the Midwest. Davenport succeeded, in Dreiser's opinion, in satirizing the pretence, dishonesty, and unnaturalness of a refined society. "One would suspect," Dreiser observed, "that he would draw roughly, for like all Westerners he has no taste for luxury, and rather pities those creatures who are so refined and re-refined that they lack vitality enough to digest a plain meal."[12] Later, in a survey of various artists, Dreiser was appalled by their blatant hypocrisy: they often formed an exclusive community for themselves by severing themselves from nature as well as from society itself.[13]

In criticizing such "anemic" and fragile artists, Dreiser pleaded for the artist's liberation from the indoor life as Whitman did in his poetry. Dreiser's fondness for the strength and roughness of nature underlay many of his remarks on painting and sculpture. After tracing the inspirations of C. C. Curran, an Ohio painter, to those of the French painter Dagnan-Bouveret, Dreiser compared Curran's painting to Robert Louis Stevenson's poetry. Curran's picture with glimpses of children digging in the earth, sailing boats, and playing on the green turf awakened such a responsive mood in Dreiser that he quoted lines from Stevenson's "Child's Garden of Verse":

> I called the little pool a sea;
> The little hills were big to me,
>   For I am very small.
> I made a boat, I made a town,
> I searched the caverns up and down
>   And named them one and all.[14]

Even as late as 1899, when he first attempted to write fiction, Dreiser was intensely curious about nature's effects on man. Lawrence E. Earle's work, Dreiser noted, abounded with aged, weather-beaten figures that suggested "the wear and nature of the various callings from which they are selected." Every time Dreiser looked at one of Earle's paintings, he was reminded of Thoreau's description of "the old, quiet fisherman in his worn brown coat, who was so regularly to be found in a shady nook at a certain bend in the Concord River." Earle's figures, like Thoreau's, became part of the soil and landscape like the stumps and bushes. The garments the men in the pictures wear, in Dreiser's words, "are queer baked products of sun and rain; quaint, pleasant old creatures, selected by a feeling mind. In a way, they seem to illustrate how subtle are the ways of nature; how well she coats her aged lovers with her own autumnal hue."[15]

A more direct study of man in the natural state, Dreiser wrote, could be accomplished artistically in the nude as a genre. Discussing the works of Fernando Miranda, a Spanish-born sculptor, Dreiser quoted Miranda's defense of the human form in its natural beauty as "God's greatest work." Dreiser despised those who disliked nudes; with approval he repeated Miranda's comment that they were "misled by narrow conceptions of what is noble and good in the universe."[16] In such remarks, Dreiser hastened to point out the misguided concept of the viewer who was tempted to seek only the prurient from the nude. According to Dreiser, clothes distorted and concealed the beauty of form. The success of Frederick W. MacMonnies's masterpiece, *Bacchante and Child,* was the result of the sculptor's momentary capture of the pose upon one foot. The sculptor's motive, Dreiser suggested, "has plainly been to represent the beauty of a sudden and spontaneous movement, and not to glorify either inebriety or wantonness."[17]

These magazine contributions seldom gave a sign of the pessimism that, from time to time, marked his own fictional writings. This might well have been the result of the "success story" pattern Dreiser was asked to follow by the magazines. In this connection one must recall his disposition of mind during his editorial days. The columns he wrote in *Ev'ry Month* show that he was a disciple of Herbert Spencer and most notably that he interpreted the Spencerian cycle of existence as a progress for man. Nothing since then seemed to have altered his view, and he readily applied the theory to the artist's mission in life. Dreiser's faith in man's worth remained unshaken for a long time, as evidenced by the statement he made in 1909 as editor of *The Delineator.* His policy then was to accept only those contributions that were tinged with idealism and optimism and, in the case of a story, with a "truly uplifting character."[18] In a brief sketch of Bruce Crane, who was then recognized as a leading successor to the famous landscape artist George Inness, Dreiser praised Crane's work not because it adhered to nature but because it displayed a joyous and hopeful atmosphere.[19] In "E. Percy Moran and His Work," Dreiser cited Moran's view of an artist's function as "to make it [life] better, handsomer, more pleasing."[20] In surveying the gifted young portrait painters of the day, he came to this conclusion: "Intellectually, they are men of broad minds, and look upon art with clean, wholesome spirits."[21]

Only one short year before his actual writing of *Sister Carrie,* what he learned from these artists was not merely the attitude or personality of a true artist. It was also the technique of delineating how man delighted in a modern city and yet, when luck turned against him, was baffled by the complexity, impersonality, and loneliness that the city presented. Alfred Stieglitz, a contemporary artist-photographer, became one of the individuals who provided Dreiser with this technique and vision. In an essay on Stieglitz, Dreiser explained in detail how such well-known photographs as *A Rainy Day in Fifth Avenue* and *The L in a Storm* had been produced. Stieglitz was the first photographer to perfect the techniques of night pictures.[22] He would stand for hours at night in order to capture photographic impressions of some of the glittering night scenes in New York. Although Dreiser says that the famous *Winter on Fifth Avenue* was called "a lucky hit," he adds: "The driving sleet and the uncomfortable atmosphere issued out of the picture with uncomfortable persuasion. It had the tone of reality. But *lucky hit* followed *lucky hit,* until finally the accusation would explain no more, and then *talent* was substituted."[23]

By far the most influential artist for Dreiser in these years was William Louis Sonntag, Jr. The inspiration Dreiser received from Sonntag was so personal that Dreiser wrote a poem about him—and published it as an obituary in *Collier's Weekly* in 1898—when Sonntag, like Stephen Crane and Frank Norris, died an early death. Years later Dreiser's short biography of Sonntag, "The Color of To-day," became one of the chapters in *Twelve Men* under the anonymous title "W. L. S."[24] The sense of insecurity and loneliness that Carrie and Hurstwood experience in Chicago and New York, Dreiser tells us, derived from his newspaper experiences. But his actual portrayal of the scenes in the novel could not have been accomplished without the ideas of Sonntag.

Dreiser's first acquaintance with this artist goes back to his editorial days with *Ev'ry Month* in the winter of 1895. At that time, looking for striking illustrations of city life for the Christmas issue of the magazine, Dreiser paid a visit to Sonntag's studio. Dreiser had earlier been attracted to him not only by reputation but also by his colored drawings depicting night scenes of New York that appeared in one of the Sunday newspapers. These pictures, in Dreiser's recollection, "represented the spectacular scenes which the citizen and the stranger most delight in—Madison Square in a drizzle; the Bowery lighted by a thousand lamps and crowded with 'L' and surface cars; Sixth Avenue looking north from Fourteenth Street" (*Harper's Weekly* 45:1272). Dreiser's interest in Sonntag—a member of the Ashcan School noted for street scenes—is demonstrated by Dreiser's later drawing of Eugene Witla in the novel *The "Genius"*. The characterization of Dreiser's hero in that novel derives as much from Sonntag as from Dreiser's friend Everett Shinn, another Ashcan School painter. In any event, in the mid-nineties Sonntag's reputation outweighed Dreiser's. Instead of getting realistic pictures from Sonntag, Dreiser received only the romantic ones—a serious looking woman with beautiful hair flowing on the one side of the page, and a pretty fur-coated girl caught in a snowstorm.

In the late nineties what struck Dreiser's eyes in the works of Sonntag was the artist's use of color. Good coloring, as Dreiser often maintained, was above all the first element of a successful painting after idea, form, or purpose.[25] What was to become Dreiser's own use of color in describing urban scenes—streetlights, carriages, department stores, restaurants, luxurious garments—was acquired through his apprenticeship under Sonntag. On one drizzly autumn night Sonntag took Dreiser to such a scene on their way to the theater, Dreiser recalled, while they were in the midst of a serious discussion of art and life:

> He took me to a point where, by the intersection of the lines of the converging streets, one could not only see Greeley Square, but a large part of Herald Square, with its huge theatrical sign of fire and its measure of store lights and lamps of vehicles. It was, of course, an inspiring scene. The broad, converging walks were alive with people. A perfect jam of vehicles marked the spot where the horse and cable cars intersected. Overhead was the elevated station, its lights augmented every few minutes by long trains of brightly lighted cars filled with truly metropolitan crowds.
> "Do you see the quality of that? Look at the blend of the lights and shadows in there under the L."
> I looked and gazed in silent admiration.
> "See, right here before us—that pool of water there—do you get that? Now, that isn't silver-colored, as it's usually represented. It's a prism. Don't you see the hundred points of light?"
> I acknowledged the variety of color, which I had scarcely observed before.
> "You may think one would skip that in viewing a great scene, but the artist mustn't. He must get that all, whether you notice or not. It gives feeling, even when you don't see it." (*Harper's Weekly* 45 : 1273)

This is evidence that Dreiser was indebted to a practicing artist of the day and, more importantly, indicates how strongly Dreiser committed himself to capture an incisive vision of the contemporary scene. Furthermore, what fascinated Dreiser at this time was the artist's amazing versatility. Not only was Sonntag well versed in fiction, drama, music, history, and politics, but he surprised Dreiser by revealing the fact that he was an engineer (competent to handle marine, railroad, and other machinery), architect, mathematician, and philosopher. Dreiser was closely drawn to Sonntag's unique talents and experiences; during this period Dreiser himself was similarly conscientiously pursuing his apprenticeship not only as a critic in art and literature but also as a journalist who addressed himself to facts and ideas in science, technology, agriculture, commerce, politics, and many other fields. The intensity and width of vision that Dreiser achieved as a commentator on art and artists was to have a pervasive effect on his own writing as a novelist.

III

Although Dreiser vigorously pursued art criticism in these years (at times with immature haste), he did not present literary criticism with equal enthusiasm. It is common knowledge that Dreiser was incidentally a literary critic during his entire career. Interestingly, also, he was always conscious of his fellow writers and quite sensitive to their remarks on his own writing. As his numerous letters clearly indicate, Dreiser took his critics seriously. Many of his periodical writings in the nineties thus contained his views on men of letters in the past as well as in the present. In his interviews with successful men in various walks of life, Dreiser was, of course, curious as to how one would achieve eminence in the literary profession. Sometimes he violently disagreed with a theory of literature he came across. Later in his career Dreiser often confessed his aversion to many of his contemporaries because he felt that their works did not square with life as he himself experienced it. Such a distaste for much of American writing may have been part of the reason for his relative silence about his fellow writers during his free-lance period. But whenever he found an attitude or personality he felt an affinity with, he never failed to applaud it. Despite the small number of articles he wrote on this subject, he seems to have been testing his hand as critic in these years for the long literary career he was to make for himself later.

His first attempt came with a nostalgic description of Tarrytown with its world-renowned Sleepy Hollow, where Washington Irving's tombstone is located. Dreiser's interest was not so much in the famous storyteller and the legend that surrounded him as in the history of the region, particularly the Dutch settlement, and the feeling and color of this locale. In spite of his usual excitement over modern technology, Dreiser was vocal in his criticism of such an "incongruous trick" as arc lights with their unseemly glare that had invaded the Hollow road.[26] Dreiser's homage to the American past came to a climax with a long article on Hawthorne, which was published in two separate issues.[27] As in his article on Sleepy Hollow, this biographical sketch of the haunting romancer opens with reference to the undesirable effects of the modern era on the town of Salem—railroads, electric lights, and trolleys which "glared upon and outraged its ancient ways" (*Truth* 17:7).

Similar in kind to this sketch is a well-detailed account of William Cullen Bryant, which appeared in *Munsey's* in the following year.[28] The thrust of Dreiser's commentary was given to Bryant's courageous activities as journalist and poet during his last thirty-five years in the Long Island town of Roslyn. Dreiser astutely observed that although it was an old settlement with high "hopes and pretensions" years earlier, the town had "faltered and lagged in the race of modern progress" (*Munsey's,* 21:240). Dreiser's fondness for the poet is clearly shown by his frequent quotations of Bryant's poetry in this article and elsewhere. Dreiser admired Bryant for "a deep seated, rugged Americanism, wholly unconventionalized by his success in the world" (ibid., 245). Dreiser could have felt that Bryant's often-quoted lines from "To a Waterfowl"—"Lone wandering, but not lost"—would also refer to his own disappointments and hopes as journalist and future writer. To Dreiser, Bryant was "intrepid, persistent, full of the love of justice, and rich in human sympathies," a simple statement of what were to become his own qualities as a novelist (ibid., 244).

All of these literary essays contained the two leading and inseparable themes of his free-lance work: disillusionment with city life and longing for the beauty of nature. When he turned to contemporary authors, he searched for some transcendental reality beyond material appearances. He was surprised and at the same time gratified to discover that the commercial environment of Wall Street had no mark in Edmund Clarence Stedman's creative work.[29] The work and career of the travel writer Bayard Taylor, who is rather forgotten today, provided Dreiser with quiet reflections and warm sentiments.[30] Unlike Stedman, Taylor was born on a farm and struggled for existence in his early years. Much like Dreiser himself, Taylor was a self-made man, having left his native place in youth and built up a literary career in the city. Taylor, Dreiser learned, was not a materially successful man, and in his old age Taylor achieved happiness and peace of mind by retiring to Cedarcroft, his birthplace. The most significant point of a tribute to Taylor written by Dreiser comes toward the end, where Dreiser, foreshadowing his own characteristic turn of thought, portrays the old writer, who "drew out his rocking chair in the evening, and swayed to and fro as the light faded and sights and sounds gave place to the breath of night and the stars." Dreiser infuses the scene with an Emersonian, mystic quality that one frequently finds later in the novels: "The pale moonlight flooded all the ground, and leaves gained voices from the wind, and over them all brooded the poetic mind, wondering, awed, and yearning" (*Munsey's* 18:601).

Dreiser was more impressed by a mystic poet of an older generation such as Taylor than by a contemporary analytical critic who, Dreiser felt, often smacked of egotism. This is why when he encountered an influential British critic, Israel Zangwill, Dreiser became most indignant in his attack on the man and his philosophy.[31] Zangwill's critical tenets, Dreiser believed, were not entirely original, and Dreiser was indeed prepared to criticize those tenets for his American audience. Zangwill's rule was not to criticize a book for not being some other book, and yet his first criterion was that a book must be worth criticizing. What irritated Dreiser was a dogmatism that underlay Zangwill's standard of judgment. "All that remains," Zangwill said, "is to classify it [the work]. It is of such and such a period, such and such a school, such and such merit." Dreiser realized that, in Zangwill's criticism, judgment necessarily preceded classification and analysis. In any event, Dreiser argued that what was lacking in such criticism was the heart of a critic. To him, Zangwill's criticism demonstrated

> . . . the great analytical spirit, useful no doubt, but the world loves an enthusiast better, who criticizes not at all, but seizes upon the first thing to his hands and toils kindly, if blindly, in the thought that his is the great and necessary labor. Certainly such a life bespeaks a greater soul, if keen sympathies make soul, than does that of the man who can sit off and eternally pass judgment, unmoved forever to ally himself heart and hand with any one great effort for the uplifting of humanity. (*Ainslee's* 2:355–56)

Another eminent critic whom Dreiser met was William Dean Howells, "the Dean of American Letters," as he called him.[32] Before the interview Dreiser had read *My Literary Passions* and found his image of the great novelist readily confirmed. He found Howells "one of the noblemen of literature"—honest, sincere, and generous. Such laudatory remarks sound incongruous today since it has become legend that the two men never liked each other. We know from what Dreiser said later that Howells's novels failed to give him a sense of American life. Dreiser confided to one critic: "Yes, I know his books are pewky and damn-fool enough, but he did one fine piece of work, *Their Wedding Journey,* not a sentimental passage in it, quarrels from beginning to end, just the way it would be, don't you know, really beautiful and true" (Dudley, p. 143). On numerous occasions Dreiser revealed to his friends that *Their Wedding Journey* was the only work of Howells that he liked,[33] but he did admire Howells for championing young talents. In *Ev'ry Month* and again in *Ainslee's,* Dreiser called Howells a "literary Columbus" for discovering Stephen Crane and Abraham Cahan. Howells's support for Hamlin Garland and Frank Norris is well known, but Howells was blind to *Sister Carrie* and never tried to appreciate Dreiser during the rest of his life.

In order to understand Dreiser's "change of heart" as regards Howells, we must look into a transformation that took place in Howells's later years. The Howells whom Dreiser met in New York was not an aloof, genteel novelist, the product of New England culture. A decade earlier Howells had witnessed the suppression of justice in the wake of the Haymarket massacre. With a vehemence that was reminiscent of Zola, Howells protested against the incident, which he felt destroyed forever "the smiling aspect" of American life. With this social and political upheaval which shook his conscience, Howells was also under an important literary influence that subsequently was to change him. Dreiser's "The Real Howells" thus concluded with a personal tribute that Howells made to Tolstoy:

> Tolstoi's influence had led him back, as he puts it, "to the only true ideal, away from that false standard of the gentleman to the Man who sought not to be distinguished from other men, but identified with them, to that *Presence* in which the finest gentleman shows his alloy of vanity, and the greatest genius shrinks to the measure of his miserable egotism." (*Ainslee's* 5 : 140)

For the sixty-three-year-old novelist, such a revelation came rather belatedly, but for Dreiser, the unpublished novelist, it served to strengthen the already hardening literary foundation he had been building all these years.

IV

In the period immediately preceding the publication of *Sister Carrie*, the lives of various artists and writers strongly captured Dreiser's interest, and at times he envied them. He was always fascinated by their unique concept of beauty and their sympathetic treatment of life itself. Dreiser was convinced more than ever of the inseparable ties between art and ordinary human life. One of the dominant subjects in his magazine writing was, therefore, American life as he saw it. And one common theme Dreiser was consciously developing was American progress.

This theme scarcely sounded humanistic at that time, nor does it today; it was a journalist's attempt to provide the public with information on technology as it affected the urban scene. Disillusionment with science and distrust of progress were, in fact, common reactions in many quarters in American intellectual life. But Dreiser in the late nineties was undoubtedly an optimist; he had earlier interpreted the Spencerian law of existence as inevitable progress for mankind. "The world," he had earlier quoted another journal as declaring, "is not going downward to ruin. . . . Everything in this splendid country has an upward trend, despite the wail of the cynics."[34] As the editor of a new national magazine Dreiser thus urged his readers: "We will be concerned with making things good, and with living so that things shall be better . . . there will be naught but hope, unfaltering trust and peace" (*Ev'ry Month* 3, no. 2:7). Later as a free-lance writer Dreiser discussed, for example, the impact which the recent development of "motor carriages" made on transportation in the city. Using specific details and designs in the manner of an engineering journal, Dreiser demonstrated how electricity had been converted to motor power. He even projected the invention of "motor cars," as he called them, which would be operated by gasoline engines in the near future. After spelling out the enormous economic gains such development would generate for the country, he concluded the article with what must seem to modern readers a partially false prediction: "The saving of time, the added comfort and the improved health which would result from the system can hardly be overestimated."[35]

The introduction of automobiles into American life must have given such a compassionate man as Dreiser a sense of relief, because watching clattering horses in the streets was "itself too often an object of real and piteous interest" (*Demorest's* 35:154). As a naturalist in the vein of John Burroughs, Dreiser could hardly promote the cause of man's happiness on earth without due consideration for the welfare of other creatures. This is perhaps why Dreiser was curious about the intelligence and efficiency of pigeons as they were used for secret communications. But at the same time he expressed his idiosyncratic concern for pigeons as he concluded his essay with a quotation from Bryant's "To a Waterfowl."[36] His expression of sympathy was extended not only to animals but also to plants. Discussing the importance of studying plant roots scientifically, Dreiser illustrated how a microscope could trace down their "infinitesimal . . . threads as light as gossamer, almost—they did not naturally end." "In that unseen part," he interjected, "there was a friendly union between the life of the plant and the life of the earth, and the latter had given some of itself to course up the hair-like root and become a part of the plant."[37] On the basis of new research on the relationship of weeds to the soil, Dreiser even pleaded for the preservation of some weeds: "There are weeds that are soil renewers, weeds that are food for man and beast, and weeds without which thousands of acres of our most fertile lands would be wastes to-day."[38]

Such sensitive treatments of plant and animal life in the light of human progress were characteristic of Dreiser the philosopher. But as a historian Dreiser paid far more attention to the various technological innovations being made in the American 1890s. Thus, the development of transportation in the urban and rural areas became a focal point of his argument for progress. In "The Railroad and the People: A New Educational Policy Now Operating in the West," his purpose was to correct the term "soulless corporation" that was often used to describe the nature of the largest commercial organization then existing in the United States.[39] The railroads were usually described as "dark, sinister, dishonest associations which robbed the people 'right and left,' . . . and gave nothing in return" (*Harper's Monthly* 100:479). But like Shelgrim, the railroad president in Norris's novel *The Octopus,* Dreiser put forward an argument in favor of the industry's "cordial and sympathetic relationship with [the] public" and, with meticulous details, illustrated how both would benefit under such an enterprise. Dreiser's view of capitalism in this instance is evenhanded. "For if the public has had nothing save greed and rapacity to expect of its railroads," he went on, "the sight of the latter adopting a reasonable business policy, whereby they seek to educate and make prosperous the public in order that they in turn may be prosperous, is one which, if not inspiring, is at least optimistic" (ibid., 479).[40] A sense of optimism could even be detected in his account of manufacturing small arms. The evil connected with weapons moved him to despair, but his explanation of this sinister enterprise became a curious rationalization: the ultimate purpose of weapon production is to build peace.[41]

The jubilant mood in which he dealt with the events of the day seemed to have touched almost all of his writings in this period. In explaining how battleships were built, he even failed to reflect on the baleful purposes for which technology was used; instead, he dramatized the majesty of ships and the ingenuity involved in constructing them. As for road construction, Dreiser contrasted the enterprise to that of Imperial Rome, which thrived on slavery. American roads came into being, he emphasized, "with awakening reason and sympathy in all the hearts of men"; true greatness lay in the fact that the roads were built by the people and for the people. "Unlike the magnificent public structure of the empires long since departed," he asserted, "they will neither conceal squalor nor want, nor yet a race of whip-driven Helots, but rather bespeak a nation of free men and beauty lovers—men strong in the devotion and enjoyment of good."[42] Whether Dreiser was describing how the Chicago drainage canal was completed, how trains were manufactured in the Midwest, how pilot boats were operated in New York harbor, how trolleys ran between New York and Boston, or how the subway was laid in New York City— in these spectacles, Dreiser's vision of progress always dramatized the excitement of the people involved.[43]

In reporting America's industrial development, Dreiser suspected that some people had built their personal fortunes in the name of progress for all men. Earlier, when he was a newspaperman, Dreiser observed successful men such as Andrew Carnegie and Joseph Pulitzer, but he was somehow compelled to be reticent about their private conduct, which he could not admire. Now as a free-lance writer he was able to write about these wealthy men as he pleased. Consequently, through his magazine work, Dreiser became acquainted with Dr. Orison Swett Marden, the founder and editor of *Success,* the first issue of which appeared in December 1897. Trusting Dreiser's abilities to brighten up the contemporary scene, Marden engaged his services to interview successful men in business, industry, science, art, and literature. Although Marden's format for these articles does not seem to have restricted Dreiser's ideas on the subject, Dreiser's writing nevertheless lacked the sensitive approach that marked his best essays. Indeed, traditional success stories that dramatized the rags-to-riches ideal were still popular. It was easy for Dreiser to follow the well-established pattern of a Horatio Alger story; one could hardly expect any originality from his treatment of this theme.

The rapidity with which Dreiser composed these pieces was indicated by the fact that an interview by him appeared almost every month in the first two years of *Success.*[44] The monotonous similarity of these articles stemmed from several identical questions he put to the men he wrote about: "What quality in you was most essential to your success?" "Were you rich or poor before starting a career?" "Were reading and school work necessary for your success?" "What is your concept of happiness?" To these stock questions there were stock answers. All the men, of course, said that hard work led to their success. To this they added such traits as "perseverance" and "consistency" in their work; they all emphasized "honesty" and "integrity" as the moral scruples rewarded by success. Except for Thomas Edison, however, they did not believe in "overwork." All were convinced that the fewer advantages one had in his youth, the greater chances for success one could hope for. Even a man coming from a relatively distinguished family such as Joseph H. Choate, a leading lawyer and later an ambassador, stated: "I never met a great man who was born rich" (*Success* 1 [January 1898]:41). They all advocated thrift, saving, and investment as means to accumulate wealth. They also replied that education and book learning had little influence on their careers, a point with which Dreiser could certainly agree.

Finally, despite the prestige and glory accorded to successful men, Dreiser learned that only constant labor, not luxury and wealth, constituted their happiness. "When it is all done and is a success," Edison confessed, "I can't bear the sight of it. I haven't used a telephone in ten years, and I would go out of my way any day to miss an incandescent light" (*Success* 1 [February 1898]:9). Once these men achieved their eminence, most of them looked for satisfaction in their humanitarian cause, but to them labor itself preceded such happiness. Philip D. Armour, a businessman and philanthropist, explained: "If you give the world better material, better measure, better opportunities for living respectably, there is happiness in that. You cannot give the world anything without labor, and there is no satisfaction in anything but labor that looks toward doing this, and does it" (*Success* 1 [October 1898]:4). Dreiser also interviewed another famous industrialist and philanthropist, Andrew Carnegie, whose words on humanitarianism are questionable in view of the various reservations Dreiser had earlier expressed about him. In *Success* magazine, Dreiser somewhat inflated Carnegie's motive for a large-hearted liberality.

V

Among Dreiser's thirty *Success* articles, exactly half were later reprinted in three separate volumes edited by Marden, as mentioned earlier: *How They Succeeded* (1901), *Talks with Great Workers* (1901), and *Little Visits with Great Americans* (1903). One could easily wonder why the other articles were not selected by Marden, but there were some obvious reasons to be found. In each case, Marden certainly wanted to dramatize the life story of a single figure; seven of the articles that were not selected by Marden, such as "American Women as Successful Playwrights" and "America's Greatest Portrait Painters," dealt with more than one individual and did not suit Marden's purpose. The rest of the articles were left out for some other reasons. Whether or not the editor disagreed with Dreiser's point of view on the subject of the unselected articles is unknown, but it is interesting to note that most of the eliminated articles from the volumes of reprints lacked a sense of glamour often associated with the American Dream of Success. Marden's intention in this project was to inspire young men and women who wanted to be somebody but felt that they had no chance in life. However, the list of Dreiser's *Success* stories that were omitted—for instance, interviews with Alice B. Stephens (a well-known woman painter), H. Barrington Cox (an inventor), Clara S. Folts (a leading woman lawyer), Edward Atkinson (a food scientist), and Thomas B. Reed (a one-time Speaker of the House)—

demonstrated, contrary to common belief, that success was necessarily derived from one's advantages over others at the start of life including a solid educational background.[45]

Perhaps the most significant point to be drawn from Marden's selection is that he did not approve of Dreiser's interest in humanistically oriented portrayals of successful men. Two articles of this nature were carefully omitted from Marden's reprints: "A Cripple Whose Energy Gives Inspiration" and "A Touch of Human Brotherhood." In the first piece Dreiser, as if writing a story, describes how bleak a small fishing town on the coast of Connecticut had become through a decline in the whaling business and ship-building industry. "A friend of mine and myself," Dreiser begins the tale, "were sitting on the lawn surrounding the local Baptist church, one morning, discussing the possibilities of life and development in so small and silent a place, when a trivial incident turned the arguments to the necessity of doing something to promote the organization and intelligence of the world." The author's ensuing narration reveals an idea which would later clarify the meaning of struggle in his novels: while other young boys, complaining about their unfortunate social and economic conditions, cursed the world and idled away their energy and ambition, a physically handicapped youth, persisting in his labor and winning public trust and love, achieved happiness and success in life.[46]

The second story was concerned with the concept of success and happiness according to a less glamorous and totally strange figure whom Dreiser had found on Broadway and Fifth Avenue in New York. This man's story was so striking that Dreiser used it toward the end of *Sister Carrie,* where a lone, poverty-stricken man known only by his title of Captain created a job for himself.[47] In both versions, the Captain solicits passersby to contribute money to shelter bums during nights when the cold was like that pictured in Alfred Stieglitz's photograph. In the eyes of this self-styled philanthropist, people think that life is beautiful outside rather than inside. They would regard as happiness the "hotels and theaters, the carriages and fine homes— they're all in the eye . . . it's only for a season" (*Success* 5 [March 1902]: 176). The same scene had earlier appeared in another magazine article entitled "Curious Shifts of the Poor."[48] To Dreiser's surprise, many of the poor in the streets, though they appeared helpless and isolated, were not complaining as common people were. These seemingly victimized men, Dreiser discovered, were merely indifferent, if not cheerful, toward their conditions; in fact, they were far more stable mentally than the rich.

Another *Success* article which failed to be reprinted by Marden was

"The Tenement Toilers," one of several reports on the seamy side of city life Dreiser wrote shortly after *Sister Carrie*. In it, in contrast to his other *Success* stories, Dreiser dispassionately told how city workers for cheap labor lived in inhumanly crowded tenements and taught their young children that money was all they must aim at in life.[49] "Christmas in the Tenements" also discussed a contrast between the rich and the poor, but here he joyfully observed that despite their wretched living conditions in the tenements, Christmas brought the poor a temporary relief.[50] And curiously he proposed a *carpe diem* theme for them: "Eat, drink, and be merry, for to-morrow you must die" (*Harper's Weekly* 46:53). A little earlier his essay on "The Transmigration of the Sweat Shop" (*Puritan* 8:498–502), which was to serve him for Carrie Meeber's sweatshop in the novel, disclosed how such conditions did indeed exist in the factories he had visited in New Jersey. Dreiser's argument here was interesting because he presented himself as a reformer, not merely a compassionate and philanthropic observer but one who believed that these conditions could be eliminated by men of good will, honesty, and justice—by employees as well as employers. Society was full of inadequacies and inequalities, but now he could suggest positive remedies for society to use in coping with the problem. Man, Dreiser began to see, was not necessarily a victim of his conditions; it would be possible for man himself to ameliorate them. Similarly, "Little Clubmen of the Tenements" served Dreiser for a counter argument to Stephen Crane's "An Experiment in Misery."[51] The subtitle of Dreiser's piece reads "A remarkable boys' club established in Fall River, Massachusetts, for the children of the slums who find there the resources of a city and the pleasures of a home" (*Puritan* 7:665). His experiment showed that no matter how poorly such children were brought up in the tenements, they could still acquire good manners and attitudes once they were placed in the club. In the past some of the boys had lived with alcoholic parents; others had been orphans, motherless, fatherless, had been turned out to roam the streets at night. Scars of environment on the children were deep enough, yet he learned that they could be healed.

What emerged from such social criticism was that Dreiser was not easily swayed by the appearances of reality. Although the dreams of contemporary Americans were dramatized in his account, it was still possible for him to delve into their miseries and fears as well. He could now look at social phenomena from the vantage points of a worker and a capitalist. As a social critic, he was not superficial; his analyses and details were balanced by his arguments and points of view. "Man's ingenuity," he opened a report on the cartridge factory, "finds many contradictory channels for its expression. The labor to perfect those sciences which tend to save human life goes on side by side with the labor to create new and more potent methods for its destruction."[52] From a commercial point of view, the Chicago River provided him with a symbol of progress. The river not only gave the corporations the most efficient services but also offered the city its beauty: "At night, when the heavy traffic ceases and the bridges lose their throngs of vehicles and pedestrians, it glows beneath the lamps and sky like a stream of silver."[53] But, from a citizen's point of view, it was already the most polluted river in the country despite the federal laws which should have protected this navigable stream. Dreiser also had his second thoughts on the sacred Mississippi River, still fresh with its echoes from Mark Twain. Though aware of its scenic charms and literary memories, Dreiser thought its traditions to be an anachronism in the light of later and more civilized conditions:

> The overseers howl terribly without taking breath, brandish sticks, wave their arms, stamp their feet, and make startling lunges in all directions. They threaten the idle, curse the active, bluff the bystanders, and add prodigiously to the tumult of the scene without otherwise affecting it. Regardless of these busy-bodies that buzz about like gnats, the darkies shuffle here and there, rolling with rhythmic motions and with more rests than efforts the cotton bales. The character of the negro in the situation is no doubt picturesque, but the fact that the business is more or less dependent upon such labor, and the impossibility of securing active, systematic, skilled service forms one of the serious problems in the commerce of the river.[54]

In his discussion of successful public figures Dreiser was also critical, often undercutting their image and reputation. In "The Real Choate," the celebrated lawyer-diplomat was assailed, for Dreiser believed that Choate was unworthy of his reputation. In another article on Choate, published a few months earlier in *Success,* Dreiser was unable to criticize him freely because of Marden's theory of success. In that article Choate's assiduity and skill as a lawyer were generously praised, but in the later article Dreiser could not help pointing out his inadequacies as a human being.[55] Choate was known for his brilliant quotations from Shakespeare; indeed, his New England name and background brightly shone in the minds of many people. But Dreiser hastened to add: "There is not enough of that radiant humanity in him which the common people understand and make fellowship with" (*Ainslee's* 3:324). The problem with Choate's personality,

Dreiser argued, derived not so much from his intellect and air of superiority as from his profession itself, in which his mind was preoccupied with the cold corporations, his time spent "with entanglements never seen of the people" (ibid., 326). Englishmen, to whom Choate represented Americans, would admire "his brilliancy, his unfailing humor, his persuasive powers, and his fine show of courage and chivalry"; but for American purposes, Dreiser insisted, Choate needed other qualities, the chief of which should have been "a craving for distinction at the hands of the people" (ibid., 326). What was worse, Choate was attacked on moral grounds. "It is curious," Dreiser wondered, "that this powerful analytical sense is seldom joined with any tenderness of heart, or with any defined leanings to right or wrong" (ibid., 328). That man must be judged not by what he says but by what he does was Dreiser's reminder to his readers. Dreiser's conclusion was simple: "he has done for himself nobly, not for others" (ibid., 333). For Dreiser, then, Choate's talents—"arrayed in all their subtlety in defense of some execrable Tammany scapegoat, some organized industry seeking to avoid the fulfillment of its just obligations, some corporation caught in act of the false dealing with the State"— served to symbolize the evil forces that were to dominate the American political system for generations to come. And the portrayal of the underdog in the rising civilization which Dreiser later wove into his fiction was to be a faithful reflection of reality in America.

VI

Dreiser's understanding of and feeling for American life were shown in full force in his novels. That picture of American life, some critics argued, was distorted, but Dreiser spoke the truth as he saw it. In "True Art Speaks Plainly" published in 1903, shortly after the turmoil over the publication of *Sister Carrie,* Dreiser wrote: "The extent of all reality is the realm of the author's pen, and a true picture of life, honestly and reverentially set down, is both moral and artistic whether it offends the conventions or not."[56] It is now easy to see that Dreiser's magazine writings in the 1890s show a characteristic reverence for his material. Whether he was commenting on artists, writers, or society in general, this attitude resulted from his lifelong conviction that "the surest guide is a true and responsive heart."[57]

Qualities of sympathy and compassion indisputably characterize his fiction, but what his magazine work indicates is the fact that Dreiser was not a simple "commiserator" as Edward D. McDonald portrayed him in a picture attached to an article in *The Bookman*: Dreiser, in tears, devouring a tragic story in the newspaper.[58] His compassionate appreciation of all stories of human interest cannot be doubted, but more importantly Dreiser before *Sister Carrie* also acquired a capacity for detachment and objectivity; rarely did his magazine essays display passionate outbursts. In effect, Dreiser was a literary realist in the best sense of the word. These magazine contributions suggest that although he was eager to learn from literary and philosophical sources, he trusted his own vision and portrayed life firsthand.

H. Alan Wycherley has maintained that Dreiser's nonfiction after 1900 fluctuated between "mechanism" and "vitalism."[59] If one agrees with Wycherley's assessment, Dreiser was clearly a vitalist in his freelance work of the 1890s. This vitalist philosophy was so deeply rooted in the most important period of his development that it likely remained with him for the rest of his career. In his novels Dreiser often writes of the apparently indifferent and uncontrollable forces that sweep over man's life, but in reality he does not seem to have abandoned a belief in man's capacity to determine his own destiny. Although Dreiser has often been labeled as a literary naturalist in the manner of Zola and the other French naturalists, his magazine writing suggests that he was perhaps—at least in his early years—a naturalist in the vein of Thoreau and John Burroughs rather than a literary naturalist. Many of his early writings reveal that Dreiser was genuinely an American patriot; he was unabashedly an advocate of American values and an exponent of national character. His writing in this period constantly stressed the value of contentment in one's daily living; Dreiser was not a religionist or mystic as he was characterized toward the end of his life. Whatever assessment a modern reader may make of Dreiser's magazine writing, the fact remains that it was indeed comprehensive. And what we have here is a substantial portion of the vital impressions a major American writer received from his environment at the dawn of the twentieth century in America.

Notes

1. Dorothy Dudley, *Dreiser and the Land of the Free* (New York, 1946), p. 142.
2. See, for instance, W. A. Swanberg, *Dreiser* (New York, 1965), p. 76. A notable exception is Ellen Moers; see Moers, *Two Dreisers* (New York, 1969), pp. 32–69.
3. Frank L. Mott, *A History of American Magazines, 1885–1905* (Cambridge, Mass., 1957), pp. 6–8.
4. *Crumbling Idols*, ed. Jane Johnson (Cambridge, Mass., 1960 [1894]), p. 116.
5. *Critic*, o. s. 25 (11 August 1894): 97.

6. *Fortnightly Review* 93 (May 1910): 921–32.

7. See Isaac F. Marcosson, *Adventures in Interviewing* (New York, 1923), pp. 60–61.

8. Dreiser, *A Book About Myself* (New York, 1922), p. 178.

9. See Letters of J. Scott Hartley to Dreiser in the University of Pennsylvania Library Dreiser Collection.

10. *Metropolitan* 7 (April 1898): 359.

11. "Benjamin Eggleston, Painter," *Ainslee's* 1 (April 1898): 45.

12. "A Great American Caricaturist," *Ainslee's* 1 (May 1898): 340.

13. "A Notable Colony: Artistic and Literary People on the Picturesque Bronx," *Demorest's* 35 (August 1899): 240–41.

14. "C. C. Curran," *Truth* 18 (September 1899): 228.

15. "Lawrence E. Earle," *Truth* 20 (February 1901): 27–30.

16. "The Sculpture of Fernando Miranda," *Ainslee's* 2 (August 1898): 113–18.

17. "The Art of MacMonnies and Morgan," *Metropolitan* 7 (February 1898): 143–51.

18. See *Letters of Theodore Dreiser*, ed. Robert H. Elias (Philadelphia, 1959), 1:94.

19. "Concerning Bruce Crane," *Truth* 18 (June 1899): 143–47.

20. *Truth* 18 (February 1899): 35.

21. "America's Greatest Portrait Painters," *Success* 2 (11 February 1899): 184.

22. "A Master of Photography," *Success* 2 (10 June 1899): 471.

23. "The Camera Club of New York," *Ainslee's* 4 (October 1899): 329.

24. See "The Color of To-day," *Harper's Weekly* 45 (14 December 1901): 1272–73; *Twelve Men* (New York, 1919), pp. 344–60.

25. See, for instance, "Benjamin Eggleston, Painter," *Ainslee's* 1 (April 1898): 41.

26. "Historic Tarrytown," *Ainslee's* 1 (March 1898): 25–31.

27. "Haunts of Nathaniel Hawthorne," *Truth* 17 (21 September 1898): 7–9; (28 September 1898): 11–13.

28. "The Home of William Cullen Bryant," *Munsey's* 21 (May 1899): 240–46.

29. "Edmund Clarence Stedman at Home," *Munsey's* 20 (March 1899): 931–38.

30. "The Haunts of Bayard Taylor," *Munsey's* 18 (January 1898): 594–601.

31. "The Real Zangwill," *Ainslee's* 2 (November 1898): 351–57.

32. "The Real Howells," *Ainslee's* 5 (March 1900): 137–42.

33. In a letter of 15 October 1911 to William C. Lengel, Dreiser wrote: "You will not be surprised when I tell you that few American books if any interest me. I've enjoyed *Uncle Tom's Cabin* and *Huckleberry Finn* and *Roughing It* and *Ben-Hur* as a boy. More recently or rather somewhat later I liked *The Red Badge of Courage* (Crane) [,] *Main-Travelled Roads* (Hamlin Garland) [,] *With the Procession* (H. B. Fuller) [,] *McTeague* (Frank Norris) [,] *The 13th District* (Brand Whitlock) [,] *The Story of Eva* (Will Payne) [,] *Quicksand* (Henry White) & *Their Wedding Journey* (W. D. Howells). These are quite the sum total of my American literary admirations." *Letters*, 1:121. As late as 1942 Dreiser told George Ade: "In fact I entered it [the "gay nineties"] with your *Fables in Slang*, Finley Dunne's *Philosopher Dooley*, Frank Norris' *McTeague* and Hamlin Garland's *Main-Travelled Roads*. And I stored it—or thought I had—along with these and a very few others of that time or earlier:—Howells' *Their Wedding Journey*, for example. These were the beginning of my private library of American Realism." *Letters*, 3:949. Dreiser was possibly thinking about *A Modern Instance* when he kept referring to *Their Wedding Journey*, for his remark about the constant quarreling does not describe *Their Wedding Journey*.

34. *Ev'ry Month* 3, No. 4 (January 1897): 7.

35. "The Horseless Age," *Demorest's* 35 (May 1899): 155.

36. "Carrier Pigeons in War Time," *Demorest's* 34 (July 1898): 222–23.

37. "Plant Life Underground," *Pearson's* 11 (June 1901): 861–62.

38. "The New Knowledge of Weeds," *Ainslee's* 8 (January 1902): 533.

39. *Harper's Monthly* 100 (February 1900): 479–84.

40. One example of the educational policy advanced by the railroads around the turn of the century was mapping and examining the soils for the benefit of farmers as well as for industry. See "The Problem of the Soil," *Era* 12 (September 1903): 249.

41. "The Making of Small Arms," *Ainslee's* 1 (July 1898): 549.

42. "The Harlem River Speedway," *Ainslee's* 2 (August 1898): 56.

43. See "Where Battleships Are Built," *Ainslee's* 1 (June 1898): 433–39; "The Chicago Drainage Canal," *Ainslee's* 3 (February 1899): 53–61; "The Town of Pullman," *Ainslee's* 3 (March 1899): 189–200; "The Log of an Ocean Pilot," *Ainslee's* 3 (July 1899): 683–92; "From New York to Boston by Trolley," *Ainslee's* 4 (August 1899): 74–84; "New York's Underground Railroad," *Pearson's* 9 (April 1900): 375–84.

44. See "A Talk with America's Leading Lawyer [Choate]," *Success* 1 (January 1898): 40–41; "A Photographic Talk with Edison," *Success* 1 (February 1898): 8–9; "Life Stories of Successful Men—No. 10, Philip D. Armour," *Success* 1 (October 1898): 3–4; "Life Stories of Successful Men—No. 11, Chauncey M. Depew," *Success* 1 (November 1898): 3–4; "Life Stories of Successful Men—No. 12, Marshall Field," *Success* 2 (8 December 1898): 7–8; "A Leader of Young Manhood, Frank W. Gunsaulus," *Success* 2 (15 December 1898): 23–24; "A Monarch of Metal Workers [Carnegie]," *Success* 2 (3 June 1899): 453–54.

45. See "A High Priestess of Art," *Success* 1 (January 1898): 55; "A Vision of Fairy Lamps," *Success* 1 (March 1898): 23; "The Career of a Modern Portia," *Success* 2 (18 February 1899): 205–6; "Atkinson on National Food Reform," *Success* 3 (January 1900): 4; "Thomas Brackett Reed: The Story of a Great Career," *Success* 3 (June 1900): 215–16.

46. *Success* 5 (February 1902): 72–73.

47. "A Touch of Human Brotherhood," *Success* 5 (March 1902): 140–41, 176; cf. *Sister Carrie* (New York, 1900), pp. 517–25. Whether the article was written before *Sister Carrie* or possibly extracted from the novel is difficult to determine.

48. "Curious Shifts of the Poor. Strange Ways of Relieving Desperate Poverty. —Last Resources of New York's Most Pitiful Mendicants," *Demorest's* 36 (November 1899): 22–26. "Curious Shifts of the Poor" is also the title of Chapter 45 in *Sister Carrie.*

49. "The Tenement Toilers," *Success* 5 (April 1902): 213–14, 232. The same article appeared as "The Toilers of the Tenements" with some stylistic changes in *The Color of a Great City* (New York, 1923), pp. 85–99.

50. *Harper's Weekly* 46 (6 December 1902): 52–53; reprinted in *The Color of a Great City.*

51. See "Little Clubmen of the Tenements," *Puritan* 7 (February 1900): 665–72; cf. "The Transmigration of the Sweat Shop," *Puritan* 7 (July 1900): 498–502.

52. "Scenes in a Cartridge Factory," *Cosmopolitan* 25 (July 1898): 321.

53. "The Smallest and Busiest River in the World," *Metropolitan* 8 (October 1898): 363.

54. "The Trade of the Mississippi," *Ainslee's* 4 (January 1900): 742–43.

55 *Aislee's* 3 (April 1899): 324–33; cf. "A Talk with America's Leading Lawyer," *Success* 1 (January 1898): 40–41.

56. *Booklover's Magazine* 1 (February 1903): 129.

57. "Reflections," *Ev'ry Month* 2, No. 6 (1 September 1896): 2.

58. See Edward D. McDonald, "Dreiser Before 'Sister Carrie,'" *The Bookman* (U. S.) 67 (June 1928): facing p. 369.

59. "Mechanism and Vitalism in Dreiser's Nonfiction," *Texas Studies in Literature and Language* 11 (1969): 1039–49.

Selected
Magazine Articles
of THEODORE DREISER

Part One

LITERARY HERITAGE

The Haunts of Bayard Taylor[1]

The quiet Pennsylvania village which was the home of the famous American author and traveler's boyhood, and to which, in the days of his celebrity, he loved to return from the travels and labors of his wandering life.

In the valley of the Brandywine, which, as all good Americans know, lies in Chester County, Pennsylvania, not far from Philadelphia, and which was the scene of a Revolutionary battle, in which we did not trounce the British to any noticeable extent, there is the home of a famous American poet.

When men who are now fifty years old were boys, there was not a youth in the country who did not know of Bayard Taylor and hope to do as he had done. The fact that he was a poor lad who had earned his own way, and traveled and distinguished himself by his own efforts, made him an excellent example for parents to hold up to children. His newspaper letters gave him a wonderful, though ephemeral, popularity, and when a boy grew restless and urged his parents for permission and means to travel, it was very easy to cite Bayard Taylor. His fine poems thrilled men also.

Kennett Square, which is but a few miles from Chester, is a mere handful of houses lying along clean roadways. Bayard Taylor was born there in 1825, in a house which preceded the corner grocery in its present location; a little way from the village is the old farm of his parents, and on the other side of the road the sixty acres of the estate of Cedarcroft, which he bought when he had grown to manhood, and gained fame and money.

When the poet was a little fellow, still performing, or dodging, the arduous duties of the farm, this estate of Cedarcroft was thicket and bramble, and in a swampy portion of it the boy often went bare legged at morning and came out when his stomach urged him, loaded with such spoils and treasures as blue mud, black turtles with orange spots, and baby frogs the size of chestnuts. He rode along the turnpike to

Bayard Taylor, printer, traveler, poet, and novelist. Born at Kennett Square, Pennsylvania, January 11, 1825; died in Berlin, December 19, 1878.

and from the old stone mill at Chaddsford, bringing home bags of flour now and again. It is mournfully told by him somewhere that when the flour bags would fall off he "would sit in mute despair beside the giant sacks, awaiting the coming of a stronger arm." But the boy who, in thirty years, could edit and translate over fifty volumes, and write half as many more, was not, we may imagine, much given to mute despair.

Cedarcroft, which the poet built, is a splendid old house, rather striking in such a far away, inconvenient locality, but really beautiful to look on. Taylor had coveted the ground when he was a boy, and in 1853 he purchased the tract of eighty acres on which the house stands. In 1855 he added to it about forty five acres which he bought from his father, and forty acres, with an ancient stone farm house, obtained from his uncle. Then he traveled and lectured, and in 1858 found himself with money enough to begin building Cedarcroft. He put his weariness of lecturing and earthly struggle in its humorous form when he said, in reference to sleeping car berths and traveling, that his "legs were too long for lecturing," and that he would give up that business as soon as Cedarcroft was finished. It was built with lecture money, every brick of it.

It is something to think over, this warm affection that Bayard Taylor bore for Chester County and the place of his birth. He left its rural beauty when only seventeen years old, and had begun his travels into the outer world even before then.

He had traveled over Europe at eighteen, and written his "Views Afoot," had returned, and been country editor, and then editorial writer on the New York *Tribune,* and in that connection lived the life of a Bohemian and literary struggler in New York with Stedman,[2] Stoddard,[3] Fitzjames O'Brien,[4] and their comrades. Still the beautiful valley of the Brandywine was in his mind. His tastes and labors led him to the gold fields of California, the lands of Europe and Africa, the scenes of the far north, and the distant plains of Asia, and yet he found no spot that suited him better. Whenever he thought of rest, he thought of Kennett Square.

There are one or two places in New York where Taylor held forth. One is an old building in Murray Street not far from Broadway, where he had his room during his early *Tribune* days. Mr. Stoddard, the poet, has often told the story of the Saturday evenings when Taylor, Stedman, Willis,[5] Fitzjames O'Brien, and himself gathered in this room and enjoyed themselves with literary talk.

"He had a beautiful and pathetic voice," said Stoddard of Taylor, "and an enthusiasm for poetry that was pleasant to see. He loved to read, and there was scarcely a week that he did not have a new poem ready for us."

Amid these attractions and distractions at the beginning of a literary life, the poet wrote to his Mary Agnew: "Would to heaven I could drop down in Kennett for an hour or two these delicious evenings. I am shut up in these brick walls, and, like Sterne's starling, 'I can't get out.'"

There really is no other spot on earth identified with him. He traveled so much and so far, and was so little in one place during those years, that one who tries to find his haunts must come to Kennett, whence he first departed, and to which at last his body was returned.

The place is now kept in condition by the owners. The great arched window in the south front was the one which Taylor designed to enframe a lovely view. At the base of the tower there is the great cornerstone, which he personally placed with all due ceremony. Under it, in a box of zinc, are a copy of "Views Afoot," and an original poem by him, to be read, as he said, "four hundred years hence by some one who never heard of me"; a *Tribune*; some coins; a poem by R. H. Stoddard, in his own handwriting, and so on. "I broke the neck of a bottle on the stone," wrote Taylor, "poured a libation to all good Lares and Penates, and then gave the workmen cake and ale." Thus Cedarcroft was builded for him and others.

He moved into it in 1859, dreaming of years of peace, and hours in which the greatest of his poetic conceptions could be set down. Like all men who build homes, he thought his a haven of rest. Stoddard came to visit him, a house warming was given, and an original play performed entitled "Love at a Hotel," which was announced as the joint work of "The World Renowned Dramatic Authors, B. T. Cedarcroft and R. H. S. Customhouse."

If there were no other record but the few poems of "The Poet's Journal," which Bayard Taylor wrote in the old house, a realization of all that his valley meant to him could be gained. Here at evening he looked out from his wide library across the ground which his toil had prepared, and in the quiet joy of peace and possession wrote:

> The evening shadows lengthen on the lawn.
>   Westward our immemorial chestnuts stand,
> A mount of shade; but o'er the cedars drawn,
>   Between the hedge row tree, in many a band
> Of brightening gold, the sunshine lingers on,
>   And soon will touch our oaks with parting hand;
> And down the distant valley all is still,
> And flushed with purple smiles the beckoning hill.

Here were no outer distractions, no hurry of travel, no apparent need of lecturing, no meetings or partings. Life flowed on, quiet and still. The great world of which he was so much a factor seemed distant enough.

At Kennett he wooed his first love. In those days he walked the country so familiar and dear to his heart. There is an old meeting house at Longwood—where he now lies buried—which was the place of worship of the family. To this he went on a Sunday morning in the days of his courtship, his young sweetheart on his arm, and afterward, when the love days and the bride who made them glorious had gone the way of all things earthly, he remembered. May days came again when he was installed at Cedarcroft, but they only inspired him to write:

> When buds have burst the silver sheath,
>   And shifting pink, and gray, and gold
> Steal o'er the woods, while fair beneath
>   The bloomy vales unfold;
>
> Then from the jubilee I turn
>   To other Mays that I have seen,
> Where more resplendent blossoms burn
>   And statelier woods are green.

> For she whose softly murmured name
> The music of the month expressed,
> Walked by my side, in holy shame
> Of girlish love confessed.

That Taylor had made up his mind to reap all the advantages of so delightful a retreat shows itself in his "Home Pastorals," which he wrote while at Cedarcroft:

Here will I seek my songs in the quiet fields of my boyhood;
Here, where the peaceful tent of the home is pitched for a season.

And often he drew out his chair on the broad veranda, and viewed the scene so familiar in poetic content. There is a picture of this in a poem to his wife, of which one verse runs:

> Come, leave the flowery terrace, leave the beds
>   Where Southern children wake to Northern air;
> Let yon mimosas droop their tufted heads,
>   These myrtle trees their nuptial beauty wear.

> And while the dying day reluctant treads
>   From tree top unto tree top, with me share
> The scene's idyllic peace, the evening's close,
> The balm of twilight, and the land's repose.

Poor Taylor! The world was not idyllic peace for him. There is something tragic in the change of his early view to that which he expressed in later years. As an editor in the printing office at Phœnixville, in 1847, he wrote to his Mary Agnew: "Sometimes I feel as if there were a Providence watching over me, and as if an unseen and uncontrollable hand guided my actions. I have often dim, vague forebodings that an eventful destiny is in store for me, that I have vast duties yet to accomplish, and a wider sphere of action than that which I now occupy."

In 1873, five years before his death, writing from Gotha to a friend who had congratulated him on his success in life, the poet replied in the saddest letter he ever wrote:

You exaggerate what you consider my successes. From 1854 to 1862, or thereabouts, I had a good deal of popularity of the cheap, ephemeral sort. It began to decline at the time when I began to see the better and truer work in store for me, and I let it go, feeling that I must begin anew and acquire a second reputation of a different kind. For the last five years I have been engaged in this struggle, which is not yet over.

I am giving the best blood of my life to my labors, seeing them gradually recognized by the few and the best, it is true; but they are still unknown to the public, and my new claims are fiercely resisted by the majority of the newspaper writers in the United States. "Lars" is the first poem of mine ever published in England, and I hoped for some impartial recognition there. Well, the sale is just 108 copies! My translation of "Faust" is at last accepted in England, Germany, and America as much the best. It cost me years of the severest labor, and has not yet returned me $500. The "Masque of the Gods" has not yet paid expenses. The sale of my former volumes of travel has fallen almost to nothing. For two years past I have had no income of any sort from property or copyright, and am living partly on my capital and partly on mechanical labor of the mind. I am weary, indeed, completely fagged out, and to read what you say of my success sounds almost like irony.

The ashes of Dead Sea fruit were upon his lips.

In 1878 the poet was appointed minister to Germany by President Hayes, and on October 19 of the same year he died. In March of the following year the body arrived in New York, where it lay in state in the governor's room in the City Hall, and was then removed to Cedarcroft, and from thence a few miles away to Longwood Cemetery. There were four thousand friends and neighbors present when the body was deposited in its last resting place and the poet Stedman spoke.

Within the iron railing around the burial plot stands a Greek altar of Doric order, which bears a medallion of him and the words, "He being dead yet speaketh." At his side lie his first wife, Mary Agnew, his parents, and his brother Frederick.

The place is secluded and out of the way. He who was heralded the world over sleeps unminded here. The summer that he loved with his Mary comes in all her glory. Her scarf is loosened on the hills, and all the wide landscape is flecked with gold. A blue smoky haze fills the air, and the heat grows stifling and oppressive, but he is not there to see.

There is nothing about Cedarcroft that is inconsistent with the references made to it by Taylor. The splendid trees and spread of foliage are all that trees and foliage could be. No sky is bluer than the sky is here on a summer day. Nowhere does the sun pour its golden flood more copiously than upon these green fields. The hills rise gently, and the Brandywine flows over its pebbly bed with the softest ripple conceivable. When evening comes and the stillness seems to gather with the long shadows of the trees, the scene will soothe the most restless heart.

On the piazza at Cedarcroft Bayard Taylor drew out his rocking chair in the evening, and swayed to and fro as the light faded and sights and sounds gave place to the breath of night and the stars. Here he gazed dreamily at heaped up shadows where trees had stood before. The pale moonlight flooded all the ground, the leaves gained voices from the wind, and over them all brooded the poetic mind, wondering, awed, and yearning. His was a fleeting day—a few years of longing and pleasure and loving, a few hours in which the heart struggled to grasp all the meaning of the beauty, and then he passed on. But the fields he loved are still there, and the sights and sounds are as before. Nature has not changed in light or in shadow, and where Bayard Taylor dreamed and loved others may dream anew and love as though there were no ending.

Notes

1. "The Haunts of Bayard Taylor," *Munsey's* 18 (January 1898): 594–601. On (James) Bayard Taylor (1825–1878).

2. Edmund Clarence Stedman (1833–1908), critic and businessman. See Dreiser's article, "Edmund Clarence Stedman at Home," reprinted in this volume.

3. Richard Henry Stoddard (1825–1903), poet and critic. Stoddard, along with Taylor, Stedman, George Henry Boker, and Thomas Baily Aldrich, formed a group of five close literary friends.

4. Fitz-James O'Brien (1828–1862), Irish-American poet and story-writer, wrote *The Diamond Lens and Other Stories.*

5. Nathaniel Parker Willis (1806–1867), editor and writer, best known for many volumes of letters of travel and personal experience, such as *Pencillings by the Way* and *The Convalescent.*

Fame Found in Quiet Nooks[1]

John Burroughs, the Apostle of "Plain Living and High Thinking," Interviewed for "Success" in his Hut on the Hill-top

"I Was Raised Among the Fields"

"Money-Getting is Half a Mania"

When I visited the hilltop retreat of John Burroughs, the distinguished lover of nature, at West Park, New York, it was with the feeling that all success is not material: that mere dollars are nothing, and that the influential man is the successful man, whether he be rich or poor. John Burroughs is unquestionably both influential and poor. On the wooden porch of his little bark-covered cabin I waited, one June afternoon, until he should come back from the woods and fields, where he had gone for a ramble. It was so still that the sound of my rocker moving to and fro on the rough boards of the little porch seemed to shock the perfect quiet. From afar off came the plaintive cry of a wood-dove, and then all was still again. Presently the interpreter of out-door life appeared in the distance, and, seeing a stranger at his door, hurried homeward. He was without coat or vest, and looked cool in his white outing shirt and large straw hat. After some formalities of introduction, we reached the subject which I had called to discuss, and he said:—

"It is not customary to interview men of my vocation concerning success."

"Any one who has made a lasting impression on the minds of his contemporaries," I began, "and influenced men and women—"

"Do you refer to me?" he interrupted, naively.

I nodded and he laughed. "I have not endowed a university nor made a fortune, nor conquered an enemy in battle," he said.

"And those who have done such things have not written 'Locusts and Wild Honey' and 'Wake, Robin.'"

50

"A feeling that I want to write"

"I recognize," he said, quietly, "that success is not always where people think it is. There are many ways of being successful and I do not approve of the mistake which causes many to consider that a great fortune acquired means a great success achieved. On the contrary, our greatest men need very little money to accomplish the greatest work."

"I thought that anyone leading a life so wholly at variance with the ordinary ideas and customs would see success in life from a different point of view," I observed. "Money is really no object with you?"

"The subject of wealth never disturbs me."

"You lead a very simple life here."

"Such as you see."

The sight would impress anyone. So far is this disciple of nature away from the ordinary mode of the world that his little cabin, set in the cup-shaped top of a hill, is practically bare of luxuries and the so-called comforts of life. His surroundings are of the rudest, the very rocks and bushes encroaching upon his back door. All about, the crest of the hill encircles him, and shuts out the world. Only the birds of the air venture to invade his retreat from the various sides of the mountain, and there is only a straggling, narrow path, which branches off a dozen times before it takes the true direction. In his house are no decorations but such as can be hung upon the exposed wood. The fireplace is of brick, and quite wide; the floor, rough boards scrubbed white; the ceiling, a rough array of exposed rafters, and his bed a rudely constructed work of the hand. Very few and very simple chairs, a plain table and some shelves for books make the wealth of the retreat and serve for his ordinary use.

"Many people think," I said, "that your method of living is an ideal example of the way people ought to live."

"There is nothing remarkable in that. A great many people are very weary of the way they think themselves compelled to live. They are mistaken in believing that the disagreeable things they find themselves doing, are the things they ought to do. A great many take their idea of a proper aim in life from what other people say and do. Consequently, they are unhappy, and an independent existence such as mine strikes them as ideal. As a matter of fact, it is very natural."

"Would you say that to work so as to be able to live like this should be the aim of a young man?"

"By no means. On the contrary, his aim should be to live in such a way as will give his mind the greatest freedom and peace. This can be very often obtained by wanting less of material things and more of intellectual ones. A man who achieved such an aim would be as well off as the most distinguished man in any field. Money-getting is half a mania, and some other 'getting' propensities are manias also. The man who gets content comes nearest to being reasonable."

"I should like," I said, "to illustrate your point of view from the details of your own life."

"Students of nature do not, as a rule, have eventful lives. I was born at Roxbury, New York, in 1837. That was a time when conditions were rather primitive. My father was a farmer, and I was raised among the woods and fields. I came from an uncultivated, unreading class of society, and grew up amid surroundings the least calculated to awaken the literary faculty. Yet I have no doubt that daily contact with the woods and fields awakened my interest in the wonders of nature, and gave me a bent toward investigation in that direction."

"Did you begin early to make notes and write upon nature?" I questioned.

"Not before I was sixteen or seventeen. Earlier than that, the art of composition had anything but charms for me. I remember that while at school, at the age of fourteen, I was required, like other students, to write 'compositions' at stated times, but I usually evaded the duty one way or another. On one occasion, I copied something from a comic almanac, and unblushingly handed it in as my own. But the teacher detected the fraud, and ordered me to produce a twelve-line composition before I left school. I remember I racked my brain in vain, and the short winter day was almost closing when Jay Gould,[2] who sat in the seat behind me, wrote twelve lines of doggerel on his slate and passed it slyly over to me. I had so little taste for writing that I coolly copied that, and handed it in as my own."

"You were friendly with Gould then?"

"Oh, yes; 'chummy,' they call it now. His father's farm was only a little way from ours, and we were fast friends, going home together every night."

"His view of life must have been considerably different from yours."

"It was. I always looked upon success as being a matter of mind, not money; but Jay wanted the material appearances. I remember that once we had a wrestling match, and as we were about even in strength, we agreed to abide by certain rules,—taking what we called 'holts' in the beginning and not breaking them until one or the other was thrown. I kept to this in the struggle, but when Jay realized that he was in danger of losing the contest, he broke the 'holt' and threw me. When I remarked that he had broken his agreement, he only laughed and said, 'I threw you, didn't I?' And to every objection I made, he made the same answer. The fact of having won (it did not matter how) was pleasing to him. It satisfied him, although it wouldn't have contented me."

"Did you ever talk over success in life with him?"

"Yes, quite often. He was bent on making money, and did considerable trading among us schoolboys,—sold me some of his books. I felt then that my view of life was more satisfactory to me than his would have been. I wanted to obtain a competence, and then devote myself to high thinking instead of to money-making."

"How did you plan to attain this end?"

"By study. I began in my sixteenth or seventeenth year to try to express myself on paper, and when, after I had left the country school, I attended the seminary at Ashland and at Cooperstown. I often received the highest marks in composition, though only standing about the average in general scholarship. My taste ran to essays, and I picked up the great works in that field at a bookstore, from time to time, and filled my mind with the essay idea. I bought the whole of Dr. Johnson's works at a second-hand bookstore in New York, because, on looking into them, I found his essays appeared to be of solid literature, which I thought was just the thing. Almost my first literary attempts were moral reflections, somewhat in the Johnsonian style."

"You were supporting yourself during these years?"

"I taught six months and 'boarded round' before I went to the seminary. That put fifty dollars into my pocket, and the fifty paid my way at the seminary. Working on the farm, studying and teaching filled up the years until 1863, when I went to Washington and found employment in the Treasury Department."

"You were connected with the Treasury then?"

"Oh, yes; for nearly nine years. I left the department in 1872, to become a receiver of a bank, and subsequently for several years performed the work of a bank examiner. I considered it only as an opportunity to earn and save up a little money on which I could retire. I managed to do that, and came back to this region, where I bought a fruit farm. I worked that into a paying condition, and then gave all my time to the pursuit of the studies I like."

"Had you abandoned your interest in nature during your Washington life?"

"No. I gave as much time to the study of nature and literature as I had to spare. When I was twenty-three, I wrote an essay on 'Expression,' and sent it to the 'Atlantic.' It was so Emersonian in style, owing to my enthusiasm for Emerson at that time, that the editor thought some one was trying to palm off on him an early essay of Emerson's which he had not seen. He found that Emerson had not publishd any such paper, however, and printed it, though it had not much merit. I wrote off and on for the magazines."

The editor in question was James Russell Lowell, who, instead of considering it without merit, often expressed afterwards the delight with which he read this contribution from an unknown hand, and the swift impression of the author's future distinction which came to him with that reading.

"Your successful work, then, has been in what direction?" I said.

"In studying nature. It has all come by living close to the plants and animals of the woods and fields, and coming to understand them. There I have been successful. Men who, like myself, are deficient in self-assertion, or whose personalities are flexible and yielding, make a poor show in business, but in certain other fields these defects become advantages. Certainly it is so in my case. I can succeed with bird or beast, for I have cultivated my ability in that direction. I can look in the eye of an ugly dog or cow and win, but with an ugly man I have less success.

"I consider the desire which most individuals have for the luxuries which money can buy, an error of mind," he added. "Those things do not mean anything except a lack of higher tastes. Such wants are not necessary wants, nor honorable wants. If you cannot get wealth with a noble purpose, it is better to abandon it and get something else. Peace of mind is one of the best things to seek, and finer tastes and feelings. The man who gets these, and maintains himself comfortably, is much more admirable and successful than the man who gets money and neglects these. The realm of power has no fascination for me. I would rather have my seclusion and peace of mind. This log hut, with its bare floors, is sufficient. I am set down among the beauties of nature, and in no danger of losing the riches that are scattered all about. No one will take my walks or my brook away from me. The flowers, birds and animals are plentifully provided. I have enough to eat and wear, and time to see how beautiful the world is, and to enjoy it. The entire world is after your money, or the things you have bought with your money. It is trying to keep them that makes them seem so precious. I live to broaden and enjoy my own life, believing that in so doing I do what is best for everyone. If I ran after birds only to write about them, I should never have written anything that anyone else would have cared to read. I must write from sympathy and love,—that is, from enjoyment,—or not at all. I come gradually to have a feeling that I want to write upon a given theme. Whenever the subject recurs to me, it awakens a warm, personal response. My confidence that I ought to write comes from the feeling or attraction which some subjects exercise over me. The work is pleasure, and the result gives pleasure."

"And your work as a naturalist is what?"

"Climbing trees to study birds, lying by the waterside to watch the fishes, sitting still in the grass for hours to study the insects, and tramping here and there, always to observe and study whatever is common to the woods and fields."

"Men think you have done a great work," I said.

"I have done a pleasant work," he said, modestly.

"And the achievements of your schoolmate Gould do not appeal to you as having anything in them worth aiming for?" I questioned.

"Not for me. I think my life is better for having escaped such vast and difficult interests."

The gentle, light-hearted naturalist and recluse came down the long hillside with me, "to put me right" on the main road. I watched him, as he retraced his steps up the steep, dark path, lantern in hand. His sixty years sat lightly upon him, and as he ascended I heard him singing. Long after the light melody had died away, I saw the serene little light bobbing up and down in his hand, disappearing and reappearing, as the lone philosopher repaired to his hut and his couch of content.

Notes

1. "Fame Found in Quiet Nooks," *Success* 1 (September 1898): 5–6. On John Burroughs. Reprinted as "John Burroughs at Home: The Hut on the Hill Top" in *How They Succeeded,* pp. 327–40; also as "Jay Gould's Chum Chooses 'High Thinking, Not Money-Making,' and Wins Success without Riches—John Burroughs" in *Little Visits with Great Americans,* pp. 402–12. John Burroughs (1837–1921).
2. Jason Gould (1836–1892), American financier.

Haunts of Nathaniel Hawthorne[1]

However Salem may have looked in the days when the numerous craft of the old colonies harbored in the smooth waters of its bay, and when, as one humorist has put it, "Witch Hill was its chief centre of amusement," it has to-day many of the ear-marks of a modern city. The railroad, electric light and trolley have so threaded, glared upon and outraged its ancient ways, that you, who are only familiar with all that is historic and quaint in its affairs, stay in disappointment and chagrin, to exclaim, "Can this be?" It is so modern in parts. Why, only a block from the now large and grimy railroad station, there stood in Hawthorne's time "the town pump," which gave forth such a dainty and inspiring rill of thought concerning its own vocation. Some seven trolley lines pass around that identical corner now! The very bowels of the earth from which it drew the sparkling liquid, have been torn out to make way for a smoky two-track tunnel, and steam cars now pass where once the darksome well held its cool treasure in store for man and beast.

It is the public square and the newer portions of Salem which stir the feeling that all the quaintness and charm have departed, and, on the whole, it is well, for after the first cursory glance, expecting little, there is a reviving pleasure in finding a great deal.

While there are new streets, new homes and new interests, there are still the old streets and the old homes, now dark, and tottering, and bleak. In Charter Street, only a few blocks from the depot, in what is not the "old portion" of the town, lies the little cemetery familiar to the readers of "Dr. Grimshaw's Secret" and "The Dolliver Romance." Such an ancient, moss-grown burying ground it is a melancholy pleasure to look upon, for it smiles sadly with the memory of the burials of hundreds of years. Here, among the sunken and turf-grown graves, reposes the dust of many a worthy colonial dignitary, all solemn in his living pretensions, and grimly written over as befits his chill and sanctimonious ashes. Some of the graves contain Hawthorne's mariner ancestors, some of whom sailed forth on the ocean of eternity nearly two centuries ago. Among the curiously carved gravestones of slate, we see that of John Hawthorne, the "witch-judge" of Hawthorne's note books, and close at hand are the graves of the ancestors of the novelist's wife. The sombre house which encroaches upon a corner of the cemetery enclosure, with the green willows surging about it so closely, that its side windows are within our reach from the grave-stones, was the home of the Peabodys, whence Hawthorne wooed the amiable Sophia, and where in his tales he domiciled Grandsir "Dol-liver" and "Dr. Grimshaw." You find it rather a poor mansion, big-roofed and low studded, with small windows and weather-beaten sides. Evidently once a very respectable "mansion" after the New England acceptance of the word, but now exceedingly humble and the abode of many a hidden grief, no doubt.

Only a few blocks further off is the Custom House where Haw-thorne did irksome duty as "Locofoco Surveyor," its exterior being, except for the addition of a cupola, essentially unchanged since his description was written. The wide, worn granite steps still lead up to the entrance portico, and above hovers the same enormous gilded eagle, " a shield before her breast, and, if I recollect aright, a bunch of intermingled thunderbolts and barbed arrows in each claw." In Haw-thorne's time, the customs collections amounted to about $50,000 a year, where now they scarcely average $10,000, and Derby wharf, which once was alive with merchantmen from all parts of the world, now stretches for an eighth of a mile, a dilapidated and partially deserted structure, with bleak sheds and decaying structures on every hand. It was in this Custom House, in an old baggage room, that the old scarlet letter A was found by Hawthorne, and subsequently used as the basis, in idea, of his romance.

Still a little way on, and in a side street called Turner, which runs directly down to the water-side, we find the much disputed "House of the Seven Gables," with its peaked roof, small glazed windows and wealth of overhanging trees. Whether this is for certain the identical house of Hawthorne's romance or no, is a subject not broachable here for discussion. Certainly it originally had many gables, which have now disappeared, and it answers more nearly the description given in the book than any other in Salem or elsewhere.

Sauntering along the "Main Street" of Hawthorne's sketch, and the other shady avenues he knew so well, the curious old tower, which in the discontent of arrival we called tame and unattractive, seems to grow more and more picturesque, and even beautiful. If we follow "the long, lazy street," Witch Hill, which the novelist describes in "Alice Doane's Appeal," we may behold from that unhappy spot, where men and women suffered death for imagined misdoings, the whole of Hawthorne's Salem, with the environment he pictures in "Sights from the Steeple." We see the house-roofs of the town—half hidden by clustering foliage—extending now from the slopes of the fateful hill to the glistening waters of the harbor, the farther expanse of field and meadow, dotted with white villages and scored with shadowy waterways; the craggy coast with the Atlantic thundering endlessly against its headland.

It was here that Hawthorne began his life and achieved his distinction. And the number of pilgrims from all parts of the world who go to Salem to look at the old, brown, gambrel-roofed house, numbered 21 Union Street—because here nearly a century ago, in 1804, Nathaniel Hawthorne was born in its northwest corner, second story room—is very large, and each year increasing. It is the same old house, with the same monster chimney, that it was in 1804, or for that matter, in 1704, so long has it been in existence. It is said to have been built by Capt. Benjamin Pickman, who was a Salem shipmaster in 1700. At all events, Nathaniel Hawthorne's grandfather lived in it as early as 1772, and it was the home of his father and mother from their marriage until 1808, when the father, also a shipmaster, died in foreign parts. The house is now the home of a "family of foreign extraction," but is well preserved, neat and tidy.

It was only for four short years that Hawthorne lived here. Immediately upon the death of Robert Hawthorne,[2] Mrs. Hawthorne

The birthplace of Hawthorne, No. 21 Union St., Salem

moved to No. 12 Herbert Street, a house owned and partly occupied by her father, Richard Manning. This is, and was then, the next street east of Union, and the backyards of the two houses joined. Mr. Manning had a large stable and a stage office near by on Union Street. The Manning house was a large, three story one, severely plain. To-day it is a common tenement house. Once it was Hawthorne's home for nearly a quarter of a century in all; now a strange assortment of humanity fills it and gives an atmosphere of narrow means and depressing difference to the entire scene.

It is not difficult, however, to identify the haunted chamber which was Hawthorne's bedroom and study. The little dark, dreary apartment under the eaves, with its multi-paned window looking down into the room where he was born, is to all of us one of the most interesting of the Hawthorne shrines. Here the magician kept his solitary vigil during the long period of his literary probation, shunning his family, declining almost all human fellowship and sympathy, and for some time going abroad only after nightfall. Here he studied, pondered, wrote, revised, destroyed, day after day, as the slow months went by; and here, after ten years of working and waiting for the world to know him, he triumphantly recorded, "In this dismal chamber fame was won." He had completed the first volume of "Twice-Told Tales."

His first period of residence here lasted from 1808 to 1818, when the family moved to Raymond, Maine, for four years. Hawthorne was away scarcely twelve months when he returned to Salem to fit for college early the next fall, his college expenses being defrayed by his maternal uncle, Robert Manning, a brother of Richard Manning, who owned the No. 12 Herbert Street house, and permitted his sister, Hawthorne's mother, to dwell there, rent free.

It was in his year at Raymond that Hawthorne began his life of restlessness. Here, he says he "got his cursed habit of solitude. He would skate for hours on the great lake in the solitude" of night, and if he got too far away from home to return, would seek shelter in some logger's cabin and there pass the night, warmed by a roaring wood fire, watching the silent stars.

After his two years' preparation in Salem, he entered Bowdoin, where he remained four years, returning to Salem and the Manning house during vacation. The habit of roaming the country, begun at Raymond, was continued in Brunswick. The companionships there formed are as widely known almost as is the story of Hawthorne's own life. There were Longfellow, Franklin Pierce[3] and Horatio Bridge.[4] With Bridge, Hawthorne explored the country road for many miles. There is even to-day the Hawthorne brook at Brunswick. In that then unnamed stream "we often fished for the small trout," says Bridge, "that were to be found there; but the main charm of these outings was in indolent loitering along the low banks of the little stream."

When Hawthorne left college, his mother had removed from Raymond, Maine, to the house at 12 Herbert Street, and here he returned. For some little time thereafter he seems to have drifted. It was of his life at this time, from 1825 to 1828, that Hawthorne himself, wrote: "I had always a natural tendency toward seclusion; and this I now indulged to the utmost, so that, for months together, I scarcely had human intercourse outside my own family, seldom going out except at twilight, or only to take the nearest way to the most convenient solitude, which was often at the seashore."

From Herbert Street, sometime in 1828, the Hawthornes moved to Dearborn Street, in North Salem, remaining there four years in comparative comfort. In 1832, the family left this house and moved downtown again into dingy Herbert Street. I take it these frequent changes were the result of Mrs. Hawthorne's dependency, and their living at all times in Mr. Manning's houses, and were made to accommodate him or his family. This time Hawthorne lived at 12 Herbert Street, most of the next seven years. He boarded in Boston a few months at a time, on one or two occasions, while engaged in editorial and other literary work there, but came down to Salem every week or two. During this time also, his contributions to magazines were becoming notable, and the Peabody girls of Salem, one of whom was to become his wife, were attracted by them, although they did not discover that he was the author until 1837, and it was nearly a year later that they made his acquaintance. From that time until Dr. Peabody and his family moved to Boston, Hawthorne was a frequent visitor to the Charter Street house, which I have already spoken of as "Dr. Grimshaw's" abode. During these years Hawthorne also completed the first volume of "Twice-Told Tales," which gained him recognition as the greatest master of pure English living.

In 1838, he became engaged to Miss Peabody, and under stress of shortly needing to provide a home for his wife to be, he secured a position as weigher and gauger in the Boston Custom House, which he held from January, 1839, to April, 1841. His diary and letters bear evidence of his distaste for his duties, and he decided not to trust to that for a livelihood, in view of his matrimonial venture. When he began his work there, he wrote to Longfellow, telling how many and what kind of sketches he intended to produce as a result of his leisurely official life, but he did absolutely nothing of that kind. A few lines from the notebook will show how irksome to him was the weighing of coal on an old schooner. "April 19, 1840. What a beautiful day yesterday! My spirit rebelled against being confined in my darksome dungeon at the Custom House. When I shall be again free, I will enjoy all things with the fresh simplicity of a child five years old. I will go forth and stand in a summer shower, and all the worldly dust that has collected on me shall be washed away at once, and my heart will be like a bank of fresh flowers for the weary to rest upon."

His duties finally ended here with a political change in the Government, and the young romancer now indulged in that venture into communism which is really too well known to require repetition. It was in 1841–42 that he was a member of the Brook Farm community, and it scarcely need be remarked that his joining it was but one more mark of his restlessness of spirit. He joined the company the year before his marriage, thinking to bring his wife there the next year should his own experiment prove satisfactory. It did not. There was too much restraint, or not enough freedom for a man of his roving disposition, and he produced nothing at all in a literary way. His diary records an occasional walk and general complaints.

There was once more a return to Salem, then, and Herbert Street, where he married Miss Peabody, and where he brought her to board for the first seven months of his married life. After that, in July, 1842, having hired the Old Manse at Concord, of Dr. Ripley,[5] he removed there, and the most delightful period of his life began. It was a beautiful old house which his modest income permitted him to support. The picturesque old mansion stands amid greensward and foliage, its ample grounds divided from the highway by a low wall, its northernmost lawn washed by the quiet waters of the Concord River. "It was created," he wrote at the time, "by Providence expressly for our use, and at the precise time when we wanted it," and then added, with his frequent twists of humor, "it contains no water either fit to drink or bathe in. Only imagine Adam trudging out of Paradise with a bucket in each hand, to get water to drink, or for Eve to bathe in. Intolerable!"

His diary reeks with the delights of the new life. After breakfast one morning, he took his fishing-rod and went down through the orchard to the riverside, but as three or four boys were already in possession of the best spots, he did not fish. He swam in it from time to time, and was three weeks in discovering which way the tide moved. Once he declared, "I bathe once and often twice a day in our river but one dip into the salt of the sea would be worth more than a whole week's soaking in such a lifeless tide."

At Concord Hawthorne found many friends, among whom were Emerson, Thoreau, Bronson Alcott[6] and his family, including Louisa May,[7] Ellery Channing, the poet, Margaret Fuller[8] and others. Naturally where so many literary celebrities were located there was a procession of distinguished visitors, and we hear of almost every great American literary personage as having called at the house at sometime or other during Hawthorne's stay. He explored the surrounding territory with Thoreau and Ellery Channing, and the volumes of those gentlemen, who make it a point to seek out and weep over every nook wherein those noble souls disported themselves, tell us of dozens of shadowy places along the river where Hawthorne frequently went to drowse and ponder. He was conspicuous as a character to Concord residents, who often observed the darkly clad figure of the recluse hoeing in his patch, where he went to destroy what he spoke of as "weeds," next "more weeds," then a "ferocious banditti of weeds," with which "the other Adam," could never have contended.

His stay in the old Manse was for an all too brief period of four years, when financial circumstances dictating, he accepted the office of Surveyor of the Port of Salem. When he left Concord, he resided for a few months on Carver Street, Boston, where the first child, a son, was born. In November the family entered Salem, and took the house which is now numbered 18 Chestnut Street, but soon changed to decidedly less pretentious quarters on a downtown side street; having accomplished no literary work of whatsoever character at the other place.

14 Mall Street (the less pretentious spot) is, to many, the most noted of all the Hawthorne houses in America or Europe, because in it he wrote his masterpiece, "The Scarlet Letter." The house dates back into the last century, but is still well preserved and even charming in appearance, being quite large, three stories, and surrounded by trees and shrubbery. Hawthorne's study was in the third floor front room, but the room where he kept the manuscript of "The Scarlet Letter" is believed to have been on the second floor. It was in this house, in the winter of 1849–50, that James T. Fields[9] found Hawthorne "alone in a chamber over a sitting-room of the dwelling, and as the day was cold he was hovering near the stove." After trying to get from him some statement as to what he had been writing, and failing of a satisfactory answer, Fields started to go downstairs, having bade his host good-by and shut the door. Hawthorne came running quickly after with a manuscript in his hands which he handed to the publisher, and hurried back to his chamber. The result is a matter of common knowl-

edge. "The Scarlet Letter" made its author famous—the most noted man of letters of his time and country. It was substantially the only work he did while living in the Mall Street house, but if it had been all that he ever did, his name would be imperishable, and the house in which he penned it, of the greatest historic interest.

Hawthorne evidently had this story in mind sometime before he began to write it. He really dawdled through his Custom House years, and did little or no literary work until after his removal from the surveyorship through the trickery and betrayal of professing friends. He had saved nothing from his salary, and, but for the forethought of his wife in laying aside a hundred or two dollars of the money given to her for household expenses, they would have been penniless. As it was, sickness in the family, and the death of Hawthorne's mother, reduced them to straitened circumstances. This set the author to work. A liberal contribution from admiring and appreciative friends relieved them for the while, and until "The Scarlet Letter" was published. From that time to the end, Hawthorne's reputation enabled him to earn enough with his pen to provide the necessaries of life and much more, if he would work. From Mall Street, in the summer of 1850, the Hawthornes went to live in Lenox. It was then that they left Salem for good.

At Lenox he produced his other great romance, "The House of Seven Gables." The success of "The Scarlet Letter" contributed, no doubt, very largely to Hawthorne's incentive to do other literary work, and then, he needed the money. He had a small, red house at Lenox, near the Stockbridge Bowl, and although far from comfortable, he had no means of obtaining a better one. He only dwelt in Lenox one year, but in that time produced "The House of Seven Gables," and the "Wonder Book." In November, 1851, he removed to West Newton, where he set to work upon "The Blithedale Romance," and completed it by the last of the following April. In 1852 he returned to Concord, after a winter in Newton, having bought a modest house which he named the Wayside, and where, last summer, I saw as many as twenty-seven sightseers lined up before it, gazing in upon the affairs of the present quailing resident. It was in the house once occupied by the good Bronson Alcott, and where Louisa May, really lived out the story of "Little Women."

Hawthorne dwelt here in much dignity during the remainder of his days, excepting, of course, the seven years in which he traveled abroad, first as Consul at Liverpool, and then as our foremost man of letters. He resumed all his relations with his old Concord friends, and busied himself with many a literary affair. It was during his first year at the Wayside that he wrote "Tanglewood Tales" and "The Life of Franklin Pierce," his life-long friend. Besides some papers for the *Atlantic* he wrote "Our Old Home," "Dr. Grimshaw's Secret," "Septimius Felton" and "The Dolliver Romance" fragment.

For some months after the election to the Presidency of his friend, Franklin Pierce, the Wayside was frequented by office-seekers, but ordinarily Hawthorne had few visitors besides his Concord friends. Fields, Holmes,[10] Hilliard, Whipple,[11] Longfellow, Howells,[12] Horatio Bridge, the poet Stoddard, Henry Bright[13] and others visited him. Yet his own visits were very infrequent, and Alcott said that in the several years he lived next door Hawthorne came but twice into his house, good friends as they were; the first time he quickly excused himself because "the stove was too hot"; next time "because the clock ticked too loud."

This "Wayside" was the only home Hawthorne ever owned. To it he came from the "little red house" in Berkshire, and to it returned from his sojourn abroad. Here, with failing health and desponding spirits, he lived the gloomy war days—writing in his study, or, with step more uncertain, pacing his hill-top; from here he set out with Pierce on the last pleasure trip, which ended in his death, and from this house his body was taken to the old colonial church in Concord and thence to "Sleepy Hollow," the beautiful graveyard where all the whole Concord company now sleep.

The funeral took place on the 23d of May, 1864, and was conducted by the Rev. James Freeman Clark, who had performed Hawthorne's marriage service two-and-twenty years before. It was a mild, sunny afternoon, "the one bright day in the long week of rain" as Longfellow said, and the cemetery at Sleepy Hollow was full of the fragrance and freshness of May. The grave was dug at the top of the little hill, beneath a group of tall pines, where Hawthorne and his wife had often sat in days gone by and planned their pleasure hours. When the rites at the grave were over, the crowd moved away, and at last the carriage containing Mrs. Hawthorne followed. But at the gate of the cemetery stood, on either side of the path, Longfellow, Holmes, Whittier, Lowell, Pierce, Emerson, and a half dozen more; and as the carriages passed between them they uncovered their honored heads in honor of Hawthorne's widow.

If there be any solace for the bereaved in this transient world of ours, I think it must be in some such expression of reverence and honor. It surely can be found in nothing less.

Notes

1. "Haunts of Nathaniel Hawthorne," *Truth* 17 (21 September 1898): 7–9; (28 September 1898): 11–13. Published as one article in two separate issues. Nathaniel Hawthorne (1804–1864).

2. Robert Hawthorne, Hawthorne's father, was a sea captain and died of yellow fever at Surinam.

3. Franklin Pierce (1804–1869), fourteenth president of the United States (1853–57), appointed Hawthorne, who had written Pierce's campaign biography, as consul at Liverpool in 1853.

4. Horatio Bridge (1806–1893), author of *Journal of an African Cruise,* with whom Hawthorne formed a lifelong friendship at Bowdoin College.

5. George Ripley was a prominent native citizen of Concord.

6. Amos Bronson Alcott (1799–1888), teacher and philosopher.

7. Louisa May Alcott (1832–1888), author of *Little Women.*

8. Margaret Fuller (1810–1850), critic and reformer.

9. James Thomas Fields (1817–1881), American poet and editor of the *Atlantic Monthly* (1861–71). His wife held a literary salon in their home.

10. Oliver Wendell Holmes (1809–1894).

11. Edwin Percy Whipple (1819–1886) contributed his critical essays to the *North American Review.*

12. See Dreiser's article, "The Real Howells," included in this collection.

13. Henry Arthur Bright (1830–1884), educated at Cambridge, was a regular contributor of literary criticism to the *Athenaeum,* and wrote hymns and religious poems for Unitarian collections. He was an intimate friend of Hawthorne, and his name is often mentioned in the *English Note-Books.*

The Real Zangwill[1]

In this our day of quickly-made reputations and rapid declines, when the world, so anxious to seize upon a doer of deeds, examine him, estimate his worth and classify him, we see strange things. All our promising youths of the time have scarce a season in which to mature before they are plucked green, as one might say, and sunned, lauded, idolized, until what with their achievement of this public recognition, so often the only or chief incentive to great endeavor and labor, they become perverted from silent but glorious tasks and for want of other aspiration or inspiration, decay. That it is true that you cannot eat your cake and have it, too, meets daily its exposition in the literary world. You cannot be lauded as a genius, a world wonder, see all your dreams of distinction realized and still dream of distinction. Once you have had it the haunting desire to obtain it, the great desire *to do*, and be honored therefore passes, and genius too quickly hailed, withers and decays, a victim of the overestimate.

I shall not say this with any particular emphasis of its relation to the present subject, but merely as a general truth, which borne in mind, makes for a clearer and more honestly critical atmosphere, and helps each to decide with the aid of the evidence presented, what the value of a man may be.

The readers of many magazines and reviews have heard of Mr. Zangwill—I. Zangwill[2]—and of late in our own country the general public has caught the name from the daily papers, and bandied it, without further knowledge, from mouth to mouth, as the general public is very often wont to do. We have asserted, as accepted, that he has talent; fine critical ability, wit, good nature and even sympathy. Accepted as of great value in the critical world, he is also read as a novelist, admired as a contributor and railed at for what is so common a failing to-day, excessive egotism. You will find him, said a writer of the *Critic*[3] to me, "a most self-assured individual. Heaven save young men from modesty, but there are limits. This man is as peculiar as he is able, and you will find him possessed of most extraordinary conceit."

This I knew before was a characteristic of his books, but never having met him, I did not know it extended to his person. In "Without Prejudice," we find, "I know I am cleverer than the man in the street," and not said in a way that can be modified or softened by the context. Whatever we may think of this and other sentences, men usually halt before saying so disputable a thing. To write smartly is but a peculiarity, some maintain—a thing apart from greatness, and the humblest may meditate such heights of truth perennial that no reviewer great or small could say "I am cleverer," without convicting himself of smallness in being so. The very ignorant sympathies of the poorest of the unwashed are often more holy in tendency than the finer analyses of the egotist, devoid of sympathies, small or large.

However, this is of the book, not the man, and there endeth the charge. Concensus of opinion has not rendered to Mr. Zangwill's literature the highest, though a high, place. The critics of the world have said "The Ghetto Tragedies" were well done, "Flutterduck," too, was excellent work. We have laughed at the "King of the Schnorrers," and there have been one or two other short stories since, and what else is there? Nothing save some witty, precise and keenly analytical essays, in which we cannot expect to find great heart or soul because these qualities are not usually put there, forsooth.

Good fortune blessed me with a happy day. I saw him fresh from the boat, a slow, peculiar man. He looked tired, he was in tow, there was neither wish nor intention on my part to speak with him, but there he was. Readily came the thought, he ignores smooth dressing. As striking as a celebrity with long hair, he still did not wear his hair long. With trousers loose and baggy, a commonplace frock coat, hat indifferent, loose flowing tie, he glanced as with a heavy head, and shuffled with his feet at times, peculiarly. Nothing strange about this, if a man so chooses, but it is not common to all literary men and therefore mentionable. It would be impossible to say *affected,* for he. looked too serious, his head is too large, his features too marked, there is a stillness in the eye, and an altogether physical ugliness, so modified by intellect as to become wholly interesting and strange. If he were poor, ignorant, divested of that critical light of reason and forward self-assertiveness of wisdom, you would turn him out of doors for his looks. As it is, you draw near and listen.

Next he appeared at the Tolstoi dinner. Seated at the right hand of the spokesman of the evening, a guest of honor but little changed in dress. A sea of white shirt-fronts danced before his eyes. The gentlemen were in black, solemn and in perfect order, but not so the young English Jew, so peculiar unto himself. Everything was quite conventional, but there he sat, loose tie, a sort of short coat of many wrinkles indicating long and comfortable adjustment to his person, a plain vest and trousers of some light check, which might have been faint green in color, or some other shade belied by the lamps. Others ate comfortably while he listened and talked; others eulogized Tolstoi most unaffectedly and some gushingly. When he arose, however, tall, thin, his shoulders stooping, his large near-sighted brown eyes looking through and around a pair of drooping noseglasses, and his mop of kinkiest black hair standing out about his head in a surprised manner, it was to say in a thin, unoratorical voice that he disagreed somewhat with what had been said.

He spoke facetiously, with a shaft of plain wit ever and anon, and a tendency to pun a little, as Englishmen do. Tolstoi was not wholly glorified. Not altogether were the white shirts, he said, honoring the Russian author, for if great honor were done him his admirers would abandon white shirts and wear blouses. So fine a repast was no honor, since Tolstoi believes in plain living, and he continued, showing wittily the incongruity of a feast in honor of the opponent of feasts, as well as pointing the limitations and failings of the Great Peasant, while admitting his sincerity. He divorced the man from his art, and admitted partial good in him, sitting down, only to hear the next speaker eulogize where he had but analyzed.

Great is the art of analysis, for it sits in judgment upon the heart. I was prepared for this facility of adopting and twisting facts in droll and convincing manner, but not for the conviction that he sees truth clearly, until he said: "Nature is a great effort to express truth. The constant changing, shifting, appearing and disappearing material is the effort of the spirit to express itself more and more clearly—more and more perfectly—that is beautifully." Afterward I decided that he sees truth as one sees an appearing man or bird or other moving object in the distance. You can easily imagine him saying: "Ho! there goes truth. See it. Do you follow quickly, it is good," and then calmly sitting still himself and looking for some other interesting object. That is the way his Tolstoi address affected me.

The last time I saw him we came straight up against each other, he self-absorbed, careless, indifferent, ready to get rid of another dull thing quickly, and I careful, curious and quite humble.

"Well," he said, brusquely, in a manner soon to change, "what will you have—what do you want to know?"

I explained a moment, and then we strolled roomward, his feet shuffling occasionally. Evidently he expected the machinery of thought to begin at once, and there was something of condescension and a "I will assist the nervous and bashful" in the way in which he said, "Well, begin. Why—um, you are as bashful as a young girl with her first sweetheart," whereupon I laughed.

"Not wholly—considerate, let us say."

He fumbled for a key, but being nearsighted could not find the keyhole, so I took the matter in hand and opened the door.

"Now, then," he said, when the lamps were turned up.

But not to be hastened, I let him work off the interest he manifested in an open portmanteau, loaded with a confusion of letters and papers, out of the jumble of which he sought something. When deepest in his search I said:

"I want to know about your critical point of view."

He stopped and straightened up out of the depths of letters, holding many in his hand and surveying the walls blankly.

"My point of view. Well, I have certain literary canons, certain canons of art, by which I measure things. It is one of my rules that you must never blame a book for not being some other book, a work of art for not being like something else. If you criticize it at all, that should be a warrant that the thing is worth criticizing. All that remains is to classify it. It is of such and such a period, such and such a school, such and such merit."

I wish every one who admires Zangwill sincerely could hear his voice. I wish they could feel how pleasant it is, how measured, how cadenced. It is but justice to offer praises here, when so little can be said for his oratorical ability. His "Well" is something fine, and the "I have my" is soft and not exasperating, however often repeated. The head is so solid, the bones so marked, the chin receding and therefore should be the augur of sensitiveness and a readiness to weep genuinely. It is the grace of learning he has with him, the music of refinement in motion, in voice, in glance. He appeals as grotesque old porcelain appeals, after a little while, but, ah! it is not always the artistic, the intellectual, that satisfies. We accept all these things as fine premonitions and then seek and seek. But if we find not the heart, if we find not the heart!

"You find many good things that way," I said.

"All that I criticize has its place," he answered.

"Under such a system as that it seems to me you should find a place for everything and quite a respectable word for everything if you chose."

He turned on me a quizzical glance, which did not rest long. The truth is, he sees so poorly through glasses that it does not repay him to stare.

"No. A work once classified must be judged in relation to its value to the world in its particular field. There are still ample grounds for praise or condemnation."

"You have noted, of course, the tendency of the literati to grow more and more mournful, more pessimistic? One of your Englishmen, Hardy, strikes a peculiarly despairing note."

"Yes, every age has its pessimism. Pessimism is not a sign of despair but discontent. Now we know, of course, that discontent is the lever that moves the world, and the greater the pessimism the surer is the approach of change, for pessimism means that one order is bad and must give way to something else. Therefore it is a hopeful sign."

"What do you admire most in literature—what spirit or attitude?"

"The hopeful defiant one, of course. Such a note as we find in Shakespeare."

"And you consider great literature to be always hopeful literature?"

"Well, if a poem is inspiring, if it lifts you up and makes you strong, it is certainly the best thing."

"That may be, but we have still to say whether the great literature is hopeful. Take the world novels, the world poems—are not the masterpieces sad, the most thrilling passages those of agony undergone?"

"Well," he said, pausing with a critical air and extending one hand with that argumentative grace common to lawyers, "of course the note of bitterness, the wail is always the most moving. We cannot deny that the grand things are spoken of human sorrow and human suffering. It is so in all nations and all literatures."

"Yet you count this general acclaim of the works which are most sorrowful, which drag down the spirit and often compel tears, a hopeful sign?"

"Yes, in the main, the grand passions which move the heart, uplift and strengthen and broaden."

"And still the hopeful defiant note which sees only good in life is best?"

"I think so."

"We are confronted at this day and date by what I choose to call Omarism—the vast and growing delight of the many in the pathetic and despairing verses of the Persian Poet.[4] You have noted it, of course?"

"Poor poem it is—poor in philosophy, I mean. That is a kind of weakling view to take of life to say, 'I cannot understand it, we are victims of fate, therefore I will drown the memory of it in drink.' Quite a poor view I should say."

"And what of the many who read it with delight, take it to heart, and call it a true exponent of the real conditions?"

"They share a poor view."

"Then you would call it anything but a hopeful sign?"

"I must."

The conversation languished at this time, owing to the arrival of a bellboy, who lorded the situation for a moment and patronized us both.

"I believe," said the eminent critic, "I shall have a stimulant of some kind," and therewith glanced at me.

"Thanks, I never do," I smiled.

"How curious, and an American journalist, too; how curious!" he drawled. "I thought you all did."

"You were saying in your Tolstoi address," I went on when the boy had departed, "that the relationship between a man and his work means nothing either for the merit of the man or the merit of the work."

"Exactly. You would not call a good pair of shoes bad because they were made by a drunken, swearing shoemaker, nor a poor pair good, though they were made by one who devoutly practices the Christian code of morals. Neither can you condemn a book for any failing of its author."

"How," said I, "about the works of Paul Verlaine, Oscar Wilde, or the historic Villon?[5]—would you accept their work as valuable, and preserve it as a part of the world's treasure?"

"Um—assuredly. What would we say of their work, if nothing were known of their personality—as is the case with Shakespeare?"

"Then a man may degrade himself as he pleases and still be accepted on his literary side."

The critic halted, looking upward with one eye, his mental machinery fully at work.

"Pray do not misinterpret me. Understand I speak from the purely critical point of view. I speak of the works as divorced from the man, you know. They could be accepted where the man could not. What the moralist would say of the man, how his personality might or should be treated by the religionist, the lover of pure society and so on, need not concern the critic. It is the work he deals with."

"True at least to your philosophy," I answered, and not without discretion, for I spoke from knowledge of Mr. Zangwill's writings.

He is a man who sees all that is to be done, the politics that are to be purified, the religions revised or swept away, the art to be renovated, the social inequalities to be adjusted, and yet, who seeing the need in each particular field for a man to lay hold and help improve—who hearing the call for enthusiasts, prophets, reformers—men to put their shoulder to the separate wheels, prefers where there are so many things that need attention, to sit critically at the centre and observe them, judging of the efforts of those who come with separate convictions, to toil with various aims. One can imagine this man saying to the reformer: "Ah! you have only one portion of the question. You ignore all the other things done, you are narrow," and so going the rounds, while doing absolutely nothing himself but criticizing. It is the great analytical spirit, useful no doubt, but the world loves an enthusiast better, who criticizes not at all, but seizes upon the first thing to his hands and toils kindly, if blindly, in the thought that his is the great and necessary labor. Certainly such a life bespeaks a greater soul, if keen sympathies make soul, than does that of the man who can sit off and eternally pass judgment, unmoved forever to ally himself heart and hand with any one great effort for the uplifting of humanity. If no cause ever appeals to him sufficiently to enlist all his effort, he has not the wealth of sympathy, which the other man has who can be moved to so ally himself—is in other words the pure critic.

Zangwill was born thirty-three years ago in London. He was the son of a poor Jew, and went to the free Hebrew schools in the Ghetto neighborhood. He was the brightest pupil they had ever had there and took all the prizes that were to be taken.

He became a teacher in these schools finally and during that time studied and obtained his degree at the London University. He has been writing now for eight years. From the first his books were discussed in England, and his brilliant *causerie* in the *Pall Mall*[6] every month was one of the most attractive and popular features of that magazine.

Mr. Zangwill is a prominent feature of London literary life, and one must admit, after conversation with him, that his rare magnetism and brilliant gifts as a talker are made still more attractive by an almost womanish sweetness of manner and of speech. He is not guilty of monologues—it seems impossible to entice him into one. If you are worth talking to you are worth listening to in his estimation, and he develops conversation easily. Also, he rights himself quickly when his various views clash, and will when faced by a direct question, which if answered according to natural expectations might entrap him, execute some of the most marvelous mental gymnastics, always landing safely with an answer, which opens up a new avenue of thought.

His whimsical fancies are many. It is told of him that one day he was discoursing on the difficulty people of liberal tendencies experience when they go to church. The music and chanting appeal strongly to their senses, he declared, but they were pained by the dogma, or, from their point of view, the untruth contained in the words of the music. "Why," he asked, "cannot something be sung that we all feel convinced is true? For instance: 'The square of the hypothenuse of a right angle triangle is equal to the sum of the squares of the other two sides. Praise be unto Euclid, etc.'"

"We were," says the writer who first retailed it, "in the old Jesuit chapel in Antwerp when he chanted this blasphemy, and I wondered that the walls didn't fall on him before we could get away."

His absence of modesty is notorious. On one occasion its absence prompted him to propose at a London banquet the toast of literature, coupled with the name of Mr. Zangwill. "I said," thus runs his own description, "that I could wish that some one more competent and distinguished than myself had been chosen to do justice to such a toast (to himself) and to such a distinguished man of letters, but I did my best to pay him the tribute he deserved ere I sat down amid universal applause. When I arose amid renewed cheers to reply, I began by saying that I could wish that some one more competent and distinguished than myself had been chosen to respond to so important a toast—the last speaker had considerably over-rated my humble achievements in the fields of literature. So you see," he added in his account, "that I could easily master the modest manner if I took any pains to set any store by it."

We had got now to American literature and other things American, and I asked him with some interest:

"You realize that we have no distinctive poet in this our excellent land."

"There is no name, it is true, that stands out with any distinctness at present."

"Will you give your opinion as to why the multitude of minor poets all strike a pathetic note in their verse?"

"Your question is a confusion of terms, you see," he said, blandly. "It answers itself. The word minor really means the sorrowful chord and therefore——"

"I understand," I interrupted, "your interpretation of the word, but I use it in the popular sense, meaning the poets who write but one or two excellent things and are no more heard of."

"I cannot make ready answer. I have observed the melancholy of our minor English poets also. The explanation is, I suppose, that the predominant thought in the world is of the sorrow endured, the separations borne, the losses incurred. It has been so since the world began and I judge always will be while love and death continue."

"There is another discussion here, concerning the value of poetry. A number of our leading newspapers now maintain that poetry is no longer needed, that it is passing, and that there never will be another great poet."

"So? I had not heard of it."

"Do you subscribe to that opinion?"

"Oh, there will always be the need of the poetic. We will have it in some form or other. It may not survive in its present shape. Every race has a peculiar form of it and always will have, I should say. Now, the Jews had the poetry of repetition—the repeating the same idea over and over with emphasis as, for instance, in the Psalm, 'My soul thirsteth for thee—my flesh longeth for thee in a dry and thirsty land,' which is really the same thought twice repeated. So we to-day have our poetry, not of that form, but still poetry."

"The idea as set forth by our journals is that the poetry of our kind, the metrical form now so common, will pass entirely, and that we will have only prose, with fine passages of a poetic nature here and there—do you believe that?"

"No; I think poetry will survive as long as the language: that great poets will appear from time to time. The separate form is capable of such exquisite use that it will not soon be abandoned without great loss to the race."

"I have not discussed your own life much—how is it with you?"

"Well, I see so many plays each month, review so many books, write so many criticisms for the magazines and so live—nothing more."

"We hear much of your crowded and disorderly desk, your method of working."

"Yes. They often discuss those things. Will they publish what we have talked about in a magazine here?" he added in a rather surprised tone.

"Oh, yes," I answered, "interwoven. Your personality will carry it."

He made no answer to this, but looked with peculiar force, and I rose to go.

"You are destined to create much comment, no doubt."

"Yes," he said, with that pleasant inoffensive way with which he accepts his own laurels, "yes," and there was an end of studying him.

But I could not help reflecting as I went out into the night, that this man of the wondrous self-assertiveness, who affects and probably does feel himself to be a type or spirit representative of a whole time or era, is yet so solemn, so odd-shapen, and a not over-strong combination of flesh and bone. He seeks happiness also, via this abundant raillery and sharp mannerisms.

He also, sitting off alone, unallied in heart or soul with any distinct separate effort or movement, because he sees so many efforts and movements, still wishes his own privileges and blessings however they may come.

And wishing these things, it becomes also plain that he finds himself urged to work and goes on toiling willy-nilly, that he may be what he desires to be. However, though he may consider it all for his own good or otherwise, Nature uses him as a great force, and he helps mankind even in the delusion that he honors and helps himself alone.

Critic though a man may be—thinking as he may, that he is sitting apart, (as he actually does from a certain few), still is he bound up in Nature, and other men rise by the aid of the very wit and wisdom with which he distinguishes himself. And all his exclusiveness, all his "I am cleverer than the man in the street" makes him no less a toiler in the great eventual cause with that man in the street, which uses genius as it uses stone, to build and build—whereunto we know not, and neither need we care.

Notes

1. "The Real Zangwill," *Ainslee's* 2 (November 1898): 351–57. Reprinted in part in Donald Pizer, ed., *Theodore Dreiser: A Selection of Uncollected Prose* (Detroit: Wayne State University Press, 1977), pp. 124–30.
2. Israel Zangwill (1864–1926).
3. The London *Critic* was one of the most prestigious literary journals of the day in England.
4. Omar Khayyam, also an astronomer, died in about 1123.
5. François Villon (1432?–1464?), the greatest French poet of the fifteenth century, wrote the famous "Ballad of Hanged Men" during his imprisonment.
6. The *Pall Mall Gazette* (1865–1923), founded by Frederick Greenwood (1830–1901), was intended to combine the features of a newspaper with the literary features of the *Saturday Review* and the *Spectator.*

Amelia E. Barr and Her Home Life[1]

Her Early Struggles and Final Success—What She Thinks of Men, Women, and Things.

Novel readers are familiar with the name of Amelia E. Barr. She has a record which makes less energetic women stand aside in awe. She has been the mother of fourteen children, has written thirty-two novels, has prepared a professor for Princeton College, and at sixty years of age is fresh and bright, and devotes nine hours daily to her work.

Mrs. Barr's Country Home

Every resident of Cornwall-on-the-Hudson knows Mrs. Barr, and can point the way of the winding road which ascends in long lines and curves 1,750 feet above the level of the river before it passes her gate. The mountain side is broad and green, and from the wide veranda, which encircles three sides of the house, the peaks of the Adirondacks can been seen in fine weather and miles and miles of the Hudson. There are orchards and cultivated fields above and below. Comfortable residences of men with plenty of money sit in staid dignity among fine old trees, and an air of reserve in comfort permeates the entire landscape.

Mrs. Barr's home is a house of plenty. It has a dozen or more large rooms, gables and striped awnings, a display of green plants in bright porcelain, and the windows are hung with good lace. Rugs and bric-à-brac, fine pictures and sketches, long shelves of elegantly bound volumes set in polished cases, and great solid pieces of furniture are arranged to invite to comfort and ease. There are servants, both men and women, and last of all Mrs. Barr, as hostess, dressed richly, as becomes her means, and of much amiability, as befits one who is successful.

On the veranda

Her Early Work

This is a very fine picture of success in letters, but fifteen years ago it was very different. Then it was a small apartment in a New York flat-house, a scarcity of even poor furniture, no means of support except a daily round of hack work for the papers, and a number of daughters to support. Mrs. Barr was then not many years in New York. She had been in Texas with her husband, a Scotch Presbyterian minister, who had brought her as his wife from a quiet English home. She had learned the calamitous lesson which love and death can often teach. Yellow fever had killed her husband and all her sons, leaving her helpless with her daughters looking to her for support. She had begun writing, and at the time of the turn in affairs had been writing for fifteen years. Not novels, however, for she did not know she could write a novel, but short stories, poems, editorials, and articles on every conceivable subject, from Herbert Spencer's theories to gentlemen's walking sticks.[2] During the earlier years of this hard apprenticeship she worked on an average for fifteen hours a day.

Her First Novel

Then came an accident. She fell and both dislocated and broke a leg. It was no time to be ill, but ill she was and the ability to earn anything temporarily cut short. Her strongest connection was with

the *New York Times,* and after ten days of absence they sent to her for
"copy." It was a friendly inquiry, however, and accompanied by the
comforting assurance that her salary would go on, such as it was. The
emissary who called asked about what she had on hand and learned of
a story which she had started, the pages of which lay in the drawer of
a wash-stand, also used for a writing-desk. These he surreptitiously
took away, and did her the service of conferring with a New York
publisher concerning the tale. She had quite a reputation as a contributor, poor as she was, and the book company, seeing indications of
great merit in these opening chapters of the story, sent an agent to
bargain for its completion and purchase. He set out with a $200 check
in his pocket, but was refused admission to the sick chamber. He
insisted, however, brushed past the guardian daughter, came to where
the invalid lay, and explained his errand. The story had merit; the
publishers wanted it; would she take $200 on account and finish it?
She distinctly would and did. Incapacitated as she was, a writing chair
was brought in and she began toiling to conclude "Jan Vedder's
Wife," which she finished in six weeks. The publishers thought it fine
and rushed it on the market. There was a big sale, some additional
checks for royalty, and then the tide turned. She launched out as a
novelist.

Those who visit the author's pleasant home at Cornwall will find no
trace of all this struggle. The shadow of grief has passed. Instead,
there are merriment and good dinners. Mrs. Barr moves in the picture as the most natural and important thing in it. She even takes a
philosophical view of the past, and if asked about the old days, sees
only their training influence.

"The fifteen years," she said to the writer once, "which I spent
working for the weekly and monthly periodicals were all for good.
They gave me the widest opportunities for information. I was amass-
ing facts and fancies, and developing intelligence. Struggles and sufferings were doing me good. You can't form many characters for
successful labor without the aid of much suffering. I had an alcove in
the Astor Library, and I practically lived in it. I slept and ate at home,
but I practically lived in that City of Books. I was in the prime of life,
but neither society nor amusements of any kind could draw me away
from the source of all my happiness and profit. Why, at the time when
I broke my leg, and said to myself, 'I shall lose all I have gained, I shall
fall behind in the race, all things are against me,' they were even then
all for me, only I did not know it."

Thus one may see how time can change an individual's point of
view.

Her Views of Life

"What do you think of life now?" I asked her.

"It's a very good thing. If you have thought it a very hard thing and a very bad thing, and then matters swing around and the causes of your ill feeling and suffering are taken away, you naturally have, or should have, a better feeling about it. I have. It isn't so much that one has extra to eat or wear, but the approbation, which is pleasant. You toil, and are rewarded by praise, let us say. That makes toil pleasant."

"You believe, of course, that everyone should work to remove the things that are in the way of happiness?"

"Why, of course. Only I feel also that it is a pleasant thing to help people who are trying to help themselves. The people who are closest to me are young strugglers who are trying to get up in the world. You can interest yourself in and do things for young strugglers which make them dear to you, wherever they come from."

There may be a touch of pathos in this, but with Mrs. Barr it is of a wholesome kind. She has just such a company of "young strugglers," as she calls them, who look up to her with affection and whom she does for, in the way of advice and literary assistance. Young people take to her in a most interesting manner, and it is truthfully related of her that during the last winter, spent at one of the fashionable hotels at Old Point Comfort, the most attended woman of the company of fair young ladies and gracious dames of fashion was Mrs. Barr. She was invariably accompanied by a train of young men, who basked in the sunshine of her radiating good nature, until the younger set remarked it, and common gossip demanded to know why. Finally, one of the more daring asked her: "How is it, Mrs. Barr, that you have so many young men to dance attendance on you all the time?"

"Why?" she answered; "why? Because I understand them and their aspirations. Young women don't. Young men come where they can hear the best sentiments expressed and where they will be encouraged in their ideals." And then she added one of her strongest thrusts at women in general: "Young men are better than young women. They have aims in life and they want to hear what to do. That's what I am constantly telling them."

What She Says of Women[3]

Her views concerning women are rather severe. She has the idea that most women are more or less vain, that they are *poseurs* and lack the fine aspiration and spiritual beauty of men. This is, of course, a prejudice, but interesting nevertheless.

"They are a queer lot," she said to me. "Not as good as men, by half; not as developed. They expect everyone to consider their feelings without examining their motives. To-day they are paddling in the turbid maelstrom of life and dabbling in unwomanly affairs and the most unsavory social questions, and yet they still think that men, at least, ought to regard them as the sacred sex. Men are noble about this thing and still generous believers in them. But women are not sacred by grace of sex if they voluntarily abdicate its limitations and its modesties, and make a public display of unsexed sensibilities and unabashed familiarity with subjects they have nothing to do with. If men criticise such women with asperity, it is not to be wondered at; they have so long idealized women that they find it hard to speak moderately. They excuse them too much, or else they are too indignant at their follies. Women want to be criticised by women, and then they will hear the bare uncompromising truth, and be the better for it. But it is good that women should be idealized, for in a measure they are elevated by it."

Rewards of Literature

On the subject of rewards of literature Mrs. Barr holds very interesting views. The discussion came about by the asking of whether she wrote a novel a year.

"Just about," she said. "I do fragmentary things between times, such as essays and so on, but manage to finish a novel with some regularity."

"The royalties on all the novels of yours that have been successful ought to make a handsome income by this time?"

"Well, they don't. I never published my books on royalty. I did my first one, which sold immensely well, and got a little over five hundred dollars out of it in dribs and drabs, which I spent as fast as they came. After that I demanded a lump sum of $5,000, selling the work outright. I don't worry over how much the publishers make. I get my $5,000 in such a shape that I can do something with it—buy property or bonds, and that pays; whereas, if I took royalty it would come dribbling in, $300 to $800 the quarter. I would spend it and always be poor."

"Your novels have a great sale in England. Don't you sell the English right for a good sum?"

"No; $5,000 covers everything. I give the American publisher all the rights. If I am going to be swindled I would rather be swindled by an American than an Englishman."

"I don't see the logic of that."

"Well, you would if you were an American author. For years I kept the English rights and sold them to an English publisher. When the year was up I would write and write for a settlement, but no answer. Never a word heard I, until I took a ship and strolled into the London office, defiant. Then there was a counting up and a payment, which just about covered my expenses, while my time and trouble went for nothing. Finally I decided not to run any more, and simply sold the whole thing out on this side."

"I count that truckling to injustice."

"Well, maybe so. Anyhow, the English house will have more trouble swindling my American publisher, and I gain some good will here by being liberal. It's the only way."

This system has been profitable in Mrs. Barr's case, anyhow, for with the "lump sums" annually she has been able to buy property and bonds of various kinds until now she has a tidy income and a dignified position in the world of finance. Her Cornwall place is large and well taken care of, the grounds beautiful, the house ornamental, and her style of living fashionable. In winter it is the Fifth Avenue Hotel, in New York, or the Hygeia, at Old Point Comfort, for her, with receptions and social calls, and the concluding of some work to pass away the day. She is a good manager in a way, and holds everything in hand with unrelaxing energy.

Mrs. Barr attributes her vitality and good spirits to her determination to be a philosopher and to her system of work. The quiet country life she finds best suited to her temperament. When she has a book on hand she devotes all her time to it, and she never writes at night. The early morning hours find her up and at work. She writes through the whole forenoon. After dining at noon she sleeps two hours, takes a cold plunge—the second of the day—and then carefully typewrites her morning's work. She never allows anyone to handle her manuscripts. Late in the afternoon come tea, callers and pleasure, but, no matter what is going on, Mrs. Barr is off to bed at nine o'clock. This routine is carefully followed all the while a book is being written, and after the book is out of the way the author gives herself up to pleasure. Her summers are usually spent in England, or were up to a year ago, though she has decided that she will trouble herself to leave America no more.

Notes

1. "Amelia E. Barr and Her Home Life," *Demorest's* 35 (March 1899): 103–04. On Amelia Edith Barr (1831–1919).

2. In the late 1890s Dreiser himself was engaged in writing short stories, poems, editorials, and articles on numerous subjects including Herbert Spencer. Like Barr, he had not yet tried his hand at the novel; shortly after writing this article he began writing his first novel *Sister Carrie* in earnest.

3. Dreiser similarly deals with the woman question in *A Gallery of Women* (New York: Liveright, 1929), a two-volume collection of fifteen semifictional portraits of women.

Edmund Clarence Stedman
at Home[1]

The veteran poet and critic who has won success in Wall Street and fame in the world of letters, and his home in the artistic colony at Lawrence Park, in New York's northern suburbs.

Not all poets have pleasant rural residences. Few of the high priests of song possess a wealth of books and paintings to shield them from an irritating sense of the outer bookless, paintingless world. But Edmund Clarence Stedman is a business man, as well as a poet and a critic, and combines artistic talent and critical judgment with commercial instinct.

Personally Stedman is a fine American type, young and handsome at sixty five years of age; active, bright eyed, witty, and generous. It is true that his full beard is silvery white, but in his vigor of mind and body he gives the lie to years and speaks the strength that scarce another score of them could undo.

But this is no place for expression of original opinions concerning the poet. Whittier, Bayard Taylor,[2] Frank Stockton,[3] Eugene Field,[4] William Dean Howells,[5] all have expressed their thought of him in prose and verse, and "poems to Stedman" are frequent enough. He seems to have inspired undying regard in those fine ethereal minds that have crossed his path. Whittier's last collection of poems, entitled "At Sundown," shows something of this, as the dedication to Stedman runs:

To E. C. S.

Poet and friend of Poet, if thy glass
Detects no flower in winter's tuft of grass,
    Let this slight token of the debt I owe
Outlive for thee December's frozen day,
    And, like the arbutus budding under snow,
Take bloom and fragrance from some morn of May

84

When he who gives it shall have gone away
Where faith shall see and reverent trust shall know.

And Frank Stockton sent this quatrain on the occasion of Stedman's sixtieth birthday:

Good friend—from me—"Good Afternoon!"
May all thy coming days atune
Themselves to one fair day in June
With longest, brightest afternoon.

The writer who comes at this late day to look into the beautiful home of Mr. Stedman must be content, in a measure, to leave the account of the poet's long, active life as it has been written down by other pens. When he dwelt in Fifty Fourth Street, and later in Thirtieth Street, New York, his home was, as it is today in Lawrence Park, the center of literary New York.

Before Mr. and Mrs. Stedman began gathering their friends about them, years ago, it had pleased the humor of Boston to speed its arrows of wit at New York's claim to the possession of literary circles and coteries. But when Boston's men of letters were invited to the Stedman's to dinner, the satirical arrows seemed of a sudden to lose their edge. On Sunday evenings, in the Stedman house, there was such a varied assemblage of guests as only a metropolis can bring together. Not only authors and artists, critics and professional men, but such votaries of fashion and society as really possessed culture, found their way there. At the weekly dinners were to be met the distinguished foreigner, the latest successful novelist or young poet, and the wittiest and most beautiful women.

Nowadays New York has made good its claim to supremacy in the world of American letters, but the home of the Stedmans is still its literary center, if any one spot can claim that distinction. It is a fine old two story structure, architecturally suggestive of the manors of our comfortable forefathers, and it stands in the center of the literary and artistic colony at Bronxville. Lawrence Park, the headquarters of the colony, is ninety acres in extent, and the dozen or so artists and writers who have their homes therein are all distinguished in their special fields. There are no fences, and the lawns are unbroken except for splendid trees, beds of bright colored flowers, and a winding road leading to the lodge gate. No mark of any kind indicates where Mr. Stedman's possessions end and those of William H. Howe, the cattle painter, or Will H. Low, the decorative artist, begin. It is all common property.

From the many windows of the twenty rooms of this delightful home, there are landscape pictures without number. The balcony from the second floor looks away over the tree tops to where the convent of St. Joseph, on the shores of the Hudson, lifts its tower towards the sky. The view is a sea of green in the summer, a valley of many colors in the fall, and a hollow of leaden, frosted twigs in winter. Lawrence Park is a colony set on a hill, and the crown of the hill is the Stedman house.

Once across the wide lawn and broad piazza, and within the broad front door, the sense of light and comfort irresistibly takes hold of the visitor. The furnishings are not heavy or gorgeous. They are light, warm in color, pleasing in outline, delicate in arrangement, and, above all, abundant and serviceable.

The reception room, into which the front door opens, shows the staircase to the rear and doorways to the right and left leading to the library, the poet's study, and the diningroom. The windows, with the light colored walls, make the room impressively bright. There comes a feeling of pretty tables and chairs, more tables and chairs, bookcases, still other tables, then walls covered with pictures, and everywhere books—volumes of white and gilt, and green and gilt, and white and green, and other volumes of varied colors. There are rich draperies and soft toned carpets, with which everything seems to harmonize; and the sudden appearance of the poet himself suggests that he matches with everything also, and that somehow the whole house is curiously like him.

Howells, in his impressions of "Literary New York," tells how he found Stedman "of a worldly splendor of dress" and envied him, as much as he could envy him anything, the New York tailor whose art had clothed him. Says Howells: "He had a worldly dash along with his supermundane gifts, which took me almost as much, and all the more because I could see that he valued himself nothing upon it." And that is the way Edmund Clarence Stedman dawns upon you in his own house.

One is made sensible, by means of the most pleasing devices, that in this home the arts and not the upholstery are called upon to do the honors. This admirable result is due in great part to the taste and skill of Mrs. Stedman, who possesses a genuine artistic instinct for grouping and effect. A tour of the house is a passing in review of trophies won at sales, bits picked up in foreign travel, a purchase now and then of some choice collection, either of glass or china, or of prints and etchings.

The reception room in Mr. Stedman's house
"Within the broad front door, the sense of light and comfort irresistibly takes hold of the visitor." From a photograph by Bennett, New York

In the poet's study is a noted portrait of Miss Fletcher, the author of "Kismet" and "Vestigia," painted by her stepfather, Eugene Benson, and here also one of the very earliest of the late A. H. Wyant's paintings,[6] "An Irish Bog," the first work that that talented artist sold in the East. Mr. Stedman bought it when the painter was very much of an unknown. In the same room is an old portrait of Edgar Allan Poe, which shows the dual qualities of the gifted author's intellect very plainly. While you are considering it, the poet can produce a splendid daguerreotype of Poe, and a manuscript roll of his just as he wrote it—the only one in existence—with its sheets wafered together after the old style.

Over the mantelpiece in the diningroom are bronze medallions of Bayard Taylor and Stedman, by O'Donovan. That of Bayard Taylor is a replica of the memorial that graces the library of Cornell University. The exactness of the likeness is due in a measure to Stedman, who on finding that O'Donovan could not exactly catch, from memory, the expression of the mouth, slightly creased the lip in the clay with his fingers. Then it was exactly as Stedman remembered his friend.

All the halls and stairways, and the walls of every room, show treasures. Among the paintings are a "Lion and Lioness," by George

Butler,[7] which Barye would have applauded: Winslow Homer's "A Voice from the Cliff,"[8] with its inspiring trio of faces and its magnificent sweep of feminine arms; "Longfellow's 'Wayside Inn,'" by Bellows;[9] one of Bayard Taylor's aquarelles, and a sketch made by Henry Bacon[10] of the head of a beautiful Italian girl, a sentimental model whom hopeless love drove to suicide. There are Gifford's brushes and his palette as he left it, with its colors mixed in a glorious impression of sunset; a good and rare Seymour Haden;[11] and one of Howard Pyle's paintings,[12] bought by its present owner for the price of the poem that its reproduction illustrated.

And books—he has a legion of the elect, autographed and otherwise made sacred by ties of friendship. They are principally volumes of poetry, including scarce first editions of American, English, and French books, collected without bibliomania. Those who loved Eugene Field would delight in the little pamphlet of original verse, written and illustrated in pen and ink by Field and sent to Stedman with the most friendly dedication. They were good friends until Field's death, and the Western genius never forgot the kindly service Stedman did him in securing a Boston publisher for his first volume.

There was an amusing side to this friendship between these two men. Stedman, on urgent invitation, once visited Chicago to lecture before the Twentieth Century Club, and Field, who was then with the Chicago *Record*, sought to celebrate his arrival by making a journalistic announcement of the visit. Accordingly, he stated, in his bantering way, that the Robert Browning Benevolent and Patriotic Association of Cook County had resolved to invite Mr. Stedman to a grand complimentary banquet at Kinsley's, and that a parade was to be formed which would conduct the guest from the railroad station to his quarters, on the morning of his arrival. In the procession were to be "two hundred Chicago poets, afoot," with brass bands galore, the "Blue Island Avenue Shelley Club," and a "magnificent advertising car of Armour & Co.,[13] illustrating the progress of civilization." The line of march was to be extensive, taking in the packing houses and other notable points. At Mr. Armour's professional establishment the process of slaughtering was to be illustrated for the delectation of the honored guest, after which a poem by Decatur Jones, president of the Lakeview Élite Club, would be read, followed by Mr. Armour entertaining a select few to a champagne lunch in the scalding room!

The fact that this broad, almost crude, Western humorism, thrust forward on an occasion savoring much of dignity, was enjoyed by Mr. Stedman in accordance with the spirit in which it was written, and that he replied with a bit of drollery equally clever, expressed in a poem entitled "She Never Called Him 'Gene," is sufficient to indicate the ready sympathy of his refined nature. His relations with the author of "Little Boy Blue" became intimate.

Of a different shade, but similar texture, was his friendship with Bayard Taylor—that poetic star of the older days which gleams even now as from afar. Their connection began in Stedman's early life—the life of which he speaks in "Bohemia":

> When buttercups are blossoming,
>   The poet sang, 'tis best to wed;
> So all for love we paired in spring,
>   Blanche and I—ere youth had sped,
> For autumn's wealth brings autumn's wane.
>   Sworn fealty to royal art
> Was ours, and doubly linked the chain,
> With symbols of her high domain
>   That twined us ever heart to heart,
> And onward, like the Babes in the Wood,
> We rambled till before us stood
>   The outpost of Bohemia.

It was in Bohemia that Mr. Stedman and Bayard Taylor met:

> And one—a poet—nowise sage
>   For self, but gay companion born,
> And prophet of the golden age;
> He joined us in our pilgrimage
>   Long since, an early autumn noon
> When, faint with journeying, we sate
> Within the wayside hostel gate
>   To rest us in Bohemia.

Their friendship continued until Taylor's death in 1878. Ten years before, Mr. Stedman had visited him at his beautiful country place, Cedarcroft, which is but a little way from where he lies buried, and near the old battlefield of the Brandywine. An unpublished poem by Taylor to Mr. Stedman adorns one of the volumes in the house at Lawrence Park.

Coming back to books again, there is a first edition of Keats' "Endymion," 1818; there are all the works of Landor[14] and Horne;[15] and the best collection of Greek idyllic poems extant, including fifty editions of Theocritus, beginning with the first impression made by Aldus Manutius, in 1495.

There is a copy on vellum of "Le Tombeau de Théophile Gautier," with typographical corrections in the Latin and Greek poems, notes in the margin of the English poem, and an inscription to Stedman on the flyleaf, all in the handwriting of Swinburne. There is a copy of "Vignettes in Rhyme," by Austin Dobson,[16] edited by Stedman. The younger poets are not shunned, and on his table are verses by Bliss Carman,[17] and others by Alice and Caroline Duer.[18]

Seemingly, Mr. Stedman's life lies down in Wall Street, amid the hurrying throng of money makers, and the excitement of the Stock Exchange. And yet, either by nature or through force of circumstances, he is one of the typical literary men of the day. There is that in his personality which gives him the air of constantly pressing the electric button that puts him in relation with the civilized activities of the world. He was born man of the world as well as poet, with the sensitive response to his age and surrounding which has enabled him to touch the life of the day at many divergent points of contact. He owes it to an equally rare endowment that he has been enabled to maintain his social life free from the influences of his business career. The broker is a separate and distinct person from the writer and the poet. The two, it is true, meet as one on friendly terms, on the street or at the club. But the man of Wall Street is entertained with scant courtesy within the four walls of the poet's house. It is within them that his true life is lived.

And his has been an eventful life. He tasted court life in Italy, while his mother was wife of the American minister. He was a war correspondent in the Civil War—which inspired one of his finest poems, "How Old Brown Took Harper's Ferry." But in the end he discovered that journalism left him no time or means for his chosen literary work, and turning stockbroker and banker, secured more or less of both those requisites.

Notes

1. "Edmund Clarence Stedman at Home," *Munsey's* 20 (March 1899): 931–38. Edmund Clarence Stedman (1833–1908).
2. See Dreiser's article, "The Haunts of Bayard Taylor," included in this collection.
3. Frank [Francis] R. [Richard] Stockton (1834–1902) was a novelist best known for *The Lady or the Tiger?*
4. Eugene Field (1850–1895), poet and journalist, whose column "Sharps and Flats" made the *Chicago Daily News* famous. Field's Chicago was typically American and, as Dreiser acknowledges, it influenced his vision of American life.
5. See Dreiser's article, "The Real Howells," included in this collection.
6. Alexander Helwig Wyant (1836–1892) painted his early landscapes in the naturalism of the Hudson River School, but his later style, more personal and smaller in scale, was similar to the Barbizon School.
7. George Bernard Butler (1838–1907), American painter.

8. Winslow Homer (1836–1910), who spent his youth in rural surroundings, was recognized as the most "American" of American painters.

9. Albert Fitch Bellows (1829–1883), American painter.

10. Henry Bacon (1839–1924), American painter.

11. Francis Seymour Haden (1818–1901), English etcher.

12. Howard Pyle (1853–1911), American painter, illustrator, and muralist.

13. Philip Danforth Armour (1832–1901), American meat packer. See Dreiser's article, "Life Stories of a Successful Men—No 10, Philip D. Armour," included in this collection.

14. Walter Savage Landor (1775–1864), English poet, whom Byron called "that deep-mouthed Boeotian Savage Landor" in *Don Juan.*

15. Richard Henry Horne (1803–1884), English poet, best remembered for his poem *Orion.*

16. Henry Austin Dobson (1840–1921), English poet and essayist.

17. William Bliss Carman (1861–1929), Canadian poet.

18. Alice Duer (born 1874) and Caroline King Duer (born 1865) were known for their poetry collection for children, *Poems* (New York: Richmond, 1896).

The Home of William Cullen Bryant[1]

How the famous American poet and journalist made his home in the little Long Island town of Roslyn, where he spent the last thirty five years of his life, and where he lies buried.

At the head of one of the many bays that indent the northern shore of Long Island, at a point where the inflowing waters from the Sound narrow to a mere creek, whose wavelets wash the doorsteps of pleasant cottages, lies the village of Roslyn. It is an old settlement, and years ago it had more hopes and pretensions than it has today; but it has faltered and lagged in the race of modern progress, and in 1899 it is no more than an unimportant market town, a quiet, peaceful home dwelling community, charming in its rural qualities. A few oystermen "farm" the shallow waters of the bay, a host of clam diggers wait upon the tides in order to turn the wet sand, and fishermen put out into the Sound; but as for commerce, there is none. Such life as the village possesses is mainly due to those who come to it from the great metropolis, which lies within an hour's journey.

The beauty of the region is of the simple order which soothes rather than excites admiration. On the long arm of the sea known as Hempstead Bay, whose fingers of silvery water extend so placidly inland, many little craft sail or ride at anchor. On either hand rise low hills, festooned with the greenery of summer, their grass covered sides dotted with cottages. In the distance, on clear days, the ships of the Sound are seen to pass—some trailing long clouds of smoke, others spreading glorious white sails, like seagulls flying low to drink. Birds fill the thickets with multitudinous carolings; insects and flowers glorify the heights and hollows with sound and color, and over all a blue sky arches, making the summer day one of cheering and drowsy charm.

Into this region, some fifty six years ago, at the earliest period of his fortune, when the New York *Evening Post* began to repay him for his long devotion to its interests, came William Cullen Bryant. Through all his career as poet, lawyer, and editor he had never lost his love of rural life, nor the aptitudes that had characterized his young days in Hampshire County, Massachusetts. Almost fifty years of age, he had distinguished himself in the world of letters and the more mixed realm of politics and journalism. He had the love and respect of many of the famous men of his time, and the admiration of all who read English literature. And at Roslyn he decided to dwell for the remainder of his days, a total, as it proved, of thirty five years.

Years before, so far back as 1825, he had left the region of Plainfield and Great Barrington in Massachusetts, where he had spent the first three decades of his life, and journeyed to New York. He had been a student at Williams College, a contributor of boyish satire to local papers, a student of law at Cummington, and a practitioner at the bar in Plainfield and afterward in Great Barrington. He had also been town clerk of Great Barrington, where the record of his marriage to Frances Fairchild, January 11, 1821, is still to be seen, entered by himself in the capacity of clerk. All these facts, of course, are well known. It is also well known that he found the law unprofitable, and that he betook himself to New York and journalism in the hope of bettering his fortunes.

Once in the city his hopes were destined to suffer severe modification, for the profits of journalism proved small. There was for him nothing but a faithful knuckling down to small taskwork in various literary ways—associating now with one paper and now with another. During this period he wrote for a once lively annual, the *Talisman,* and did other fugitive work, most of which has been lost. He occupied a room in Chambers Street, a thoroughfare now clogged with wholesale merchandise, but then a quiet residence street, on the outskirts of the city.

His employment in those days was not constant, and poetry brought him scanty dollars, so that from time to time the thought came to him of returning again to the practice of law. Journalism was a hard life; and though he did not despair, some of its moodiness and gloom crept into his verse:

> The trampled earth returns a sound of fear—
> A hollow sound, as if I walked on tombs;
> And lights, that tell of cheerful homes, appear
> Far off, and die like hope amid the glooms.

In the same strain he wrote:

> How fast the flitting figures come!
> The mild, the fierce, the stony face;

> Some bright with thoughtless smiles, and some
> Where secret tears have left their trace.

Beyond doubt, Bryant was homesick, and longed for his northern hills—the hills where he had seen the water fowl, "lone wandering but not lost," which gave him the idea of that exquisite poem.

By 1828, despite the hardships of living and struggling in the metropolis, he had gained a foothold, and was able to purchase a share in the *Evening Post.* This paper, which had been established as far back as 1801, was, at Bryant's advent, controlled and largely owned by William Coleman, a New York lawyer. Mr. Coleman, who was old and crippled, no longer cared for active work, and the energetic young New Englander was soon in full charge of the *Post.*

In 1834 Bryant left his desk for a trip to Europe, where he remained for two years. On his return, and for some time afterward, the financial aspects of the paper were not inspiring. Times were bad; he would not make those many little concessions which sometimes bring patronage to a paper. His advocacy of free trade offended some friends; his outspoken hostility to slavery alienated others, and sturdy political independence robbed him of local party advertising and other profitable contracts. Still he stuck to his colors, not grieving over enemies made in fighting for what he counted good.

At one time he wrote to his brother, established in the West, asking as to the chances in that neighborhood, if he could sell out for a few thousands and transport his family there. Before 1844, however, the financial tide had turned, and in President Polk's time the net earnings of the *Post,* of which he was now half owner, were $10,000; in 1850 they had risen to $16,000; in 1860 they counted more than $70,000. After the poet's death his property in the journal he had virtually created sold for something more than $400,000.

At the lift in his fortunes, he began to look about him for a place in the country. It was not long before the beautiful bay at Roslyn caught his attention, and he decided to find on its shores an abode for his remaining years. In 1843 he bought a tract of land there, and wrote to his brother:

> DEAR JOHN: Congratulate me. I have bought forty acres of solid earth at Hempstead Harbor. There, when I get money enough, I mean to build a house.

He did not build, however, since there was a ponderous, Quaker fashioned house upon the site, which, with certain added dependencies, and some properly restrained decorative treatment, made a delightful home for the poet and his family. The place contained many rooms, was surrounded by shrubbery and fine trees, and looked over a shelving lawn to a pretty little fresh water lake. It promised snug retirement and an escape from the toil and noise of a New York newspaper office.

What store he set by this place may be gathered from almost every letter which subsequently issued from his home there. In one of these missives of 1850 he says:

> I have been passing a few days at my place on Long Island, and tomorrow must go back to the town—the foul, hot, noisy town. . . . We have quite given the world the go by today. We have been no further than the garden, from the foot of which we saw this morning a sloop go down the bay, with a fiddle on board, and a score of young women in sunbonnets. . . . The temperature all day has been delightful, and now at two o'clock a delightful breeze has sprung up, which is bringing in at the window the scent of flowrs of early summer, and some faint odor of hay fields. If you care for sea bathing, the tide is swelling up, and when it meets the grass I think I shall take a plunge myself.

In another letter, written nine years later, the same feeling holds—a feeling of constant satisfaction, for he writes: "I wish you could take a look at our little place in the country," and then goes on with a poetic description of its surroundings. A friend who visited him at Roslyn wrote:

> It is under the open sky, and engaged in rural matters, that Mr. Bryant is seen to advantage—that is, in his true character. It is here that the amenity and natural sweetness of disposition, sometimes clouded by the cares of life and the outward circumstances of business intercourse, shine greatly forth under the influences of nature, so dear to the heart and so tranquilizing to the spirits of her child. Here the eye puts on its deeper and softer luster, and the voice modulates itself to the tone of affection, sympathy, and enjoyment. Little children cluster about the grave man's steps, or climb his shoulders in triumph, and serenest eyes meet his in fullest confidence, finding there none of the sternness of which casual observers sometimes complain.

That his affection for Cedarmere, as he called his place at Roslyn, was an enduring one is testified by the genial author of "Dream Life," who visited him there about eight years before Bryant's death. From an old notebook Mr. Mitchell (Ik Marvel)[2] has transcribed some of his impressions of the pilgrimage to the veteran poet's home:

The weather is doubtful as the little steamer Seawanhaka nears the dock at Great Bay. It is questioned if we should take the open carriage, which is drawn up in waiting, or run out (by boat) to the bay of Roslyn; but the voice of that one of the party who would seem least able to brave storms decides for the drive; and away we go through the pleasant roads that skirt the north shore; now brushing the boughs of a veteran wood, now rounding a placid inlet of the Sound, passing scant, quiet hamlets, old country homesteads, orchards, grain fields, wayside churches, seven miles or more, until we rattle down into the little village of Roslyn.

Passing through the village and bearing north, we have at our right a bold, wooded bluff, and at our left a spit of land between the high road and the quiet bay, which there juts with a southward sweep into the Long Island shore. Upon this spit of land are scattered houses—three of which, by their orderly keeping, mark the beginning of Mr. Bryant's property. Farther on, the land between the road and the bay widens so as to give room for a couple of placid little lakelets, lying so high above tidewater as to supply a raceway for a picturesque mill, which stands on the farther shore of the northern pool, embowered in trees. The lands sloping to this pool are lawn-like in keeping, and a swan or two with a brood of ducks are swimming lazily over it; a post bridge spans the narrowed part, and a skiff lies moored under a boathouse under the northern bank. Eight or ten rods beyond, under the shadow of a great locust and a tulip tree, we catch a glimpse of the homestead. The carriage comes to a stand under a bower of shade.

Along the walk we pass on and up the broad veranda, which sweeps around three sides of the homestead. No martinet-like precision shows in the keeping of either lawn or walks; everywhere turf and garden carry the homelike invitingness of look which testifies to the mastership of one who loves the country and its delights.

Within doors a great welcoming blaze is upon the parlor hearth— a provision against the damp evenings of early June; piquant souvenirs of wide travel arrest the eye; dashes of watercolor, which friendly artists have contributed to the cheer of the master; a bit of ruin which may be the Roman Forum; a blaze of sunset, which may hover over the blue waters of Capri, or haply a stretch of the Rhone at Avignon; over the mantel a photograph from the fresco of the wonderful "Aurora" of Guido. In the library—no affectation of literary aplomb, or of literary disorder, but only markings of easy, every day, comfortable usage; maybe a little over heaping of such reference books as go—just at this date—to the furnishing or mending of the translation of Homer.

Thus Marvel found him, late in life, and thus he lived at Cedarmere to the end of his days. Those who knew him well counted him intrepid, persistent, full of the love of justice, and rich in human sympathies. He was rather under than over the average height, firmly knit in figure, quick in motion, capable of large fatigues, and counted, by most, an austere man. Certainly he was not given to easy and uncalled for smiles, and invariably weighed his words, except in rare moments of vexation.

Ceremony he abhorred with all its trappings, never seeking willingly the men or the occasions which involved or demanded it. Accordingly, for all his fame and influence, he was less than most men on terms of intimacy with office holders or those highly placed socially or financially. He invariably refused all chance of office. It is said by Hawthorne[3] that he affected a New England twang while abroad, which Mitchell accepts as very probable, and attributes to a deep seated, rugged Americanism, wholly unconventionalized by his success in the world. He was often acrid in his writings on public affairs. He carried his impetuosities and prejudices into battle, and this was one reason why he seldom cared to meet political leaders.

If, however, he had no worship in him for great names or great places, and though his cold, reserved manner was not calculated to extend his range of friendship, he certainly lavished his best and truest social nature on his family and a few tried intimates. Not many of those who encountered him day by day knew where the gentleness lay, or how and in what terms it declared itself. We do not need to inquire at this date, however, for we find ample evidence in his poems. "Autumn Days" is but a simple expression of his long and tender recollection of the sister whom he lost in his early life.

So, too, his deep affection for his wife is now most plain, for among the unpublished poems found at his death was one written fifty two years after his marriage, and when he had been seven years a widower, living quite lonely:

> Here, where I sit alone, is sometimes heard,
>   From the great world, a whisper of my name,
> Joined, haply, to some kind, commending word
>   By those whose praise is fame.
>
> And then, as if I thought thou still wert nigh,
>   I turn me, half forgetting thou art dead,
> To read the gentle gladness in thine eye,
>   That once I might have read.

So he lived on, realizing that the end was drawing near. In a letter to the Rev. Orville Dewey, he voices the sentiments of age when he says:

I do not know how it may be with you, but for my part I feel an antipathy to hard work growing upon me. This morning I have been laboriously employed upon the *Evening Post,* and do not like it. Did you ever feel a sense of satiety—a feeling like that of an uncomfortably overloaded stomach—at the prospect of too much to do? Does the love of ease take possession of us as we approach the period when we must bid the world good night, just as we are predisposed to rest when evening comes?

A good view of the veteran in his very last days is given in the reminiscences of Richard Henry Stoddard,[4] who was one of his friends. Quite the last picture comes in connection with a poem which Stoddard had written in 1878, to recite before the Grand Army of the Republic, and which he had requested Bryant to read and criticise. Two or three days elapsed before the two men met again. Stoddard writes:

> When we did, and had exchanged greetings, he handed me a letter containing his criticisms. I wanted to talk with him, and would have done so but for the presence of one of our impecunious poets, who had evidently called upon him in his editorial room, and who had accompanied him into the business office of the *Evening Post.*
> I knew that a money transaction was about to take place, and not wishing, for the honor of the guild, to witness it, I left Mr. Bryant and his brother poet to themselves, noting, as I did so, that the hand of Mr. Bryant was in the act of slipping into his pocket. I folded up his letter, which was the last that he wrote, went away, and never saw him more, for in a week or ten days he was dead.

On Wednesday, May 29, 1878, Mr. Bryant repaired to the office of the *Post,* and, after a morning spent at editorial labor, and an hour for lunch, was driven to Central Park, where he made an address at the unveiling of the statue to Mazzini.[5] Going after the ceremony to visit a friend whose residence was in Fifth Avenue, he stumbled at the door-step and fell, injuring his head. He recovered sufficiently to return to his New York house, where he lingered in a weak, twilight state until, on the 12th of June, he fell into a sleep and passed away.

By order of the mayor the flags of the city were placed at half mast, and draped portraits of "the good, gray head, which all men knew," were hung in many windows. Funeral services were held in All Souls' Church, after which a special train conveyed the body to Roslyn. It was laid to rest in the village cemetery, where, as he had said years before:

Through the long, long summer hours,
   The golden light shall lie,
And thick young herbs and groups of flowers
   Stand in their beauty by.

Notes

1. "The Home of William Cullen Bryant," *Munsey's* 21 (May 1899): 240–46. William Cullen Bryant (1794–1878).

2. Ik Marvel [Donald Grant Mitchell] (1822–1908), American essayist, became an overnight success with the publication of his *Reverie of a Bachelor* (1850).

3. See Dreiser's article "Haunts of Nathaniel Hawthorne," included in this collection.

4. See note 3 to Dreiser's article, "The Haunts of Bayard Taylor," p. 49.

5. Unidentified.

The Real Howells[1]

Howells, it can be truly said, is greater than his literary volumes make him out to be. If this be considered little enough, then let us say he is even greater than his reputation. Since it is contended that his reputation far outweighs his achievements, let this tribute be taken in full, for he is all that it implies—one of the noblemen of literature.

A striking characteristic of the man is that he understands himself better than any one else, and that he has the courage to write himself down without color or favor. Prof. Boyesen[2] found, when he interviewed him in 1893, that he could "portray himself unconsciously (in conversation) better than I or anybody else could do it for him." His manner is so simple, his wonder at life so fresh and unsatisfied that he appeals to the student and observer as something truly rare—a wholly honest man. He is evidently so honest at heart that he is everywhere at home with himself, and will contribute that quiet, homelike atmosphere to everything and everybody around. He will compel sincerity in you, when you talk with him, not by any suggestion from him, but by the wholesome atmosphere which he exhales, and which steals over all, and makes plain that forms and slight conventionalities are not necessary.

We will not say that he was always thus. One can easily imagine the ideality of his youth when the world seemed young and green. Never insincere, we can believe, but enthusiastic and imaginative. But youth slipped away, the days waned in weariness of work, the mystery of life did not become clearer, and duty came to look more stern. I think that the thought of the final hour is too much with him; that the "watch, for ye know not," rings too much in his ears. He appeals to me as possessing a deeply religious nature unanchored to any religious belief.

My first sight of him was on a January day in Fifth Avenue. Some one who knew him said, "Here comes Howells," and I saw a stout, thick-set, middle-aged man trudging solemnly forward. He was enveloped in a great fur ulster, and peered, rather ferociously upon the odds and ends of street life that passed. He turned out again and again for this person and that, and I wondered why a stout man with so fierce a mien did not proceed resolutely forward, unswerving for the least or the greatest.

The next time I saw him was for a favor. Some magazine wanted his opinion. A total stranger, I knocked at his door in the apartments overlooking Central Park, and gave no card—only my name. "If he is in he will see you," said the servant, and, sure enough, see me he did, after a few moments. It was with a quiet trudge that he entered the room, and in a glance everything was put at ease. Anybody could talk to him providing the errand was an honest one.

There was none of that "I am a busy man" air. The wrinkles about the eyes were plainly not evidences of natural ferocity, but of kindly age. He even smiled before hearing all my request, motioned me to a chair, and sat down himself. When I had done I arose and suggested that I would not intrude upon his time, but he only shook his head and sat still. Then he propounded some question, for all the world like a kindly bid to conversation, and we were off on an argument in a moment.

How it came around to speculation concerning life and death is almost beyond recall. Andrew Lang[3] had newly re-issued his translations of Greek odes. They deal with the passions and pains of individuals dead thousands of years ago, and I expressed wonder at the long, inexplicable procession of life.

Mr. Howells folded his hands calmly and sat quite silent. Then he said, "Yes, we never know wherefrom or whereto. It seems as if all these ruddy crowds of people are little more than plants wakened by the sun and rain."

"Do you find," I said, "that it is painful to feel life wearing on, slipping away, and change overtaking us all?"

"It is, truly. Life is fine. The morning air is good. When I stroll out of a sunny day it seems too much that it should not stay and endure. It is wistfulness that overtakes us, all the more bitter because so hopeless. Every one suffers from it more or less."

From the flight of time and ever imminent death, the conversation drifted to the crush of modern life and the struggle for existence.

"It is my belief," he said, "that the struggle really does grow more bitter. The great city surprises me. It seems so much a to-do over so little—millions crowding into to obtain subsistence in a region where subsistence is least."

"Where would you have them go?"

"There are more fertile parts of the world. This little island is cold and bleak a great many months of the year. Nothing is grown here. When you come to think, there is no reason why the people of the world should not live in the tropics. The means of subsistence there are greater. Yet here they are scheming and planning, and sometimes dying of starvation."

"You have had no direct experience of this great misery."

"No; but I have observed it. All my experiences have been literary, yet in this field I have seen enough."

"Is it so hard to rise in the literary world?"

"About as difficult as in any other field. There seems to be almost invariably a period of neglect and suffering. Every beginner feels or really finds that the doors are more or less closed against him."

"Your view is rather dispiriting."

"Life seems at times a hopeless tangle. You can only face the conditions bravely and take what befalls."

Other things were talked of, but this struck me at the time as peculiarly characteristic of the work of the man. His sympathies are right, but he is not primarily a deep reasoner. He would not, for instance, choose to follow up his speculations concerning life and attempt to offer some modest theory of improvement. He watches the changeful scene, rejoices or laments over the various and separate instances, but goes no further. He has reached the conclusion that life is difficult and inexplicable without really tracing the various theories by which it is synthetically proved. He is inclined to let the great analysis of things go by the board, sure that it is a mystery and not caring much for the proof.

And yet this attitude which looks so much like pessimism is anything but characteristic of his nature. For all that life with him is a riddle, approaching death a bane, he works and lives gladly. His heart is warm. Since he cannot explain the earthly struggle he chooses to help others make the best of it. Is it a young poet longing, verses in hand, for recognition, Howells will help him. He is not a rich man and must work for his living, yet he will take of his time to read the struggler's material and recommend him according to his merit. The country knows how often he has appeared in print with a liberal commendation of a quite unknown author. He it was who first read Stephen Crane's books and assisted him in New York. It was he who publicly applauded the ghetto story of Abraham Cahan[4] when that beginner was yet unrecognized. He has, time after time, praised so liberally that paragraphers love to speak of him as the "lookout on the watch tower," straining for a first glimpse of approaching genius.

On my first visit, and when we were discussing the difficulties beginners experience, I happened to mention what I considered to be an appropriate instance of a young man in the West who had a fine novel which no publisher seemed to want.

"You consider it good, do you?" he asked.

"Very," I said.

"You might ask him to send it on to me. I should like to read it."

I was rather astonished at the liberal offer, and thanked him for the absent one. It was no idle favor of conversation, either. The book was forwarded, and, true to his word, he read it, doing what he could to make the merit of the work a source of reward for the author. There were several similar instances within a comparatively short period, and I heard of others from time to time until it all became impressively plain—how truly generous and humane is the Dean of American Letters. The great literary philanthropist, I call him.

It is useless to go to the critics for confirmation of this view of the man. Whatever may be said elsewhere, it is better to go to the man's own account of his life and his opinions. What he has put down in "My Literary Passions" rings true as a bell. It is, aside from a record of his likes and dislikes of books, a valuable human document, and in it much of the real Howells can be found, though not so much as in conversation with him. He explains in a style whose chief charm is its evident truth how he began life in an Ohio village and practically educated himself. To any one who knows the man, his account of how he made his father's meagre library his university, how his youthful years were divided between the country schools and the printing office, and how he grew into an understanding of his sphere in life must read wholly true. He endured it all with a cavalier bearing, making the best of the worst, and even to-day shields its memory with words of noble import. When I inquired of him how much time he devoted each day to his literary aims, he answered:

"The length varied with changing conditions. Sometimes I read but little. There were years of work, of the over-work, indeed—which falls to the lot of many, that I should be ashamed to speak of except in accounting for the fact. My father had sold his paper in Hamilton, and had bought an interest in another at Dayton, and at that time we were all straining our utmost to help pay for it."

How strong was that love of literary work that could find a little time to study his favorite author, even though he sat up until midnight waiting for telegraphic news, and arose again at dawn to deliver the papers and toil anew at the case. The history of his early career has a flavor of sentiment and poetry well becoming a genius. How his literary aspirations were stirred by the great authors whom he succes-

sively read; how he was perpetually imitating the writings of these—
but never willing to own it; how he eventually came to understand
that he must be like himself and no other—all savors of the youthful
dreamer of literary fame. It was of this period that he wrote: "I had a
narrow, little space, under the stairs at home. There was a desk
pushed back against the wall which the irregular ceiling sloped down
to meet, behind it, and at my left was a window, which gave good light
on the writing leaf of my desk. This was my workshop for six or seven
years—and it was not at all a bad one. It seemed, for a while, so very
simple and easy to come home in the middle of the afternoon when
my task at the printing office was done, and sit down to my books in
my little study, which I did not finally leave until the family were all in
bed."

So went the days, with long evenings when, weary with manual toil,
he got out his manuscripts and "sawed and filed and hammered away
at the blessed poems, which were little less than imitations."

The world has not despised these poems for all the author's modesty. There are things in them which are neither sawed nor hammered nor filed, but rather done out of a sad and tender spirit
weighted down with the mistaken thought of its own inefficiency.

Then came legislative work at the state capitol, more printer's
drudgery, and, finally, for some campaign service, a consulate at
Venice, where he sojourned for four years.[5] This is not a biography,
however, but merely an attempt to get a suggestion, out of the past, of
the present helpful and sincere worker in the cause of humanity.

The most likable trait of this able writer, is his honest, open delight
in being appreciated. The driving force of his youth was this desire to
do fine things and get credit for them. The applause of the world—
what an important thing it seemed. To-day he is wiser, but the heart is
the same.

I said to him: "Have you found that satisfaction in the appreciation
of your fellowmen, which in your youth you dreamed it would give
you?"

"Yes," he answered, "truly. It is all that the heart imagines—sweet."

"Worth the toil?"

"Yes. I know of nothing more exquisite than to have labored long
and doubtingly and then to find, for all your fears, your labor com-
mended, your name on many tongues. It is reward enough."

Howells owns to this on every occasion where an expression of
opinion is necessary and appropriate, and it makes for greater dignity
in him. One of the most characteristic of these acknowledgments

occurs in some paper by him in which he says: "I came into the hotel office (at Montreal) the evening of a first day's lonely sightseeing, and vainly explored the register for the name of some acquaintance; as I turned from it two smartly dressed young fellows embraced it, and I heard one of them say, to my great amaze and happiness, 'Hello, here's Howells!' 'Oh,' I broke out upon him, 'I was just looking for some one I knew. I hope you are some one who knows *me!*' 'Only through your contributions to *The Saturday Press*,' said the young fellow, and with these golden words, the precious first personal recognition of my authorship I had ever received from a stranger, and the rich reward of all my literary endeavor, he introduced himself and his friend. I do not know what became of this friend, or where or how he eliminated himself, but we two others were inseparable from that moment. He was a young lawyer from New York, and when I came back from Italy four or five years later, I used to see his sign in Wall Street, with a never fulfilled intention of going in to see him. In whatever world he happens now to be, I should like to send him my greetings, and confess to him that my art has never since brought me so sweet a recompense, and nothing a thousandth part so much like Fame, as that outcry of his over the hotel register in Montreal."

Some may think that such open expression of sentiment and pleasure is like hanging one's heart upon one's sleeve for daws to peck at, but more will feel that it is but the creditable exuberance of a heart full of good feelings. He is thus frank in his books, his letters, his conversation. His family get no nearer in many things than those in the world outside who admire his charming qualities. He is the same constantly, a person whose thoughts issue untinged by any corroding wash of show or formality.

What more can be said of a man? He is not rich, and can therefore provide no evidence of his character by his individual disposition of money. His field of endeavor is of that peculiar nature which permits of much and effective masquerading. Many an evil heart is effectively cloaked and hidden from the world by a show of literary talent. We can look only at his individual expression of himself, the hold his nature has taken upon those who know him and the extent and use of his reputation. Fame is a very good collateral in the hands of an able man, and Howells has made good use of his fame.

If Howells, by reason of greater advantages in his youth, had been able to go farther intellectually, if he had had direction along the lines of sociology and philosophy, he might have given the world something most important in that direction. The man has the speculative, philosophic make-up. His sympathies are of a kind that produce able theories for the betterment of mankind. As it is, what he has written smacks of the social-prophetic.

How true this is the readers of "A Traveler from Altruria" can witness. Therein he sets forth his dream of universal peace and good-will. He sketches a state of utter degradation from which the brutalized poor rise to the purest altruism.

In a further sense, the socialistic-philosophic turn of his nature is evidenced by his confession of the hold the works of Tolstoi have taken upon him. "He charms me," he said, "by his humanity, his goodness of heart." And in the "Literary Passions" that fine opening to the last chapter, confirms this statement, "I come now, though not quite in the order of time, to the noblest of all these enthusiasms, namely, my devotion for the writings of Lyof Tolstoi. I should wish to speak of him with his own incomparable truth, yet I do not know how to give a notion of his influence without the effect of exaggeration. As much as one merely human being can help another, I believe that he has helped me; he has not influenced me in aesthetics only, but in ethics, too, so that I can never again see life in the way I saw it before I knew him."

Tolstoi's influence has led him back, as he puts it, "to the only true ideal, away from that false standard of the gentleman to the Man who sought not to be distinguished from other men, but identified with them, to that *Presence* in which the finest gentleman shows his alloy of vanity, and the greatest genius shrinks to the measure of his miserable egotism."

It does not matter whether Howells is the greatest novelist in the world or not, he is a great character. There are many, who find senti-ments and feelings so rich, so fair, so delicately drawn, in his work, that it seems as if he had gathered the very moonbeams out of the night to weave a wistful spell over the heart, and it is certain that these perfect parts of his work will live. About the other it does not matter, for the larger part of the work of all authors is more or less bad, anyhow. What is more important is that he has been an influence for good in American letters—that he has used his strength and popular-ity in the direction of what he took to be the right. He has helped thousands in more ways than one, and is a sweet and wholesome presence in the world of art. By the side of the egotists in his field, the chasers after fame and the hagglers over money, this man is a towering figure. His greatness is his goodness, his charm his sin-cerity.

Notes

1. "The Real Howells," *Ainslee's* 5 (March 1900): 137–42. Reprinted in *Americana* 37 (April 1943): 274–82; also in *American Thought and Writing: The 1890's*, ed. Donald Pizer (Boston: Houghton Mifflin, 1972), pp. 62–68; and in *American Literary Realism* 6 (Fall 1973): 347–51. More recently reprinted in part in *Theodore Dreiser: A Selection of Uncollected Prose*, ed. Donald Pizer (Detroit: Wayne State University Press, 1977), pp. 141–46. William Dean Howells (1839–1920).

2. Hjalmar Hjorth Boyesen (1848–1895), Norwegian-American critic and novelist, whose first novel *Gunnar* (1873), written in English, was published by Howells in the *Atlantic Monthly*.

3. Andrew Lang (1844–1912), Scottish scholar and author.

4. Abraham Cahan (1860–1951), a Jewish immigrant, became an editor and novelist, best known for *Yekl* (1899) and *The Rise of David Levinsky* (1907).

5. Howells wrote the campaign biography of Lincoln and, in return, was appointed the consulship of Venice.

Part Two

SUCCESS STORIES

A Photographic Talk with Edison[1]

A . . . Quiet Interview in His Laboratory

The . . . Story of 52 Years of Magnificent Work

To discover the opinion of Thomas A. Edison, concerning what makes and constitutes success in life is an easy matter, if one can only discover Mr. Edison. I camped three weeks in the vicinity of Orange, N.J., awaiting the opportunity to come upon the great inventor and voice my questions. It seemed a rather hopeless and discouraging affair until he was really before me; but, truth to say, he is one of the most accessible of men, and only reluctantly allows himself to be hedged in by the pressure of endless affairs. "Mr. Edison is always glad to see any visitor," said a gentleman who is continually with him, "except when he is hot on the trail of something he has been working for, and then it is as much as a man's head is worth to come in on him." He certainly was not hot on the trail of anything on the morning when, for seemingly the tenth time, I rang at the gate in the fence which surrounds the laboratory on Valley Road, Orange. A young man appeared, who conducted me up the walk to the elegant office and library of the great laboratory. It is a place, this library, not to be passed through without thought, for with a further store of volumes in his home, it contains one of the most costly and well-equipped scientific libraries in the world; the collection of writings on patent laws and patents, for instance, is absolutely exhaustive. It gives, at a glance, an idea of the breadth of the thought and sympathy of this man who grew up with scarcely a common school education.

On the second floor, in one of the offices of the machine-shop, I was asked to wait, while a grimy youth disappeared with my card, which he said he would "slip under the door of Mr. Edison's office." "Curious," I thought; "what a lord this man must be if they dare not even knock at his door!"

Thinking of this and gazing out the window, I waited until a work-

111

Thomas Edison at thirty-one

ing man, who had entered softly, came up beside me. He looked with a sort of "Well, what is it?" in his eyes, and quickly it began to come to me that the man in the sooty, oil-stained clothes was Edison himself. The working garb seemed rather incongruous, but there was no mistaking the broad forehead, with its shock of blackish hair streaked with gray. The gray eyes, too, were revelations in the way of alert comprehensiveness.

"Oh!" was all I could get out at the time.

"Want to see me?" he said, smiling in the most youthful and genial way.

"Why,—yes, certainly, to be sure," I stammered.

He looked at me blankly.

"You'll have to talk louder," said an assistant who worked in another portion of the room; "he don't hear well."

This fact was new to me, but I raised my voice with celerity and piped thereafter in an exceedingly shrill key. After the usual humdrum opening remarks, in which he acknowledged with extreme good nature his age as fifty-two years, and that he was born in Erie county, O.² of Dutch parentage, the family having emigrated to America in 1730, the particulars began to grow more interesting. His great-grandfather, I learned, was a banker of high standing in New York; and, when Thomas was but a child of seven years, the family fortune suffered reverses so serious as to make it necessary that he should become a wage-earner at an unusually early age, and that the family should move from his birth-place to Michigan.

"Did you enjoy mathematics as a boy?" I asked.

"Not much," he replied. "I tried to read Newton's 'Principia' at the age of eleven. That disgusted me with pure mathematics, and I don't wonder now. I should not have been allowed to take up such serious work."

"You were anxious to learn?"

"Yes, indeed. I attempted to read through the entire Free Library at Detroit, but other things interfered before I had done."

"Were you a book-worm and dreamer?" I questioned.

"Not at all," he answered, using a short, jerky method, as though he were unconsciously checking himself up. "I became a newsboy, and liked the work. Made my first *coup* as a newsboy in 1869."

"What was it?" I ventured.

"I bought up on 'futures' a thousand copies of the 'Detroit Free Press' containing important war news,—gained a little time on my rivals, and sold the entire batch like hot cakes. The price reached twenty-five cents a paper before the end of the route," and he laughed.

"I ran the 'Grand Trunk Herald,' too, at that time—a little paper I issued from the train."

"When did you begin to be interested in invention?" I questioned.

"Well," he said, "I began to dabble in chemistry at that time. I fitted up a small laboratory on the train."

In reference to this, Mr. Edison subsequently admitted that, during the progress of some occult experiments in this workshop, certain complications ensued in which a jolted and broken bottle of sulphuric acid attracted the attention of the conductor. He, who had been long suffering in the matter of unearthly odors, promptly ejected the young devotee and all his works. This incident would have been only amusing but for its relation to, and explanation of, his deafness. A box on the ear, administered by the irate conductor, caused the lasting deafness.

"What was your first work in a practical line?" I went on.

"A telegraph line between my home and another boy's, I made with the help of an old river cable, some stove-pipe wire, and glass-bottle insulators. I had my laboratory in the cellar and studied telegraphy outside."

"What was the first really important thing you did?

"I saved a boy's life."

"How?"

"The boy was playing on the track near the depot. I saw he was in danger and caught him, getting out of the way just in time. His father was station-master, and taught me telegraphy in return."

Dramatic situations appear at every turn of this man's life, though, temperamentally, it is evident that he would be the last to seek them. He seems to have been continually arriving on the scene at critical moments, and always with the good sense to take things in his own hands. The chance of learning telegraphy only gave him a chance to show how apt a pupil he was, and the railroad company soon gave him regular employment. He himself admits that, at seventeen, he had become one of the most expert operators on the road.

"Did you make much use of your inventive talent at this time?" I questioned.

"Yes," he answered. "I invented an automatic attachment for my telegraph instrument which would send in the signal to show I was awake at my post, when I was comfortably snoring in a corner. I didn't do much of that, though," he went on; "for some such boyish trick sent me in disgrace over the line into Canada."

"Were you there long?"

"Only a winter. If it's incident you want, I can tell you one of that time. The place where I was and Sarnier, the American town, were cut off from telegraph and other means of communication by the storms until I got at a locomotive whistle and tooted a telegraphic message. I had to do it again and again, but eventually they understood over the water and answered in the same way."

According to his own and various recorded accounts, Edison was successively in charge of important wires in Memphis, Cincinnati, New Orleans, and Louisville. He lived in the free-and-easy atmosphere of the tramp operators—a boon companion with them, yet absolutely refusing to join in the dissipations to which they were addicted. So highly esteemed was he for his honesty that it was the custom of his colleagues, when a spree was on hand, to make him the custodian of those funds which they felt obliged to save. On a more than usually hilarious occasion, one of them returned rather the worse for wear, and knocked the treasurer down on his refusal to deliver the trust money; the other depositors, we may be glad to note, gave the ungentlemanly tippler a sound thrashing.

"Were you good at saving your own money?" I asked.

"No," he said, smiling. "I never was much for saving money, as money. I devoted every cent, regardless of future needs, to scientific books and materials for experiments."

"You believe that an excellent way to succeed?"

"Well, it helped me greatly to future success."

"What was your next invention?" I inquired.

"An automatic telegraph recorder—a machine which enabled me to record dispatches at leisure, and send them off as fast as needed."

"How did you come to hit upon that?"

"Well, at the time, I was in such straits that I had to walk from Memphis to Louisville. At the Louisville station they offered me a place. I had perfected a style of handwriting which would allow me to take legibly from the wire, long hand, forty-seven and even fifty-four words a minute, but I was only a moderately rapid sender. I had to do something to help me on that side, and so I thought out that little device."

Later, he pointed out an article by one of his biographers, in which a paragraph, referring to this Louisville period, says:—

"True to his dominant instincts, he was not long in gathering around him a laboratory, printing office, and machine shop. He took press reports during his whole stay, including, on one occasion, the Presidential message, and veto of the District of Columbia, by Andrew Johnson,[3] and this at one sitting, from 3.30 P.M. to 4.30 A.M.

"He then paragraphed the matter he had received over the wires, so that printers had exactly three lines each, thus enabling them to set up a column in two or three minutes' time. For this, he was allowed all the exchanges he desired, and the Louisville press gave him a state dinner."

"How did you manage to attract public attention to your ability?" I questioned.

"I didn't manage," said the Wizard. "Some things I did created comment. A device that I invented in 1868, which utilized one submarine cable for two circuits, caused considerable talk, and the Franklin telegraph office of Boston gave me a position."

It is related of this, Mr. Edison's first trip East, that he came with no ready money and in a rather dilapidated condition. His colleagues were tempted by his "hayseed" appearance to "salt" him, as professional slang terms the process of giving a receiver matter faster than he can record it. For this purpose, the new man was assigned to a wire manipulated by a New York operator famous for his speed. But there was no fun at all. Notwithstanding the fact that the New Yorker was in the game and was doing his most speedy clip, Edison wrote out the long message accurately, and, when he realized the situation, was soon firing taunts over the wire at the sender's slowness.

"Had you patented many things up to the time of your coming East?" I queried.

"Nothing," said the inventor, ruminatively. "I received my first patent in 1869."

"For what?"

"A machine for recording votes and designed to be used in the State Legislature."

"I didn't know such machines were in use," I ventured.

"They ar'n't," he answered, with a merry twinkle. "The better it worked, the more impossible it was; the sacred right of the minority, you know,—couldn't filibuster if they used it,—didn't use it."

"Oh!"

"Yes, it was an ingenious thing. Votes were clearly pointed and shown on a roll of paper, by a small machine attached to the desk of each member. I was made to learn that such an innovation was out of the question, but it taught me something."

"And that was?"

"To be sure of the practical need of, and demand for, a machine, before expending time and energy on it."

"Is that one of your maxims of success?"

"It is."

In this same year, Edison came from Boston to New York, friendless and in debt on account of the expenses of his experiment. For several weeks he wandered about the town with actual hunger staring him in the face.[4] It was a time of great financial excitement, and with that strange quality of Fortunism, which seems to be his chief characteristic, he entered the establishment of the Law Gold Reporting Company just as their entire plant had shut down on account of an accident in the machinery that could not be located. The heads of the firm were anxious and excited to the last degree, and a crowd of the Wall Street fraternity waited about for the news which came not. The shabby stranger put his finger on the difficulty at once, and was given lucrative employment. In the rush of the metropolis, a man finds his true level without delay, especially when his talents are of so practical and brilliant a nature as were this young telegrapher's. It would be an absurdity to imagine an Edison hidden in New York. Within a short time, he was presented with a check for $40,000, as his share of a single invention—an improved stock printer. From this time, a national reputation was assured him. He was, too, now engaged upon the duplex and quadruplex systems—systems for sending two and four messages at the same time over a single wire,—which were to inaugurate almost a new era in telegraphy.

Recalling the incident of the Law Gold Reporting Company, I inquired: "Do you believe want urges a man to greater efforts and so to greater success?"

"It certainly makes him keep a sharp lookout. I think it does push a man along."

"Do you believe that invention is a gift, or an acquired ability?"

"I think it's born in a man."

"And don't you believe that familiarity with certain mechanical conditions and defects naturally suggests improvements to any one?"

"No. Some people may be perfectly familiar with a machine all their days, knowing it inefficient, and never see a way to improve it."

"What do you think is the first requisite for success in your field, or any other?"

"The ability to apply your physical and mental energies to one problem incessantly without growing weary."

"Do you have regular hours, Mr. Edison?" I asked.

"Oh," he said, "I do not work hard now. I come to the laboratory about eight o'clock every day and go home to tea at six, and then I study or work on some problem until eleven, which is my hour for bed."

"Fourteen or fifteen hours a day can scarcely be called loafing," I suggested.

"Well," he replied, "for fifteen years I have worked on an average of twenty hours a day."

That astonishing brain has been known to puzzle itself for sixty consecutive hours over a refractory problem, its owner dropping quietly off into a long sleep when the job was done, to awake perfectly refreshed and ready for another siege. Mr. Dickson, a neighbor and familiar, gives an anecdote told by Edison which well illustrates his untiring energy and phenomenal endurance. In describing his Boston experience, Edison said he bought Faraday's works on electricity,[5] commenced to read them at three o'clock in the morning and continued until his room-mate arose, when they started on their long walk to get breakast. That object was entirely subordinated in Edison's mind to Faraday, and he suddenly remarked to his friend: "'Adams, I have got so much to do, and life is so short, that I have got to hustle,' and with that I started off on a dead run for my breakfast."

"Are your discoveries often brilliant intuitions? Do they come to you while you are lying awake nights?" I asked him.

"I never did anything worth doing by accident," he replied, "nor did any of my inventions come indirectly through accident, except the phonograph. No, when I have fully decided that a result is worth getting, I go about it, and make trial after trial, until it comes.

"I have always kept," continued Mr. Edison, "strictly within the lines of commercially useful inventions. I have never had any time to put on electrical wonders, valuable only as novelties to catch the popular fancy."

"What makes you work?" I asked with real curiosity. "What impels you to this constant, tireless struggle? You have shown that you care comparatively nothing for the money it makes you, and you have no particular enthusiasm for the attending fame. What is it!"

"I like it," he answered, after a moment of puzzled expression. "I don't know any other reason. Anything I have begun is always on my mind, and I am not easy while away from it, until it is finished; and then I hate it."

"Hate it?" I said.

"Yes," he affirmed, "when it is all done and is a success, I can't bear the sight of it. I haven't used a telephone in ten years, and I would go out of my way any day to miss an incandescent light."

"You lay down rather severe rules for one who wishes to succeed in life," I ventured, "working eighteen hours a day."

"Not at all," he said. "You do something all day long, don't you? Every one does. If you get up at seven o'clock and go to bed at eleven, you have put in sixteen good hours, and it is certain with most men, that they have been doing something all the time. They have been either walking, or reading, or writing, or thinking. The only trouble is that they do it about a great many things and I do it about one. If they took the time in question and applied it in one direction, to one object, they would succeed. Success is sure to follow such application. The trouble lies in the fact that people do not have an object—one thing to which they stick, letting all else go."

"You believe, of course," I suggested, "that much remains to be discovered in the realm of electricity?"

"It is the field of fields," he answered. "We can't talk of that, but it holds the secrets which will reorganize the life of the world."

"You have discovered much about it," I said, smiling.

"Yes," he said, "and yet very little in comparison with the possibilities that appear."

"How many inventions have you patented?"

"Only six hundred," he answered, "but I have made application for some three hundred more."

"And do you expect to retire soon, after all this?"

"I hope not," he said, almost pathetically. "I hope I will be able to work right on to the close. I shouldn't care to loaf."

Shouldn't care to loaf! What a thought after fifty-two years of such magnificent achievement.

Notes

1. "A Photographic Talk with Edison," *Success* 1 (February 1898): 8–9. Reprinted as "A Talk with Edison" in *How They Succeeded,* pp. 220–40; also as "Hard Work, the Secret of a Great Inventor's Genius—Thomas Alva Edison" in *Little Visits with Great Americans,* pp. 17–34. Thomas Alva Edison (1847–1931).

2. Located halfway between Cleveland and Toledo.

3. Andrew Johnson (1808–1875), seventeenth president of the United States (1865–69).

4. Edison's harrowing experience in New York echoes Dreiser's when he himself came to New York, destitute, during the winter months of 1894–95 in the midst of the worst depression America had ever known.

5. Michael Faraday (1791–1867), English chemist and physicist.

Life Stories of Successful Men——No. 10[1]

Philip D. Armour, business man and philanthropist—the inner history of a
remarkable career, related specially for the readers of "Success"

Work   Sagacity   Honesty

Truth   Courage   Energy

I found Mr. Armour in his crowded office at 205 La Salle Street,
Chicago, an office in which a snow storm of white letters falls thickly
upon a mass of dark desks, and where brass and lamps and electrical
instruments abound, yet not much more than do the hurrying men.
Such a mobilization of energy, to promote the private affairs of one
man, I had never seen.

"Is Mr. Armour within?" I asked, supposing, since it was but 9:30
A.M., that he had not arrived.

"He is," said the attendant, "and has been since half past seven."

"Does he usually arrive so early?" I inquired.

"Always," was the significant reply.

I presented my letters, and was soon informed that they were of no
avail there. Mr. Armour could see me only after the crush of the day's
affairs,—that is, at 6 P.M., and then in the quiet of the Armour Institute, his great philanthropic school for young men and women. He
was very courteous, and there was no delay. He took my hand with a
firm grasp, evidently reading with his steady gaze such of my characteristics as interested him, and saying, at the same time, "Well, sir."

"Mr. Armour," I said, "will you answer enough questions concerning your life to illustrate for our readers what success means?"

The great Hercules of American industry visibly recoiled at the
thought of implied notoriety, having, until the present time, steadily

veiled his personality and general affairs as much as possible from public gaze.

"I am only a plain merchant," he answered.

A Boy's Chance To-Day

"Do you consider," I said, "that the average American boy of to-day has equally as good a chance to succeed in the world as you had, when you began life?"

"Every bit, and better. The affairs of life are larger. There are greater things to do. There was never before such a demand for able men."

"Were the conditions surrounding your youth especially difficult?"

"No. They were those common to every small New York town in 1832. I was born at Stockbridge, in Madison County. Our family had its roots in Scotland. My father's ancestors were the Robertsons, Watsons, and McGregors of Scotland; my mother came of the Puritans who settled in Connecticut."

"Dr. Gunsaulus[2] says," I ventured, "that all these streams of heredity set toward business affairs."

Inherited Qualities

"Perhaps so, I liked trading as well. My father was reasonably prosperous and independent for those times. My mother had been a school-teacher. There were six boys, and, of course, such a household had to be managed with the strictest economy in those days. My mother thought it her duty to bring to our home some of the rigid discipline of the school-room. We were all trained to work together, and everything was done as systematically as possible."

"Had you access to any books?"

"Yes, the Bible, 'Pilgrim's Progress,' and a history of the United States."

It is said of the latter, by those closest to Mr. Armour, that it was as full of shouting Americanism as anything ever written, and that Mr. Armour's whole nature is yet colored by its stout American prejudices; also that it was read and re-read by the Armour children, though of this the great merchant would not speak.

"Were you always of a robust constitution?" I asked.

"Yes, sir. All our boys were. We were stout enough to be bathed in an ice-cold spring, out of doors, when at home. There weren't any bath tubs and warm water arrangements in those days. We had to be strong. My father was a stern Scotchman, and when he laid his plans they were carried out. When he set us boys to work, we worked. It was our mother who insisted on keeping us all at school, and who looked after our educational needs, while our father saw to it that we had plenty of good, hard work on the farm."

"How did you enjoy that sort of life?" I asked.

"Well enough, but not much more than any boy does. Boys are always more or less afraid of hard work."

The truth is, though Mr. Armour laughs it out of court, as not worth discussing, that when he attended the district school he was as full of pranks and capers as the best, and traded jack-knives in summer and bob-sleds in winter.

Leaving the Farm

Young Armour was often to be found, in the winter, coasting down the long hill near the schoolhouse; and, later, his experience at the Cazenovia Seminary was such as to indicate that some of the brightest people finish their education rather more suddenly than their family and friends might desire.

"When did you leave the farm for a mercantile life?" I asked.

"I was a clerk in a store in Stockbridge for two years, after I was seventeen, but was mixed up with the farm more or less, and wanted to get out of that life. I was a little over seventeen years old when the gold excitement of 1849 reached our town. Wonderful tales were told of gold already found and the prospects for more on the Pacific coast. I was taken with the fever, and brooded over the difference between tossing hay in the hot sun and digging up gold by handfuls, until one day I threw down my pitchfork and went over to the house and told mother that I had quit that kind of work.

"People with plenty of money could sail around Cape Horn in those days, but I had no money to spare, and so decided to walk across the country. That is, we were carried part of the way by rail and walked the rest. I persuaded one of the neighbor's boys, Calvin Gilbert, to go along with me, and we started."

"How did you fare?"

"Rather roughly. I provided myself with an old carpet sack into which I put my clothes. I bought a new pair of boots, and when we had gone as far as we could on canals and wagons, I bought two oxen. With these we managed for awhile, but eventually reached California afoot."

A Mining Venture

He suffered a severe illness on the journey, and was nursed by his companion Gilbert, who gathered herbs and steeped them for his friend's use, and once rode thirty miles in the rain to get a doctor. When they reached California, he fell in with Edward Croarkin, a miner, who nursed him back to health. The manner in which he remembered these men gives keen satisfaction to the friends of the great merchant.

"Did you have any money when you arrived at the gold-fields?"

"Scarcely any. I struck right out, though, and found a place where I could dig, and I struck pay dirt in a little time."

"Did you work entirely alone?"

"No. It was not long before I met Mr. Croarkin at a little mining camp called Virginia. He had the next claim to mine, and we became partners. After a little while, he went away, but came back in a year. We then bought in together. The way we ran things was 'turn about.' Croarkin would cook one week and I the next, and then we would have a clean-up every Sunday morning. We baked our own bread, and kept a few hens, which kept us supplied with eggs. There was a man named Chapin who had a little store in the village, and we would take our gold dust there and trade it for groceries."

"Did you discover much gold?" I asked.

"Oh, I worked with pretty good success,—nothing startling. I didn't waste much, and tried to live as carefully as I ever had. I also studied the business opportunities around, and persuaded some of my friends to join me in buying and developing a 'ditch,'—a kind of aqueduct, to convey water to diggers and washers. That proved more profitable than digging for gold, and at the end of the year, the others sold out to me, took their earnings and went home. I stayed and bought up several other water-powers, until, in 1856, I thought I had enough, and so I sold out and came East."

"How much had you made, altogether?"

"About four thousand dollars."

"Did you return to Stockbridge?"

He Enters the Grain Market

"For a little while. My ambition was setting in another direction. I had been studying the methods then used for moving the vast and growing food products of the West, such as grain and cattle, and I believed that I could improve them and make money. The idea and the field interested me and I decided to enter it.

"Well, my standing was good, and I raised the money and bought what was then the largest elevator in Milwaukee. This put me in contact with the movement of grain. At that time, John Plankinton had been established in Milwaukee a number of years, and, in partnership with Frederick Layton, had built up a good pork-packing concern. I bought in with those gentlemen, and so came in contact with the work I liked. One of my brothers, Herman, had established himself in Chicago some time before, in the grain-commission business. I got him to turn that over to the care of another brother, Joseph, so that he might go to New York as a member of the new firm, of which I was a partner. It was important that the Milwaukee and Chicago houses should be able to ship to a house of their own in New York,—that is, to themselves. Risks were avoided in this way, and we were certain of obtaining all that the ever-changing markets could offer us."[3]

"When did you begin to build up your Chicago interests?"

"They were really begun, before the war, by my brother Herman. When he went to New York for us, we began adding a small packing-house to the Chicago commission branch. It gradually grew with the growth of the West."

"Is there any one thing that accounts for the immense growth of the packing industry here?" I asked.[4]

"System and the growth of the West did it. Things were changing at startling rates in those days. The West was growing fast. Its great areas of production offered good profits to men who would handle and ship the products. Railway lines were reaching out in new directions or increasing their capacities and lowering their rates of transportation. These changes and the growth of the country made the creation of a food-gathering and delivering system necessary. Other things helped. At that time (1863), a great many could see that the war was going to terminate favorably for the Union. Farming operations had been enlarged by the war demand and war prices. The state banking system had been done away with, and we had a uniform currency, available everywhere, so that exchanges between the East and the West had become greatly simplified. Nothing more was needed than a steady watchfulness of the markets by competent men in continuous telegraphic communication with each other, and who knew the legitimate demand and supply, in order to sell all products quickly and with profit."

Qualities That Bring Success

"Do you believe that system does so much?" I ventured.

"System and good measure. Give a measure heaped full and running over and success is certain. That is what it means to be the intelligent servants of a great public need. We believed in thoughtfully adopting every attainable improvement, mechanical or otherwise, in the methods and appliances for handling every pound of grain or flesh. Right liberality and right economy will do everything where a public need is being served."

"Have your methods improved any with years?"

"All the time. There was a time when many parts of cattle were wasted, and the health of the city injured by the refuse. Now, by adopting the best known methods, nothing is wasted, and buttons, fertilizer, glue and other things are made cheaper and better for the world in general, out of material that was before a waste and a menace. I believe in finding out the truth about all things,—the very latest truth or discovery,—and applying it."

"You attribute nothing to good fortune?"

"Nothing!" Certainly the word came well from a man whose energy, integrity, and business ability made more money out of a ditch than other men were making out of rich placers in the gold region.

"May I ask what you consider the turning-point of your career?"

"The time when I began to save the money I earned at the gold-fields."

"What trait do you consider most essential in young men?"

"Truth. Let them get that. Young men talk about getting capital to work with. Let them get truth on board, and capital follows. It's easy enough to get that."

"Did you always desire to follow a commercial rather than a professional life?"

"Not always. I have no talent in any other direction, but I should have liked to be a great orator."

The Genesis of a Great Benevolence

Mr. Armour would say no more on this subject, but his admiration for oratory has been demonstrated in a remarkable way. It was after a Sunday morning discourse by the splendid orator, Dr. Gunsaulus, at Plymouth Church, Chicago, in which the latter had set forth his views on the subject of educating children, that Mr. Armour came forward and said:—

"You believe in those ideas of yours, do you?"

"I certainly do," said Dr. Gunsaulus.

"And would you carry them out if you had the opportunity?"

"I would."

"Well, sir," said Mr. Armour, "if you will give me five years of your time, I will give you the money."

"But to carry out my ideas would take a million dollars!" exclaimed Gunsaulus.

"I have made a little money in my time," returned Mr. Armour, and so the famous Armour Institute of Technology, to which its founder has already given sums aggregating $2,800,000, was associated with Mr. Armour's love of oratory.

One of his lieutenants says that Gerritt Smith, the old abolitionist, was Armour's boyhood's hero, and that to-day Mr. Armour will go far to hear a good speaker, often remarking that he would have preferred to be a great orator rather than a great capitalist.

"There is no need to ask you," I continued, "whether you believe in constant, hard labor?"

"I should not call it hard. I believe in close application, of course, while laboring. Overwork is not necessary to success. Every man should have plenty of rest. I have."

"You must rise early to be at your office at half past seven?"

"Yes, but I go to bed early. I am not burning the candle at both ends."

The enormous energy of this man, who is too modest to discuss it, is displayed in the most normal manner. Though he sits all day at a desk which has direct cable connection with London, Liverpool, Calcutta, and other great centers of trade, with which he is in constant connection,—though he has at his hand long-distance telephone connection with New York, New Orleans, and San Francisco, and direct wires from his room to almost all parts of the world, conveying messages in short sentences upon subjects which involve the moving of vast amounts of stock and cereals, and the exchange of millions in money, he is not, seemingly, an overworked man. The great subjects to which he gives calm, undivided attention from early morning until evening, are laid aside with the ease with which one doffs his raiment, and outside of his office the cares weigh upon him no more. His mind takes up new and simpler things.

"What do you do," I inquired, "after your hard day's work,—think about it?"

"Not at all. I drive, take up home subjects, and never think of the office until I return to it."

"Your sleep is never disturbed?"

"Not at all."

A Business King

And yet the business which this man forgets, when he gathers children about him and moves in his simple home circle, amounted, in 1897, to over $102,000,000 worth of food products, manufactured and distributed. The hogs killed were 1,750,000; the cattle were 1,080,000; the sheep, 625,000. Eleven thousand men were constantly employed, and the wages paid them were over $5,500,000; the railway cars owned and moving about all parts of the country, four thousand; the wagons of many kinds and of large number, drawn by 750 horses. The glue factory, employing 750 hands, made over twelve million pounds of glue! In his private office, it is he who takes care of all the general affairs of this immense world of industry, and yet at half past four he is done, and the whole subject is comfortably off his mind.

"Do you believe in inherited abilities, or that any boy can be taught and trained, and made a great and able man?"

"I recognize inherited ability. Some people have it, and only in a certain direction; but I think men can be taught and trained so that they become much better and more useful than they would be, otherwise. Some boys require more training and teaching than others. There is prosperity for everyone, according to his ability."

"What would you do with those who are naturally less competent than others?"

"Train them, and give them work according to their ability. I believe that life is all right, and that this difference which nature makes is all right. Everything is good, and is coming out satisfactorily, and we ought to make the most of conditions, and try to use and improve everything. The work needed is here, and everyone should set about doing it."

When, in 1893, local forces planned to defeat him in the grain market, and everyone was crying that at last the great Goliath had met his David, he was all energy. He had ordered immense quantities of wheat. The opposition had shrewdly secured every available place of storage, and rejoiced that the great packer, having no place to store his property, would suffer immense loss, and must capitulate. He foresaw the fray and its dangers, and, going over on Goose Island, bought property at any price, and began the construction of immense elevators. The town was placarded with the truth that anyone could get work at Armour's elevators. No one believed they could be done in time, but three shifts of men working night and day, often under the direct supervision of the millionaire, gradually forced the work ahead; and when, on the appointed day, the great grain-ships began to arrive, the opposition realized failure. The vessels began to pour the contents of their immense holds into these granaries, and the fight was over.

The foresight that sent him to New York in 1864, to sell pork, brought him back from Europe in 1893, months before the impending panic was dreamed of by other merchants. It is told of him that he called all his head men to New York, and announced to them:—

"Gentlemen, there's going to be financial trouble soon."

Forearmed Against Panic

"Why, Mr. Armour," they said, "you must be mistaken. Things were never better. You have been ill, and are suddenly apprehensive."

"Oh, no," he said, "I'm not. There is going to be trouble;" and he gave as his reasons certain conditions which existed in nearly all countries, which none of those present had thought of. "Now," said he to the first of his many lieutenants, "how much will you need to run your department until next year?"

The head man named his need. The others were asked, each in turn, the same question, and, when all were through, he counted up, and, turning to the company, said:—

"Gentlemen, go back and borrow all you need in Chicago, on my credit. Use my name for all it will bring in the way of loans."

The lieutenants returned, and the name of Armour was strained to its utmost limit. When all had been borrowed, the financial flurry suddenly loomed up, but it did not worry the great packer. In his vaults were $8,000,000 in gold. All who had loaned him at interest then hurried to his doors, fearing that he also was imperiled. They found him supplied with ready money, and able to compel them to wait until the stipulated time of payment, or to force them to abandon their claims of interest for their money, and so tide him over the unhappy period. It was a master stroke, and made the name of the great packer a power in the world of finance.

Some Secrets of Success

"Do you consider your financial decisions which you make quickly to be brilliant intuitions?" I asked.

"I never did anything worth doing by accident, nor did anything I have come that way. No, I never decide anything without knowing the conditions of the market, and never begin unless satisfied concerning the conclusion."

"Not everyone could do that," I said.

"I cannot do everything. Every man can do something, and there is plenty to do."

"You really believe the latter statement?"

"There was never more. The problems to be solved are greater now than ever before. Never was there more need of able men. I am looking for trained men all the time. More money is being offered for them everywhere than formerly."

"Do you consider that happiness consists in labor alone?"

"It consists in doing something for others. If you give the world better material, better measure, better opportunities for living respectably, there is happiness in that. You cannot give the world anything without labor, and there is no satisfaction in anything but labor that looks toward doing this, and does it."

Notes

1. "Life Stories of Successful Men—No. 10," *Success* 1 (October 1898): 3–4. On Philip D. Armour. Reprinted as "Philip D. Armour's Business Career" in *How They Succeeded,* pp. 65–86; also as "A 'Forty-niner' Who Seized Opportunities Others Failed to See—Philip D. Armour" in *Little Visits with Great Americans,* 2d ed. (1905), pp. 541–57. Philip Danforth Armour (1832–1901).

2. Frank W. Gunsaulus, D. D. (1856–1921), preacher, orator, educator, practical reformer, and the founder of the Armour Institute of Technology. Dreiser wrote an article about him, "A Leader of Young Manhood," *Success* 2 (15 December 1898):23–24.

3. Armour's financial dealings, to which Dreiser refers in his interview, were later to become a prototype of his business novel *The Titan* (1914).

4. See Dreiser's article, "Great Problems of Organization III: The Chicago Packing Industry," included in this collection.

Life Stories of Successful Men——No. 12[1]

Marshall Field, one of America's greatest merchants, gives to the world the history of his life for the first time—an example for everyone ambitious to succeed in business

"I Determined Not to Remain Poor"

How He Saved His First $5,000

Marshall Field, one of the greatest merchants of the United States, and that means of the world, is not readily accessible to interviews. He probably feels, like most men of real prominence, that his place in the history of his time is established, and he is not seeking for the fame that is certain to attend his name and his business achievements. This very fact, however, makes it all the more desirable for the readers of Success that they should have as a conspicuous study from life the story of Marshall Field related by himself. No more significant story, none more full of stimulus, of encouragement, of brain-inspiring and pulse-thrilling potency has been told in these columns. It is grand in its very simplicity, in its very lack of assumption of special gifts or extraordinary foresight. The Phoenix-like revival from the ashes of ruined Chicago is spoken of by Mr. Field as an incident in the natural and to be expected order of events. In Marshall Field it was no doubt natural and to be expected, and it touches the very keynote of the character of the celebrated Western merchant, sprung from rugged Eastern soil, whose career is an example to be studied with profit by every farmer boy, by every office boy, by every clerk and artisan,—yes, and by every middle-aged business man, whether going along smoothly or confronted by apparently ruinous circumstances, throughout our broad land.

I was introduced to Mr. Field in the private office of Mr. Harry G.

Selfridge, his most trusted lieutenant, and this first of interviews with the head of Chicago's greatest mercantile house followed.

"My object," I said to Mr. Field, "is to obtain your opinion as to what makes for and constitutes success in life."

"That can be quickly given," said Mr. Field; "what would you like to know?"

"I wish to know something of your early life, and under what conditions you began it."

"I was born in Conway, Massachusetts, in 1835. My father's farm was among the rocks and hills of that section, and not very fertile."

"And the conditions were?"

"Hard."

"You mean that you were poor?"

"Yes, as all people were in those days, more or less. My father was a farmer. I was brought up under farming conditions, such as they were at that time."

His Parents Helped Him

"Did the character and condition of your parents tend in any way to form your ambition for commercial distinction?"

"Yes, somewhat. My father was a man who, I consider, had good judgment. He made a success out of the farming business. My mother was more intellectually bent, if anything, and, naturally, both my parents were anxious that their boys should amount to something in life. Their interest and care helped me."

"Had you early access to books?"

"No; I had but few books, scarcely any to speak of. There was not much time for literature. Such books as we had, though, I made use of."

"Were you so placed that your commercial instincts could be nourished by contact with that side of life?" I asked.

"Yes, in a measure. Not any more so than any other boy raised in that neighborhood. I had a leaning toward business, and took up with it as early as possible."

"Were you naturally of a saving disposition?"

"Oh, yes. I had to be. Those were saving times. A dollar looked very big to us boys in those days, and as we had difficult labor earning it, it was not quickly spent. I may say I was naturally saving, however, and was determined not to remain poor."

"Did you attend both school and college?"

"Only the common and high schools at home, but not for long. I had no college training.[2] Indeed, I cannot say that I had much of any public school education. I left home when I was seventeen years of age, and, of course, had not time to study closely."

"What was the nature of your first venture in trade, Mr. Field?"

"My first venture was made as a clerk in a country store at Pittsfield, Massachusetts, where all things were sold, including dry goods, and there I remained for four years. There I picked up my first knowledge of that business."

"Do you consider those years well spent?"

"I think my employer did, anyway." He laughed.

"I saved my earnings and attended strictly to business, and so made them valuable years to me."

"Was there no inducement to remain there as you were?"

"Yes; before I went West, my employer offered me a quarter interest in his business if I would remain with him. Even after I had been here several years, he wrote and offered me a third interest if I would go back. But I was already too well placed."

Marshall Field

"Did you fancy that you were destined for some other field than that in which you have since distinguished yourself?"

Always Interested in Commerce

"No, I think not. I was always interested in the commercial side of life, and always thought I would be a merchant. To this end, I bent my energies, and soon realized that, successful or not, my labor would always be of a commercial nature."

"When did you come to Chicago?" I inquired.

"I caught what was then the prevalent fever to come West, and grow up with the country, and West I came. I entered as a clerk in the dry goods house of Cooley, Woodsworth & Co., in South Water Street."

"Did you foresee Chicago's growth in any way?"

"No, there was no guarantee at that time that the place would ever become the western metropolis. The town had plenty of ambition and pluck; but the possibilities of greatness were hardly visible."

It is interesting to note in this connection that the story of Mr. Field's progress is a wonderfully close index of Chicago's marvelous growth. An almost exact parallel may be drawn between the career of the individual and the growth of the town. Chicago was organized in 1837, two years after Mr. Field was born on the far-off farm in New England, and the place then had a population of a little more than four thousand. In 1856, when Mr. Field, fully equipped for a successful mercantile career, became a resident of the future metropolis of the West, the population had grown to little more than eighty-four thousand. Mr. Field's prosperity advanced in strides parallel to those of the city; with Chicago he was stricken but not crushed by the great fire of 1871,[3] and with Chicago he advanced again to higher achievement and far greater prosperity than before the calamity.

"What were your equipments for success when you started as a clerk here in Chicago, in 1856?"

"Health, sound principles, I hope, and ambition," answered Mr. Field.

"And brains," I suggested, but he only smiled.

"What were the conditions here?"

"Well, merit did not have to wait for dead men's shoes in a growing town, of course. Good qualities were usually promptly discovered, and men were pushed forward rapidly."

"How long did you remain a clerk?"

"Only four years. In 1860, I was made a partner, and in 1865, there was a partial reorganization, and the firm consisted after that of Mr. Leiter, Mr. Palmer and myself, (Field, Palmer, and Leiter.) Two years later Mr. Palmer withdrew, and until 1881, the style of the firm was Field, Leiter & Co. Mr. Leiter retired in that year, and since then it has been as at present: (Marshall Field & Co.)

"What contributed most to the great growth of your business?" I asked.

"To answer that question," said Mr. Field, "would be to review the condition of the West from the time Chicago began until the fire in 1871. Everything was coming this way: immigration, railways and water traffic, and Chicago was enjoying what was called 'flush' times. There were things to learn about the country, and the man who learned the quickest fared the best. For instance, the comparative newness of rural communities and settlements made a knowledge of local solvency impossible. The old State banking system prevailed, and speculation of every kind was rampant. The panic of 1857[4] swept almost everything away except the house I worked for, and I learned that the reason they survived was because they understood the nature of the new country, and did a cash business. That is, they bought for cash, and sold on thirty and sixty days, instead of giving the customers, whose financial condition you could hardly tell anything about, all the time they wanted. When the panic came, they had no debts, and little owing to them, and so they weathered it all right. I learned what I consider my best lesson, and that was to do a cash business."

His Principles of Business

"What were some of the principles you applied to your business?" I questioned.

"Well, I made it a point that all goods should be exactly what they were represented to be. It was a rule of the house that an exact scrutiny of the quality of all goods purchased should be maintained, and that nothing was to induce the house to place upon the market any line of goods at a shade of variation from their real value. Every article sold must be regarded as warranted, and every purchaser must be enabled to feel secure."

"Did you suffer any losses or reverses during your career?"

"No loss except by the fire of 1871. It swept away everything,— about three and a-half millions. We were, of course, protected by insurance, which would have been sufficient against any ordinary calamity of the kind. But the disaster was so sweeping that some of the companies which had insured our property were blotted out, and a long time passed before our claims against others were settled. We managed, however, to start again. There were no buildings of brick or stone left standing, but there were some great shells of horse-car barns at State and Twentieth Streets which were not burned, and I hired those. We put up signs announcing that we would continue business uninterruptedly, and then rushed the work of fitting things up and getting in the stock.

"Did the panic of 1873[5] affect your business?"

"Not at all. We didn't have any debts."

"May I ask what you consider to have been the turning-point in your career,—the point after which there was no more danger of poverty?"

"Saving the first five thousand dollars I ever had, when I might just as well have spent the moderate salary I made. Possession of that sum, once I had it, gave me the ability to meet opportunities. That I consider the turning-point."

Perseverance, Mr. Field's Essential Trait

"What one trait of your character do you look upon as having been the most essential to your successful career?"

"Perseverance," said Mr. Field; but another at hand insisted upon the addition of "good judgment" to this, which Mr. Field indifferently acknowledged. "If I am compelled to lay claim to these traits," he went on, "it is simply because I have tried to practise them, and because the trying has availed me much, I suppose. I have always tried to make all my acts and commercial moves the result of definite consideration and sound judgment. There were never any great ventures or risks,—nothing exciting whatever. I simply practised honest, slow-growing business methods, and tried to back them with energy and good system."

"Have you always been a hard worker?"

"No," Mr. Field said, with the shadow of a smile, "I have never believed in overworking, either as applied to myself or others. It is always paid for with a short life, and I do not believe in it."

"Has there ever been a time in your life when you gave as much as eighteen hours a day to your work?"

"Never. That is, never as a steady practise. During the time of the fire in 1871, there was a short period in which I worked very hard. For several weeks then I worked the greater part of night and day, as almost anyone would have done in my place. My fortune, however, has not been made in that manner, and, as I have said, I believe in reasonable hours for everyone, but close attention during those hours."

"Do you work as much as you once did?"

"I never worked very many hours a day. Besides, people do not work as many hours a day now as they once did. The day's labor has shortened in the last twenty years for everyone. Still, granting that, I cannot say that I work as much as I once did, and I frankly admit that I do not feel the need of it."

"Do you believe," I went on, "that a man should cease laboring before his period of usefulness is over, so that he may enjoy some of the results of his labor before death, or do you believe in retaining constant interest in affairs while strength lasts?"

"As to that, I hold the French idea, that a man ought to retire when he has gained a competence wherewith to do so. I think that is a very good idea. But I do not believe that when a man retires, or no longer attends to his private business in person every day, he has given up interest in the affairs of the world. He may be, in fact should be, doing wider and greater work when he has abandoned his private business, so far as personal attention is concerned."

Qualities That Make for Success

"What, Mr. Field," I said, "do you consider to be the first requisite for success in life, so far as the young beginner is concerned?"

"The qualities of honesty, energy, frugality, integrity, are more necessary than ever to-day, and there is no success without them. They are so often urged that they have become commonplace, but they are really more prized than ever."

"I should like to know what you believe should be the aim of the young man of to-day?"

"He should aim," said Mr. Field, "to possess the qualities I have mentioned."

"By some, however," I suggested, "these are looked upon as a means to an aim only. Would you say to the young man, 'get wealth'?"

"Not," Mr. Field answered, "without practising unflinchingly these virtues."

"Would you say to him, 'acquire distinction'?"

"Not at any expense to his moral character. I can only say, 'practise these virtues and do the best you can.' Any good fortune that comes by such methods is deserved and admirable."

"Do you believe a college education for the young man to be a necessity in the future?"

"Not for business purposes. Better training will become more and more a necessity. The truth is, with most young men, a college education means that just at the time when they should be having business principles instilled into them, and be getting themselves energetically pulled together for their life's work, they are sent to college. Then intervenes what many a young man looks back on as the jolliest time of his life,—four years of college. Often when he comes out of college the young man is unfitted by this good time to buckle down to hard work, and the result is a failure to grasp opportunities that would have opened the way for a successful career."

"Would you say that happiness consists in labor, or in contemplation of labor well done, or in increased possibility of doing more labor?"

"I should say," said Mr. Field, "that a man finds happiness in all three. There certainly is no pleasure in idleness. I believe, as I have said, that a man, upon giving up business, does not necessarily cease laboring, but really does, or should do, more in a larger sense. He should interest himself in public affairs. There is no happiness in mere dollars. After they are had one cannot use but a moderate amount of them. It is given a man to eat so much, to wear so much, and to have so much shelter, and more he cannot use. When money has supplied these, its mission, so far as the individual is concerned, is fulfilled, and man must look further and higher. It is only in the wider public affairs, where money is a moving force toward the general welfare, that the possessor of it can possibly find pleasure, and that only in doing constantly more."

"What," I said, "in your estimation, is the greatest good a man can do?"

"The greatest good he can do is to cultivate himself in order that he may be of greater use to humanity."

"What one suggestion," I said, in conclusion, "can you give to the young men of to-day, that will be most useful to them, if observed?"

"Regardless," said Mr. Field, "of any opinion of mine, or any wish on the part of the young men for wealth, distinction or praise, we know that to be honest is best. There is nothing better, and we also know that nothing can be more helpful than this when combined with other essential qualities."

Notes

1. "Life Stories of Successful Men—No. 12," *Success* 2 (8 December 1898): 7–8. On Marshall Field. Reprinted as "Marshall Field" in *How They Succeeded,* pp. 19–29; also as "Determination Not to Remain Poor Made a Farmer Boy Merchant Prince—Marshall Field" in *Little Visits with Great Americans,* pp. 80–91. Marshall Field (1834–1906).

2. Dreiser was interested in finding out whether or not college education would contribute to one's success in life. Dreiser himself, coming from a poor family, attended Indiana University with a financial support by his high school teacher, but dropped out after one year to work in Chicago.

3. The fire began on Sunday evening, October 8, 1871, and burned until 10:30 the following night an area of five square miles, including the central business district of the city, destroying 17,500 buildings and rendering 100,000 people homeless.

4. The panic of 1857 followed the boom decade of railroad expansion, agricultural development in the Midwest, and gold rush in California. The depression was most serious in the rising industrial areas of the East and the wheat belt of the West. In the election of 1860, economy was no less potent an issue than the issue of slavery.

5. The panic of 1873, the causes of which were worldwide, was precipitated by the failure of many important firms, such as Jay Cooke and Company. By 1875 over 500,000 men were out of work, and in the absence of organized public relief, destitution and hunger were widespread.

The Career of a Modern Portia[1]

Mrs. Clara Shortridge Foltz, the pioneer woman lawyer of the Pacific Coast—
her struggle for recognition in her chosen profession—her success as a
pleader in the courts

One of the leading women lawyers of the United States is Clara Shortridge Foltz, who, after sixteen years of practice on the Pacific Coast,
was admitted to the New York bar in 1896. She has made money
where Belva Lockwood has not, and her preference is for criminal
cases. If distinction and a competence were all that an ambitious advocate struggles for, Mrs. Foltz could retire from practice. But, outside
of the fact that she thinks it her duty to retain all the advantages
woman has gained professionally, she has several ambitions to gratify
on her own behalf. She desires to build and endow a law college for
women, in California, the germ of which already exists in the Portia
Law Club, founded by her; and it is even said that she has in view a
judge's bench. These are not small ambitions; they require a lifetime
to gratify.

I called on Mrs. Foltz at her office in Temple Court, and found the
true barrister's suite, with all the customary show of activity common
to such offices. Mrs. Foltz was busy at the time, but promised an hour,
later. I spoke to her concerning the peculiarity of her profession. She
gravely listened with a smile, and then said:—

"It is not wholly peculiar. There is quite a large number of women
lawyers; surely enough to have dispelled the idea of novelty. Women
do not aspire to occupy the coarser ground in this line. They are not
prepared nor anxious to plead at the criminal bar, but most persons
forget that there is a vast field which requires only a thorough knowledge of law in any one, man or woman, to permit of its being lucra-
tively cultivated. The very smallest part of the business of the legal
profession is that which requires conspicuous appearances in the
courts, much pleading, or showy oratory. By far the greater part is of
a clerical character, and is as fitting for women as for men."

139

How Women Succeed in Law

"Do you think it is a profitable profession for women?"

"It is profitable for me. Making a living usually depends on energy and ability. I see no reason why a capable woman's energy should not profit as much here as elsewhere."

Mrs. Foltz's energy is only hinted at by her office hours: 10 A.M. to 7:30 P.M.; "to keep up with the men, who have had centuries the start," she solemnly avers. The pioneer Portia of the Pacific Coast, it was perhaps well for her that nature has endowed her with an attractive exterior, plenty of woman's wit, and an influential family connection.

"How did you come to take up law as a life-work?" I asked.

"It was a question of taste and necessity. I was left dependent while still a young woman, and rather than burden any relatives, I turned to aid myself in this way."

The accident of her early dependency was brought about by death. She was married when she was but fifteen, and, while still young, was left a widow with five children. She refused all offers of assistance, and declared she would study law. But it is one thing for a woman to decide on the law as a profession, and another to fit herself.

"Did you meet with any obstacles to your plan?"

"With all the obstacles, I think. At that time, twenty years ago, it was one thing for a woman to decide on the law as a profession, and another to fit herself for her labor in that field. The new constitution of California, enacted at that time, prohibited the admission of women to practice at the bar. Still, I applied to the chief law college, Hastings,[2] for admission as a student; and when I was denied, I drew up an amendment to the constitution, allowing women to practice law, and, by hard work, had my friends secure its passage in the legislature."

"Truly?"

"Yes."

"And what followed?"

"Nothing, save that I brought suit against the trustees of Hastings College, and compelled them to admit me to the law class."

"Rather a startling procedure!"

"I should qualify it, however, by speaking of my relatives. It was not so very remarkable when I tell you that law and politics were the portion of our family. My father, at the height of his legal career, left the bar to found the California branch of the Campbellite sect; my brother Samuel is an eminent corporation lawyer there, and another brother, Charles M., is editor and proprietor of the San Francisco 'Call.' A third brother, John R., is quite prominent as a lawyer and politician at Gainsville, Texas. So, you see, it runs in the family. I had to work hard for my amendment, it is true; but I had the assistance of my relatives and their friends, and so fought my battle successfully."

Business Beginnings

"Did you immediately begin practice?"

"Yes. I had some slight prestige gained in my argument with the college, and that availed me. Considerable legal business came to me, and I managed to live by my own labor, from that time on."

"Did you secure any cases which required your appearance in the courts?"

"Quite a number."

"I should like to hear you tell what your feelings were when you first appeared before a jury."

"They were not very reassuring, that you may believe. But I was well grounded in the evidence and the law of the case, and merely presented what I had thoroughly prepared, and avoided all side issues."

"Did you win?"

"In several instances. Once I secured $75,000 damages for a woman client."

"What followed this?"

Building Up a Practice

"Nothing of any importance. The next ten years I spent in building up my practice. I forgot to say that, during this time, I established a daily paper at Santiago, a small town near San Francisco, and used it as a political organ."

"Did you find that your professional work destroyed your home and social relations?"

"Not at all."

"I never neglected my children nor my friends. I had to keep a servant, to be sure; but I looked to it that my home partook of all the merits of a true home. I gave it and my children just as much time as possible, and tried to give it in the very best spirit. I think they will agree with me that it was not far short of being a happy one."

"You never entered politics?"

"Yes, in San Francisco."

"As a candidate for office?"

"Only once. At other times, I merely worked to aid the party."

"What office did you seek?"

"The city and county attorneyship, in 1880."

"You did not get it?"

"No. But I did secure a State school trusteeship,—the first ever filled by a woman."

"What were your political leanings?"

"Republican, at first."

"Are you a Republican no longer?"

"No."

"Why?"

Political Experiences

"Because I have changed in my beliefs. I am more or less independent now. At that time, I could not wholly affiliate myself with that party, because its local managers did not see the place of women in politics, and did not look with any gratification upon my services. I worked intelligently, however."

"What is the true story of it?"

"It was in 1888 that a strong mayoralty fight was on in San Francisco. I was doing a modified form of political work for the Republican candidate, when I called one day at state headquarters, for news. The state secretary was there, and, in the conversation I had with him, he took occasion to say: 'All our best women in the country take no interest in politics.' He said this in connection with other conversation, but it made perfectly plain to me what I had not known before,—that the state organization, as then constituted, took no interest in the ideal that was the base of my actions in doing political work. It did not consider the woman-suffrage question as worth serious thought. My very services were being accepted as if, in so doing, they were favoring me."

"You resented that, of course?"

"Yes. I asked the secretary whether his opinion was official or individual, and when he said that, to the best of his knowledge, it was the view of the party, I walked out of the headquarters, and remained out."

"Did you seek support for your views in any other organization, in that campaign?"

"Yes. I used my influence and that of my friends in the Democratic cause. It may not have amounted to anything, but the Republicans were unsuccessful that year."

"Why do you come to New York?"

"Because I believe the field here offers greater opportunities. I have certainly found it so. There is not the prejudice here that there is in the West, against women in professions."

This will seem to most people who believe in the broad, liberal West, as rather curious. That the distrust of her own sex should forbid the prosperity of a woman lawyer there, is rather a new fact. To hear a Western woman accused of disloyalty to her sex, as Mrs. Foltz was accused, and an Eastern woman lauded for her progress and faith in her sister's business ability, must be, indeed, a surprise to believers in the West.

"Have you found much difficulty in gaining recognition in those states in which you have desired to practice?"

Broad Avenues of Womanly Usefulness

"Not very much. I have been admitted to practice in all the state and United States courts in California, Oregon, Michigan and New York, and I have had the privilege of the United States Supreme Court since 1890."

"Do you believe that women should arouse themselves and force their way into the various professions?"

"Oh, no. I should not put it that way. I believe that where women have special aptitudes and intellectual inclinations, they should not be hampered. Most women find the home sphere enough, and a great many women who think it not enough would be much better off if they did so. But there are exceptions, and for those exceptions it is best that there should be no bars,—no legal disabilities and social prejudices to hinder them from making the utmost use of their natural gifts. To-day, a woman with any distinctive characteristics is almost sure to be frowned upon. She is apt to be cut socially, and to be ostracised, more or less."

"You believe women should vote?"

"Yes, I do. There are a great many of them who scarcely deserve to have the ballot placed in their hands, and yet the majority of women would work for the right. They would vote according to their sympathies, and their sympathies would always extend to men and measures calculated to improve the condition of society. For instance, a woman would always think of the children, and she would always vote for measures to improve and safeguard their future lives. In that way, equal suffrage, I think, would prove a blessing."

"Do you think the rules which promote the success of men, apply to women?"

"Yes. Energy, thrift, stick-to-it-iveness; they are as necessary in women as in men. I believe one thing, and that is that any woman entering any profession, will find the social prejudices and inherited opinions concerning her proper sphere in life, almost insurmountable obstacles."

Ambitious and Progressive, Courteous and Considerate

Mrs. Foltz is a handsome blonde, with a rich, strong voice, and an oratorical manner when aroused. Her dress is the extreme of style, though characterized by a quiet elegance in court; and a Redfern gown has been no unusual costume for her. She has traveled, and has had the novel experience of a shipwreck. Her manners are as courtly to her opponents as if they were guests in her parlor. "I try to live," says she, "so as to prove that woman possesses the power to master the abstruse intricacies of the law, and to skillfully practice it, without impairing her womanliness. I rejoice to follow in the steps of that magnificent woman,"—pointing to a picture of Susan B. Anthony,[3] hung over her desk,—"who struck the first blow for woman's rights at Rochester, fifty years ago. I have proven that woman possesses that quality which men have heretofore arrogated to themselves,—logic. But I have endeavored to do it in such a way as not to offend men's sensibilities."

It will be seen that Mrs. Foltz is an ardent suffragist. But she takes a modest ground, and personally prefers that women should go a little too slow, rather than too fast.

Notes

1. "The Career of a Modern Portia," *Success* 2 (18 February 1899): 205–06. On Mrs. Clara S. Foltz (1849–1934).

2. Hastings College of the Law was established as the Law Department of the University of California system in 1878.

3. Susan Brownell Anthony (1820–1906), America's best known suffragist.

The Real Choate[1]

A study of our new ambassador to the court of St. James

The name of Choate, irrespective of the several individuals whom it has served to designate, carries with it, since the days of the inspired Rufus,[2] a certain flavor of the law. Things legal are by it recalled, the subtle sarcasms of the cross-examiner, the strained pleadings of the advocate, the huge wrangles of the leading counsel and all those Protean intellectualities of that tribe whom Shakespeare dubbed

> "Windy attorneys of their clients' woes,
> Airy succeeders to intestate joys;
> Poor breathing orators of miseries."

It has meant so much in American legal history, so much of all that savors of the magnificent: wit, humor, eloquence, scholarly attainment, statesmanship, and those scintillations of intellect which, irrespective of their moral force thrill and enthrall the common mind by the very wonder of their shining. What matter whither Achilles hurls his spear—Achilles hurls it, and to the common eye the feat is pleasing. So, too, with these, the flash of wit, aimed to reveal the error of the other cause, becomes not so much an illuminant, making dull facts more clear, as a very sun whereon to gaze with wonder, and in whose brilliance it is sweet to bask. The Choates, Rufus and Joseph, have possessed this brilliant quality of wit, and first, one and now the other have risen to the very zenith of the legal heavens.

It is a matter for wonder whether, had Rufus Choate never lived, or had he been merely a reputable country lawyer, Joseph would have been more famous with the great mass of the people than he is at present. He is not a popular hero. There is not enough of that radiant humanity in him which the common people understand and make fellowship with. He is too much reserved, too much self-centered, too innately the patrician to be a man of the people. Law and the things of

145

the law are with him as our a, b, c is with us, and the refinements of belles-lettres are, as it were, graven in his likeness; but he was not born with the simpler sympathies of mankind. Many another man, far more successful with and endeared to the people, has no more of these simpler sympathies than he, but may have a meaner faculty of simulating them. Some such pretend interest and do in a measure pump up a real fellowship with the masses which carries them on to greatness in public affairs; but it is a disheartening thought. Indeed, it is a shame that a man should be master of his countenance and so compose and control it according to his mind, when that mind is not needle-true to Truth itself. While Choate lacks this moral defect in his relations to the people in general, it is not sure that with affairs of a legal nature he is not variable in his sympathies. A man to be successful as a lawyer must often be tempted by offers of fame and financial reward, to interest himself in the prosecution or defense of claims more or less at variance with the basic right of things. We must be fair, however, and extend to him, as, indeed, to all other members of his profession, that gracious tenet of the whole legal fabric, which sets forth that a man must be accounted innocent until proved guilty. There is no proof that Mr. Choate was ever arrayed in the prosecution or defense of any cause in which his sympathies and fullest sense of right were not wholly enlisted.

It is hardly fair, however, to attribute his lack of national popularity to any defect in his sympathies. The finest legal qualifications are of a nature little calculated to rank as merits in the eyes of the people. It is a profession which more often perverts and hides the finest qualities of character. Great corporate interests, also, have become so vast, so complicated, and so exacting that unless a lawyer chooses to abandon the legal profession all but nominally, and enter into the political or philanthropic-social field, he is apt to find his time wholly occupied with entanglements never seen of the people. Mr. Choate has preferred to remain wholly a lawyer. It is an admirable thing that there is nothing of the pseudo-barrister about him. He is all law, all nimbleness and reasoning; all that study and observation pursued by the broadest of intelligences can make of a man in this field. So keen he is that he seems the very essence of legality, a lord among lawyers, born to the purple, and with many generations of refined tradition back of him to make his bearing perfect.

To many outside the Eastern States Joseph H. Choate exists only as a name, or did, perhaps, before his present elevation to the Ambassadorship at the Court of St. James. Being confused with his great relative has been one cause of this, and yet it would be unjust to assign the limitations of his fame wholly to the traditional influence of his gifted cousin. His partnership with William M. Evarts[3] and that venerable gentleman's political activity are facts which have militated against his individual renown. While Mr. Evarts' powerful personality remained in public view its shadow rested upon his younger associate, obscuring him, though unintentionally, from the gaze of the multitude.

At last, however, the sun has emerged from the mist and shines at its brightest. The real Choate is being gazed upon with peculiar interest, and in the effulgence of his personality at the Court of St. James many will be able to observe the strong, distinct traits of the New Englander. His services will resemble, in character, those of Lowell, of whose aristocratic feeling he partakes in quite similar proportions; and he will be remarked for that dignity and reserve relieved by a charming urbanity, which is hereditary to the New England stock. It is safe to say that Englishmen will admire his brilliancy, his unfailing humor, his persuasive powers, and his fine show of courage and chivalry. They will not feel, like so many Americans, that he is removed from their domain of every-day life.

For American purposes Choate needs other qualities in order to become an enduring national figure. Perhaps the chief of these should have been a craving for distinction at the hands of the people. By some—Milholland,[4] for one—he has been credited with an aversion to public life; but this is scarcely true. No man is more keenly alive to his own ability, more aware of the distinguished figure he would make in the national councils of the people, and no doubt it has beén a secret thorn that his splendid talents have been thus strangely circumscribed by a disposition so reserved and a profession so inviting in its narrower way. Until nominated a member of the Constitutional Convention, in 1894, he had never been a candidate for public office. Neither had he sought appointments at the hands of the Federal, State, or City governments. But, while not an office-seeker, he has never openly held public honors in contempt. "I have made it a rule never to seek office," he once said, "or never decline; but I suppose my friends knew I did not desire office, and that is why they never nominated me." That he has been content with the honors which came to him from his remarkable professional success is questionable. What have been his occasional appearances at important public dinners to him; his duties as president of the Union League Club; and as a leading factor in the New England Society! Such activity as he has been called on to exercise in exciting campaigns and at critical stages of New York's municipal affairs has been mere grapes to this craving

Tantalus. It is more to be suspected that he has long chafed secretly at the influence of little men in these State affairs, who, fearing the influence of this giant if once he were enlisted with them, preferred, for the sake of their own prestige, to do without him and leave his magnificent powers unemployed. With them it was "better a great force left unused than awakened and uncontrolled."

This has been the drift of his life. If he has not been indifferent to the cause of good government or to the needs of the people, he has certainly been so absorbed in his professional labors as to feel that his services were not required in party management, or in the conduct of public affairs. Sometimes he has appeared before the public when the need of his aid was apparent and the public task worthy of his own estimation of his powers. When there was a Street Cleaning Commissioner to be arraigned; a member of the Bar to be saved from being sent to jail because of his reckless devotion to his client's interests;

Mr. Choate

when an arrogant element of the population was to be reminded of its faults; a theft of the State Legislature to be exposed; a Tweed ring[5] to be overthrown; a rotten Republican enrollment to be investigated; a Presidential trust to be fought in the interests of the people, or a dangerous State machine of his own party to be smashed, Joseph H. Choate was among the first to answer the clear call of duty.

Yet, for all this, there has ever been in his public movements that strange reserve and attitude of superiority, which, however natural and unconscious, has identified him in the minds of the masses with a certain exclusive and select class. Men have felt "this man is an egoist, a dweller within himself, and cares nothing for others. He is cold and superior." I can fancy many who have known him only publicly, suggesting to themselves that immortal line, "What meat hath this our Caesar fed on, that he has grown so great," and wishing, indifferently, if they wished anything at all, that he might be pulled down and humbled from his high estate for one who does not love his fellow men.

To gain a lasting impression of Mr. Choate does not require that he be seen under the various conditions of his metropolitan existence— that is, in his office, his home, in court, and before a social organization which he is addressing. If but for a moment you had seen him, the impression would linger of a man strong in the possession of those many faculties which make a ready man. His face is a striking example of what the artists call fine modeling, strong in outlines and well accorded, each part with the other, and lacking noticeable or disagreeable exaggeration of any part. He has the build of an ideal soldier—full height, broad shoulders, and, generally, a solid, firm, well-knit figure. What would be ruggedness if unschooled by the career of a student and a gentleman, has become flexibility and grace of demeanor. The eyes are large and wide-set above a powerful nose and below a forehead of most imposing dimensions. They are active and live with intelligence. A certain swiftness of glance almost unaccompanied by motion, characterizes them fixing the attention of the observer immediately. I can imagine nothing more pitiable than some shifty, hang-dog defendant suffering under the scrutiny and analytical fire of this man's eyes. He might easily read through several coats to a heart.

It is curious that this powerful analytical sense is seldom joined with any tenderness of heart, or with any defined leanings to right or wrong. It seems to be a frame of mind in which one goes about to make a display of the narrowness and meanness of another, to put forth plainly a detail of the sufferings and misfortunes and sad, hard necessities of the erring of this world, without experiencing any sensations one way or the other. A rather machine-like quality, to say the least, or, an attitude of mind allied to that of the surgeon who uses the scalpel upon a cadaver.

It has come to me, in seeing Mr. Choate in court, that this is precisely his attitude toward the individuals opposed to him, and that while it is quite the attitude of almost every lawyer, his peculiar ability and strength make it seem much more gross in the execution. The average witness, unaided by powerful counsel to interrupt and suggest, is like wax in his hands. It is marvelous to observe with what insinuating innocence of demeanor he evolves his coil of questions and winds it about his victim.

Not alone toward the unsophisticated in legal matters in this power shown. He has no fear of those above him in authority. He carries his suave manner and absolute independence into the very teeth of judges and juries. An excellent example of this happened before Justice Van Brunt,[6] who had a habit, often distressing to members of the bar, particularly young ones, of talking to his associates on the bench while the lawyers were delivering their speeches. As often as he had exasperated attorneys none of them had ever had the temerity to complain. Mr. Choate was about to make the closing speech in a highly important case. Forty minutes had been allotted him for the purpose. He had scarcely uttered a dozen words when Judge Van Brunt wheeled around in his chair and began talking to Judge Andrews. Mr. Choate ceased speaking immediately, folded his arms and gazed steadily at the judges, his handsome face a trifle paler than usual. A hush fell upon the courtroom. Judge Van Brunt, noticing the stillness, turned around and looked inquiringly at the silent advocate.

"Your Honor," said Mr. Choate. "I have just forty minutes in which to make my final argument. I shall not only need every second of that time to do it justice, but I shall also need your undivided attention."

"And you shall have it," promptly responded the judge, at the same time acknowledging the justice of the rebuke by a faint flush on his cheeks. It was an exhibition of genuine courage much appreciated by members of the profession the city over.

When the matter is thought upon it will be seen that Choate could do this. He has the confidence of his reputation. He knows, for all his show of deference, that he is a much bigger man than half the judges to whom he appeals with a sonorous, "Your Honor." His intellectual feet are firmly set upon a rock of knowledge, and he can stand defiant with every probability of coming off victorious.

His fame is built out of things of this kind. Many will recall the memorable suit in which he appeared, brought by David Stewart, in 1881, against Collis P. Huntington,[7] for the payment of a large sum of money, which the plaintiff declared was due him under the terms of agreement he made with Huntington at the time he purchased a block of Central Pacific stock from the defendant. All involved were well known, and the recital of the doings of that famous Pacific "Big Four," Huntington, Hopkins,[8] Crocker[9] and Stanford,[10] was made an entertaining chapter by Choate who appeared alone for the plaintiff.

The noted Francis N. Bangs[11] and Roscoe Conkling,[12] then in his intellectual prime, were on the other side, and they made a formidable pair of defenders. Mr. Choate made the most of this fact in almost the finest passage of his legal arguments, wherein he said:

"I doubt, gentlemen, whether any man ever had to contend alone against so powerful a combination. In the first place, there is the defendant himself, one of the three great railway monarchs of the world, all-powerful throughout the length and breadth of the land, and he has called here to aid him, as was his right, the greatest powers of the bar, the most astute, the most crafty—in the best sense of the word—the most skilful of our profession, and," with a graceful wave of the hand toward Mr. Conkling, "the very Demosthenes of our time. And yet I do not feel entirely alone or entirely unarmed. I have the evidence in this case with me, and if I can put that little weapon in my sling and aim straight at his forehead, the recent Goliath of the continent is bound to bite the dust."

The marvelous rapidity with which he takes advantage of every point and sees the elements in every situation that are favorable to him was exhibited to advantage on this trial again and again. Mr. Huntington while on the stand proved, from the layman point of view, a poor witness for Mr. Choate. He forgot everything, and Mr. Choate's most ingenious cross-questioning could elicit from him little, if any, specific information as to the operations of the famous Contract and Finance Company. His counsel smiled blandly, and the plaintiff himself looked gloomy. But observe with what telling effect Mr. Choate used this temporary triumph of his opponent.

"My learned friends upon the other side," said he, in closing, "have expressed a little regret and a kind of rebuke for me because I described their client as the Jay Gould[13] of the Pacific coast. Now, gentlemen, a great historical person like Mr. Gould we speak of without personality, and I challenge your attention to the appearance of this defendant on the stand, to say whether he has not filled the bill. Remember that dreadful Black Friday, when the wizard of the New York Stock Market pulled the wires behind the scenes that brought

destruction upon so many honest men, and afterward when called
into court of justice to describe the proceedings of that day, he knew
absolutely nothing about it, although it was all his own work. And
positively as to certain checks he had drawn, he could not say whether
it was for five or ten million dollars. When Mr. Huntington took the
stand and swore that as to the dividends he had received from the
Contract and Finance Company between October, 1867, and May,
1870, he would not tell whether they were one million or two millions,
three millions, four millions, or five millions—did he not fill the bill?"

In this same trial came another fine example of his method of
procedure at the bar. Mr. Conkling had insisted that his client was not
responsible for what his associates had done on the Pacific coast. To
this Mr. Choate responded, "Well, gentlemen, it reminds me of an
alibi that was introduced in another famous case. You remember
when Mr. Tony Weller was called in consultation about the defense of
Mr. Pickwick, in whose arms the fair widow who sued him had been
found dissolved in tears, and he said, 'Sammy, my advice to you is to
prove an *alibi*.' Some defendants, when brought to trial, believe in
character, and some in an *alibi*; but I advise you to stick to an *alibi* and
let the character go. This double of Mr. Huntington, under whose
cover he exists, and is in two places at the same time—on the Atlantic
and the Pacific coast—my distinguished friend said was a romance. I
thought, gentlemen, of that other romance, the story of 'My Double
and How He Undid Me,' and it seems that the defendant was then to
undo him in this case—this Mark Hopkins, by whom he was represented absolutely, completely, and without any limitation whatever, so
you might say that when Mr. Huntington took snuff on the Atlantic
coast Mr. Hopkins sneezed on the Pacific."

A little farther on he paid a glowing tribute to Mr. Conkling—one,
it is said, that the ex-Senator held in grateful remembrance. "However we may differ," said Mr. Choate, "one from another, or all of us
from him, we owe the Senator one debt of gratitude for standing
steadfast and incorruptible in the halls of corruption. Shadrach,
Meshach and Abednego wore immortal glory for passing one day in
the fiery furnace, but he has been twenty years there and has come
out without even the smell of smoke upon his garments."

All his great legal battles have been lightened by such passages of
oratory, such examples of nimble reasoning and flashes of witty com-
pliment and condemnation. Without hesitation he gathers the last
word of the last thought of an argument against him and using it as a
handle to tail his response, flails with that splendid sarcasm of his the
purpose that prompted it. Shakespeare, Aesop, La Fontaine[14] and the

Bible furnish him, in abundance, those splendid similes and allusions with which he graces his argument. Did his greatest opponent, Conkling, quote as he once did a published description of him which provoked a laugh, the applause had not died before he was saying, "My learned friend has been a little personal. He has seen fit to quote for your entertainment and that of the learned court and this audience, a description of my face and features that he gathered from a newspaper. I do not like to rest under this imputation, and I will return it. But, gentlemen, not from a newspaper—oh, no! I will paint his picture as it has been painted by an immortal pen. I will give you a description of him as the divine Shakespeare painted it, for he must have had my learned friend in his eye, when he said:

> See what a grace is seated on his brow;
> Hyperion's curl, the brow of Jove himself;
> An eye like Mars, to threaten and command—
> A combination and a form indeed,
> Where every god did seem to set his seal,
> To give the world assurance of a man."

In the general laugh that greeted this retort Mr. Conkling joined heartily.

In the Wall Street office of Evarts, Choate & Beaman one sees the quiet, calculating, reasoning Choate. Here the great tide of legal affairs runs deeply. His room is but simple one, out of dozens where all sorts of clerks and scriveners make haste and hubbub the long day through. The distinguished barrister has an humble desk and closets himself with his many clients one after another in that leaning, whispering attitude which lawyers adopt. He suffers no change of demeanor, however, and meets all who come with a calm, attentive bearing as though all things were of equal importance.

The firm is generally looked upon as the leading one in the country, and its business is enormous. Mr. Choate enjoys a lucrative practice, though all his fees are looked upon as modest. He works long and faithfully, rising at 6.30 a. m. every day and leaving his home at eight every morning so as to reach his office by nine. At noon he is seldom long in dining, and after an afternoon's close application leaves his desk toward five o'clock and makes his way home. He is not especially partial to street cars and "L" trains, but rides in them often, his several carriages waiting unused.

It is in his home to which he so regularly rejoices to retire that we see the more sympathetic side of the great lawyer. He has it comfortably filled with those things which interest him. A fine library, rare bric-a-brac, a few paintings, some statuary, with rugs and harmonious draperies, lend quiet and ease to the scene. Moreover the place is lightened by that sense of affection which prevails between two persons, where the glamor of a happy marriage has remained unfaded. He has the greatest comfort in the presence of his able and brilliant wife, and sets store by his glowing hearth-fire and its companionship.

I remember calling upon him once on some journalistic mission and finding him poking at a ruddy grate fire to make it burn the brighter. His arm-chair was between the lamp and the flames and a book of poems lay open at his elbow. Quite a distinguished-looking figure he made, gazing at me, poker in hand, as I collected my thoughts and addressed him on whatever subject it was. The room seemed full of an atmosphere exhaled by him, and as the light fell upon him, his fluency, wit, and humor, his sound knowledge, strength and perfect self-control, were all suggested by his face and its expression, and by the firmness of his squarely-set head and massive shoulders.

I remember asking him, under these characteristic surroundings, whether he found that long years of distinction and comfort had brought that feeling of perfect content and happiness which his youthful mind had anticipated.

"No, not exactly," he answered; "our dreams are never fulfilled. There is happiness in constant labor, or, at least, the substitute of happiness, for I find that any one who has once acquired the habit of laboring constantly will not be at peace unless he is working."

"Are not," I said, "few hours of toil, a luxuriously furnished home, hosts of friends, the applause of the people, sumptuous repasts, and content in idleness, knowing that enough has been done, the conditions of happiness?"

"We never know that enough has been done," he said, meditatively. "All that you speak of sounds pleasant, but the truth is that minds whose great exertions have made such things possible for themselves are the very last to crave or rejoice in their possession. You have described what appeals to the idler, the energyless dreamer, the fashionable dawdler, and the listless voluptuary. Enjoyment of such things would sap the strength and deaden the ambition of a Lincoln. The man who has attained to the position where such things are possible is one whose life has been a constant refutation of their need. He is one who has abstained, who has conserved his mental and physical strength by living a simple and frugal life. He has not taken more than he needed, and never, if possible, less. His enjoyment has been in working, and I guarantee that you will always find successful men plain-mannered persons of simple tastes, to whom sumptuous repasts are a bore and luxury a thing apart. They may live surrounded by these things, but personally take little interest in them, counting them mere trappings which neither add to nor detract from greatness."

It is in the social field, however, that New York has seen and heard most of him, and it must be admitted that for the mere quality of perfect humor, without moral import of any defined nature, one must hear him after dinner. The New England Society dinners are his favorites—those gatherings, as he calls them, of an "unhappy company of Pilgrims who meet annually at Delmonico's[15] to drown the sorrows and sufferings of their ancestors in the flowing bowl, and to contemplate their own virtues in the mirror of history."

It is at these meetings that he shines and the witty incidents occur. Here he encounters those old rounders of society, Senator Depew[16] and General Porter,[17] and it is with these gentlemen that he has had his liveliest social tilts. It was at one of these dinners that he greeted them by saying to the assembled company, "I am sure you would not allow me to quit this pleasing programme if I did not felicitate you upon the presence of two other gentlemen without whom no banquet is ever complete. I mean, of course, Mr. Depew and General Porter. Their splendid efforts on a thousand fields like this have fairly won their golden spurs. I forget whether it was Pythagoras or Emerson who finally decided that the soul of mankind is located in the stomach, but these two gentlemen, certainly by their achievements on such arenas as this, have demonstrated at least this rule of anatomy, that the pyloric orifice is the shortest cut to the human brain. Their well-worn title of first of after-dinner orators is the true survival of the fittest, for I assure you that their triumphant struggles in all these many years at scenes like this would long ago have laid all the rest of us under the table, if not under the sod. And so I think in your names I may bid them welcome, thrice welcome—*duo fulmina belli*."

It is always thus with these speeches—always witty. "Now," said he once, glancing up admiringly at the gallery in Delmonico's dining-room, which had just then been filled with ladies, "now I understand what the scriptual phrase means, 'Thou madest man, a little lower than the angels'"

His response to a toast to the fair sex is also well known: "And then women, the better half of the Yankee world, at whose tender summons even the stern Pilgrims were ever ready to spring to arms, and without whose aid they never could have achieved their historic title of the Pilgrim fathers. The Pilgrim mothers were more devoted martyrs than the Pilgrim fathers, because they had not only to bear the same hardships that the Pilgrim fathers suffered, but they had to bear with the Pilgrim fathers besides."

In acknowledging Mr. Choate's legal ascendency I have consciously refrained from the use of the superlative. This has been done because the conviction forces itself upon the mind that his ascendency is to be explained not wholly by superlative merits, but partially by the chance of location. Choate in Chicago or St. Louis or New Orleans—how famous would he have been? Is not New York half the battle—talent the other half? This city whose word of approval lends prestige to so many forms of effort throughout the land—how much has it given to this one of its many favorites?

As for the merit of his labor, when all is said and done, it can only be concluded that he has done for himself nobly, not for others. No great reform in the legal world is linked with his name. No truly great battle of the people has drawn forth the full resources of his splendid brain or the flashes of his oratory. He has worked for and gained a great and lucrative practice. He has laid up money, houses and lands, and has accepted the witty and fashionable characters of society as his friends. He has made himself to shine in their eyes.

Too great praise cannot be lavished upon an instinct that turns energetically to the task of acquiring culture. We can all admire his perfect familiarity with the poetry of Shakespeare. That nimbleness of mind, schooled in art and made perfect in the selection and application of the great thoughts from the master-minds of our language is a pleasing thing to contemplate. But knowledge is not all, wit is not all, analytical power is not all. Choate, the splendid talents of Choate—arrayed in all their subtlety in defense of some execrable Tammany[18] scapegoat, some organized industry seeking to avoid the fulfillment of its just obligations, some corporation caught in act of the false dealing with the State—is not wholly admirable.

But let us not be too severe in dealing with human nature—so poor at its best. For his undoubted leadership of the New York bar, for the number of causes of the first consequence with which he has been connected, for his fluency, his wit and humor, his sound knowledge and perfect self-possession—for all those qualities which make him personally liked and socially admired, let us hold him in esteem, a rare American.

Notes

1. "The Real Choate," *Ainslee's* 3 (April 1899): 324–33.
2. Rufus Choate (1799–1859), American jurist. Joseph Choate (1832–1917).
3. William Maxwell Evarts (1818–1901), American lawyer and statesman.
4. John Elmer Milholland (1860–1925), American businessman and writer, was active in World's Race Congress, London, 1911.

5. William M. Tweed, the Ward Boss in New York City, was involved in the political and industrial corruption. When Tweed was arrested, his million-dollar bond was posted by Jay Gould.

6. Charles H. Van Brunt was a justice of the Supreme Court, New York (1883–1905).

7. Collis Potter Huntington (1821–1900), American pioneer railroad builder.

8. Mark Hopkins (1802–1887), American educator.

9. Charles Crocker (1822–1888), California railroad builder and capitalist.

10. Leland Stanford (1824–1893), American financier, served as governor of California (1861–63) and U. S. Senator (1886–90), and founded Stanford University in 1887.

11. Francis Nehemia Bangs (1828–1885), New York lawyer. As an attorney in a case involving a stock brokerage firm, Bangs triggered investigations of New York's Tweed Ring in 1871 and caused the unseating of three judges.

12. Roscoe Conkling (1829–1888), corporation lawyer and campaign orator, whose control of federal patronages made him New York's undisputed GOP boss.

13. Jay [Jason] Gould (1836–1892), American financier. See note 2 to Dreiser's article, "Fame Found in Quiet Nooks: John Burroughs," included in this volume, p. 56.

14. Jean de La Fontaine (1621–1695), French fabulist. Like his contemporaries Racine and Molière, La Fontaine excelled in making new art out of old materials; his *Fables* (1668) rephrases in verse the animal fables familiar since antiquity.

15. Delmonico's was a famous hotel restaurant located on Fifth Avenue and Twenty-sixth Street in New York City.

16. Chauncey Mitchell Depew (1834–1928), American lawyer and politician. Dreiser wrote an article, "Life Stories of Successful Men—No. 11, Chauncey M. Depew," *Success* 1 (November 1898): 3–4.

17. Horace Porter (1837–1921) served under General Grant during the Civil War and as spokesman for President Grant after the war. A rival of Chauncey Depew as orator, Porter was prominent in civil affairs during the nineties.

18. The Tammany Society was a political organization in New York City that exercised or sought municipal political control by methods often associated with corruption and bossism.

A Monarch of Metal Workers[1]

The marvelous career of Andrew Carnegie—he tells "Success" how he rose
from poverty to plenty—his large-hearted liberality

"Introduced to the Broom, He Spent the Early Hours Sweeping the Office"

"He Delighted in Full Employment and a Prompt Discharge of Business"

Selfish wealth stands surprised, amazed, almost indignant, at the announcement that Andrew Carnegie, instead of resting in Olympian
luxury on the millions he has earned, and going to the grave with his
gold tightly clutched in his stiffening fingers, proposes to expend the
bulk of his riches, during his lifetime, for the benefit of his fellowmen.
Great financiers, who, if they lived to be as old as Methuselah,[2] could
not use a tithe of their vast fortunes on their own ordinary maintenance, protest against Mr. Carnegie's plan of action, and declare that
he ought to go on accumulating to the last. Others mildly suggest that
his charity will be wasted on unworthy objects, and others frankly
avow that they doubt the sincerity of his intentions. Altogether it may
be said that Mr. Carnegie has stirred the very heart of Mammon as it
has not been stirred since the Savior told the rich man to sell what he
had and give to the poor.

It is Harder Now to Get a Start

"There is no doubt," said Mr. Carnegie, in reply to a question from
me, "that it is becoming harder and harder, as business gravitates
more and more to immense concerns, for a young man without
capital to get a start for himself, and in large cities it is especially so,
where large capital is essential. Still it can be honestly said that there is
no other country in the world, where able and energetic young men

158

and women can so readily rise as in this. A president of a business
college informed me, recently, that he has never been able to supply
the demand for capable, first-class [Mark the adjective.] bookkeepers,
and his college has over nine hundred students. In America, young
men of ability rise with most astonishing rapidity."

"As quickly as when you were a boy?"

"Much more so. When I was a boy, there were but very few important positions that a boy could aspire to. Everything had to be made.
Now a boy doesn't need to make the place,—all he has to do is to fit
himself to take it."

"Did you make your high places as you went along?"

"I shouldn't call them high, and I did not make the earliest ones. In
starting new enterprises, of course, I made my place at the head of
them. The earliest ones were the poorest kinds of positions, however."

"Where did you begin life?"

"In Dunfermline, Scotland. That was only my home during my
earliest years. The service of my life has all been in this country."

"In Pittsburg?"

"Largely so. My father settled in Allegheny City, when I was only
ten years old, and I began to earn my way in Pittsburg."

"Do you mind telling me what your first service was?"

"Not at all. I was a bobbin boy in a cotton factory, then an engine-
man or boy in the same place, and later still I was a messenger boy for
a telegraph company."

Mr. Carnegie's First Wages

"At small wages, I suppose."

"One dollar and twenty cents a week was what I received as a
bobbin boy, and I can tell you that I considered it pretty good, at that.
When I was thirteen, I had learned to run a steam engine, and for
that I received a dollar and eighty cents a week."

"You had no early schooling, then?"

"None, except such as I gave myself. There were no fine libraries
then, but in Allegheny City, where I lived, there was a certain Colonel
Anderson, who was well to do and of a philanthropic turn. He announced, about the time I first began to work, that he would be in his
library at his home, every Saturday, ready to lend books to working
boys and men. He only had about four hundred volumes, but I doubt
if ever so few books were put to better use. Only he who has longed, as
I did, for Saturday to come, that the spring of knowledge might be

opened anew to him, can understand what Colonel Anderson did for me and others of the boys of Allegheny. Quite a number of them have risen to eminence, and I think their rise can be easily traced to this splendid opportunity."

"How long did you remain an engine-boy?"

"Not very long," Mr. Carnegie replied, "perhaps a year."

"And then?"

"I entered a telegraph office as a messenger boy."

Although Mr. Carnegie would not dwell much on this period, he once described it at a dinner given in honor of the American Consul at Dunfermline, Scotland, when he said:—

"I awake from a dream that has carried me away back to the days of my boyhood, the day when the little white-haired Scottish laddie, dressed in a blue jacket, walked with his father into the telegraph office in Pittsburg to undergo examination as an applicant for a position as messenger boy.

His First Glimpse of Paradise

"Well I remember when my uncle spoke to my parents about it, and my father objected, because I was then getting one dollar and eighty cents per week for running a small engine in a cellar in Allegheny City, but my uncle said a messenger's wages would be two dollars and fifty cents. . . . If you want an idea as to heaven on earth, imagine what it is to be taken from a dark cellar, where I fired the boiler from morning until night, and dropped into an office, where light shone from all sides, and around me books, papers, and pencils in profusion, and oh! the tick of those mysterious brass instruments on the desk, annihilating space and standing with throbbing spirits ready to convey any intelligence to the world! This was my first glimpse of paradise, and I walked on air."

"How did you manage to rise from this position?"

"Well, I learned how to operate a telegraph instrument, and then waited my opportunity to show that I was fit to be an operator. Eventually my chance came, as everyone's does."

The truth is that the boy had the appearance of one anxious to learn and quick to understand. James D. Reid, the superintendent of the office, and himself a Scotchman, favored the ambitious lad, and helped him. In his "History of the Telegraph," he says of him:—

"I liked the boy's looks, and it was easy to see that though he was little, he was full of spirit. He had not been with me a month when he began to ask whether I would teach him to telegraph. I began to instruct him and found him an apt pupil. He spent all his spare time in practice, sending and receiving by sound and not by tape, as was largely the custom in those days. Pretty soon he could do as well as I could at the key, and then his ambition carried him away beyond doing the drudgery of messenger work."

"As you look back upon it," I said to Mr. Carnegie, "do you consider that so lowly a beginning is better than one a little less trying?"

"For young men starting upon their lifework, it is much the best to begin as I did, at the beginning, and occupy the most subordinate positions. Many of the present-day leading men of Pittsburg, who rose with me, had a serious responsibility thrust upon them at the very threshold of their careers. They were introduced to the broom, and spent the first hours of their business life sweeping out the office. I notice we have janitors and janitresses now in offices, and our young men, unfortunately, miss that salutary branch of early education. Still I would say to the boy who has the genius of the future partner in him, that if by chance the professional sweeper is absent any morning, do not hestitate to try your hand at the broom. It does not hurt the newest comer to sweep out the office if necessary."

"Did you?"

"Many's the time. And who do you suppose were my fellow sweepers? David McBargo, afterwards superintendent of the Allegheny Valley Railroad; Robert Pitcairn, afterwards superintendent of the Pennsylvania Railroad, and Mr. Moreland, subsequently City Attorney of Pittsburg. We all took turns, two each morning doing the sweeping; and now I remember Davie was so proud of his clean shirt bosom that he used to spread over it an old silk bandanna handkerchief which he kept for the purpose, and we other boys thought he was putting on airs. So he was. None of us had a silk handkerchief."

"After you had learned to telegraph, did you consider that you had reached high enough?"

"Not in the least. My father died just at that time, and the burden of the support of the family fell upon me. I became an operator at twenty-five dollars a month, a sum which seemed to me almost a fortune. I earned a little additional money by coping telegraphic messages for the newspapers, and managed to keep the family independent."

He was an Expert Telegraph Operator

More light on this period of Mr. Carnegie's career is given by the "Electric Age," which says: "He was a telegraph operator abreast of older and experienced men; and, although receiving messages by sound was, at that time, forbidden by authority as being unsafe, young Carnegie quickly acquired the art, and he can still stand behind the ticker and understand its language. As an operator, he delighted in full employment and the prompt discharge of business, and a big day's work was his chief pleasure."

"How long did you remain with the telegraph company?"

"Until I was given a place by the Pennsylvania Railroad Company."

"As an operator?"

"At first, until I showed how the telegraph could minister to railroad safety and success. Then I was made secretary to Thomas A. Scott, then superintendent, and not long afterwards, when Colonel Scott became vice-president, I was made superintendent of the western division of the Pennsylvania Railroad."

Thinking of this period of his life, I asked Mr. Carnegie if his promotion was not a matter of chance, and whether he did not, at the time, feel it to be so. His answer was emphatic.

"Never. Young men give all kinds of reasons why, in their cases, failure is attributable to exceptional circumstances, which rendered success impossible. Some never had a chance, according to their own story. This is simply nonsense. No young man ever lived who had not a chance, and a splendid chance, too, if he was ever employed at all. He is assayed in the mind of his immediate superior, from the day he begins work, and, after a time, if he has merit, he is assayed in the council chambers of the firm. His ability, honesty, habits, associations, temper, disposition,—all these are weighed and analyzed. The young man who never had a chance is the same young man who has been canvassed over and over again by his superiors, and found destitute of necessary qualifications, or is deemed unworthy of closer relations with the firm, owing to some objectionable act, habit or association, of which he thought his employers ignorant."

"It sounds true."

The Right Men in Demand

"It is. Another class of young men attributes failure to rise to employers having near relatives or favorites whom they advance unfairly. They also insist that their employers dislike brighter intelligences than their own, and are disposed to discourage aspiring genius, and delighted in keeping young men down. There is nothing in this. On the contrary, there is no one suffering more for lack of the right man in the right place as the average employer, nor anyone more anxious to find him."

"Was this your theory on the subject when you began working for the railroad company?"

"I had no theory then, although I have formulated one since. It lies mainly in this: Instead of the question, 'What must I do for my employer?' substitute, 'What can I do?' Faithful and conscientious discharge of duties assigned you is all very well, but the verdict in such cases generally is that you perform your present duties so well, that you would better continue performing them. Now, this will not do. It will not do for the coming partners. There must be something beyond this. We make clerks, bookkeepers, treasurers, bank tellers of this class, and there they remain to the end of the chapter. The rising man must do something exceptional, and beyond the range of his special department. He must attract attention."

How to Attract Attention

"How can he do that?"

"Well, if he is a shipping clerk, he may do so by discovering in an invoice an error with which he has nothing to do and which has escaped the attention of the proper party. If a weighing clerk, he may save for the firm by doubting the adjustment of the scales, and having them corrected, even if this be the province of the master mechanic. If a messenger boy, even he can lay the seed of promotion by going beyond the letter of his instructions in order to secure the desired reply. There is no service so low and simple, neither any so high, in which the young man of ability and willing disposition cannot readily and almost daily prove himself capable of greater trust and usefulness, and, what is equally important, show his invincible determination to rise."

"In what manner did you reach out to establish your present great fortune?" I asked.

"By saving my money. I put a little money aside, and it served me later as a matter of credit. Also, I invested in a sleeping-car industry, which paid me well."

Carnegie and the Sleeping-Car

Although I tried earnestly to get the great iron-king to talk of this, he said little, because the matter has been fully dealt with by him in his

"Triumphant Democracy."[3] From his own story there, it appears that, one day at this time, when Mr. Carnegie still had his fortune to make, he was on a train examining the line from a rear window of a car, when a tall, spare man, accosted him and asked him to look at an invention he had made. He drew from a green bag a small model of a sleeping-berth for railway cars, and proceeded to point out its advantages. It was Mr. T. T. Woodruff, the inventor of the sleeping-car. Mr. Carnegie tells the story himself in "Triumphant Democracy:"—

"He had not spoken a moment before, like a flash, the whole range of the discovery burst upon me, 'Yes,' I said, 'that is something which this continent must have.'

"Upon my return, I laid it before Mr. Scott, declaring that it was one of the inventions of the age. He remarked: 'You are enthusiastic, young man, but you may ask the inventor to come and let me see it.' I did so, and arrangements were made to build two trial cars, and run them on the Pennsylvania Railroad. I was offered an interest in the venture, which, of course, I gladly accepted.

"The notice came that my share of the first payment was $217.50. How well I remember the exact sum! But two hundred and seventeen dollars and a half were as far beyond my means as if it had been millions. I was earning fifty dollars per month, however, and had prospects, or at least I always felt that I had. I decided to call on the local banker and boldly ask him to advance the sum upon my interest in the affair. He put his hand on my shoulder and said: 'Why, of course, Andie; you are all right. Go ahead! Here is the money.'

"It is a proud day for a man when he pays his last note, but not to be named in comparison with the day in which he makes his first one, and gets a banker to take it. I have tried both, and I know. The cars paid the subsequent payments from their earnings. I paid my first note from my savings, so much per month, and thus did I get my foot upon fortune's ladder. It was easy to climb after that."

"I would like some expression from you," I said to Mr. Carnegie, "in reference to the importance of laying aside money from one's earnings, as a young man."

The Mark of the Millionaire

"You can have it. There is one sure mark of the coming partner, the future millionaire: his revenues always exceed his expenditures. He begins to save early, almost as soon as he begins to earn. I should say to young men, no matter how little it may be possible to save, save that little. Invest it securely, not necessarily in bonds, but in anything which you have good reason to believe will be profitable; but no gambling with it, remember. A rare chance will soon present itself for investment. The little you have saved will prove the basis for an amount of credit utterly surprising to you. Capitalists trust the saving young man. For every hundred dollars you can produce as the result of hard-won savings, Midas, in, search of a partner, will lend or credit a thousand; for every thousand, fifty thousand. It is not capital that your seniors require, it is the man who has proved that he has the business habits which create capital. So it is the first hundred dollars saved that tell."

"What," I asked Mr. Carnegie, "was the next enterprise with which you identified yourself?"

A Fortunate Land Purchase

"In company with several others, I purchased the now famous Storey farm, on Oil Creek, Pennsylvania, where a well had been bored and natural oil struck the year before. This proved a very profitable investment."

In "Triumphant Democracy," Mr. Carnegie has expatiated most fully on this venture, which is so important. "When I first visited this famous well," he says, "the oil was running into the creek, where a few flat-bottomed scows lay filled with it, ready to be floated down the Allegheny River, upon an agreed-upon day each week, when the creek was flooded by means of a temporary dam. This was the beginning of the natural-oil business. We purchased the farm for $40,000, and so small was our faith in the ability of the earth to yield, for any considerable time, the hundred barrels per day, which the property was then producing, that we decided to make a pond capable of holding one hundred thousand barrels of oil, which, we estimated, would be worth, when the supply ceased, $1,000,000.

"Unfortunately for us, the pond leaked fearfully; evaporation also caused much loss, but we continued to run oil in to make the losses good, day after day, until several hundred thousand barrels had gone in this fashion. Our experience with the farm may be worth reciting. Its value rose to $5,000,000; that is, the shares of the company sold in the market upon this basis, and one year it paid, in cash, dividends of $1,000,000,—rather a good return upon an investment of $40,000."

"Were you satisfied to rest with these enterprises in your hands?" I asked.

"No. Railway bridges were then built almost exclusively of wood, but the Pennsylvania Railroad had begun to experiment with cast iron for bridge building. It struck me that the railway bridge of the future must be of iron, and I organized, in Pittsburg, a company for the construction of iron bridges. That was the Keystone Bridge Works. We built the first iron bridge across the Ohio."

His entrance to the realm of steel was much too long for Mr. Carnegie to discuss, although he was not unwilling to give information relating to the great subject. It appears that he realized the immensity of the steel manufacturing business at once. The Union Iron Mills soon followed as one of his enterprises, and, later, the famous Edgar Thompson Steel Rail Mill. The last was the outcome of a visit to England, in 1868, when Carnegie noticed that English railways were discarding iron for steel rails. The Bessemer process had been then perfected, and was making its way in all the iron-producing countries. Carnegie, recognizing that it was destined to revolutionize the iron business, introduced it into his mills and made steel rails with which he was enabled to compete with English manufacturers.

The Homestead Steel Works

His next enterprise was the purchase of the Homestead Steel Works,—his great rival of Pittsburg. By 1888, he had built or acquired seven distinct iron and steel works, all of which are now included in the Carnegie Steel Company, Limited. All the plants of this great firm are within a radius of five miles of Pittsburg. Probably in no other part of the world can be found such an aggregation of splendidly equipped steel works as those controlled by this association. It now comprises the Homestead Steel Works, the Edgar Thompson Steel Works and Furnaces, the Duquesne Steel Works and Furnaces, all within two miles of one another: the Lucy Furnaces, the Keystone Bridge Works, the Upper Union Rolling Mills, and the Lower Union Rolling Mills.

In all branches, including the great coke works, mines, etc., there are employed twenty-five thousand men. The monthly pay roll exceeds one million, one hundred and twenty-five thousand dollars, or nearly fifty thousand dollars for each working day. Including the Frick Coke Company, the united capital of the Carnegie Steel Company exceeds sixty million dollars.

"You believe in taking active measures," I said, "to make men successful."

"Yes, I believe in anything which will help men to help themselves. To induce them to save, every workman in our company is allowed to deposit part of his earnings, not exceeding two thousand dollars, with the firm, on which the high interest rate of six per cent is allowed. The firm also lends to any of its workmen to buy a lot, or to build a house, taking its pay by installments."

"Has this contributed any to the success of your company?"

A Strengthening Policy

"I think so. The policy of giving a personal interest to the men who render exceptional service is strengthening. With us there are many such, and every year several more are added as partners. It is the policy of the concern to interest every superintendent in the works, every head of a department, every exceptional young man. Promotion follows exceptional service, and there is no favoritism."

"All you have said so far, merely gives the idea of getting money, without any suggestion as to the proper use of great wealth. Will you say something on that score?"

"My views are rather well known, I think. What a man owns is already subordinate, in America, to what he knows; but, in the final aristocracy, the question will not be either of these, but what has he done for his fellows? Where has he shown generosity and self-abnegation? Where has he been a father to the fatherless? And the cause of the poor, where has he searched that out? How he has worshiped God will not be asked in that day, but how he has served man."

Mr. Carnegie's Philanthropy

That Mr. Carnegie has lived up, in the past, and is still living up to this radical declaration of independence from the practice of men who have amassed fortunes around him, will be best shown by a brief enumeration of some of his almost unexampled philanthropies. His largest gift has been to the city of Pittsburg, the scene of his early trials and later triumphs. There he has built, at a cost of more than a million dollars, a magnificent library, museum, concert hall and picture gallery, all under one roof, and endowed it with a fund of another million, the interest of which, (fifty thousand dollars per annum,) is being devoted to the purchase of the best works of American art. Other libraries, to be connected with this largest as a center, are now being constructed, which will make the city of Pittsburg and its environs a beneficiary of his generosity to the extent of five million dollars.

While thus endowing the city where his fortune was made, he has not forgotten other places endeared to him by association or by interest. To the Allegheny Free Library he has given $375,000; to the Braddock Free Library, $250,000; to the Johnstown Free Library, $50,000; and to the Fairfield (Iowa,) Library, $40,000. To his native land he has been scarcely less generous. To the Edinburgh Free Library he has given $250,000, and to his native town of Dunfermline, $90,000. Other Scottish towns to the number of ten have received helpful donations of amounts not quite so large.

"I should like you to say some other important things for the young man to learn and benefit by."

"Our young partners in the Carnegie company have all won their spurs by showing that we did not know half as well what was wanted as they did. Some of them have acted upon occasions with me as if they owned the firm and I was but some airy New Yorker, presuming to advise upon what I knew very little about. Well, they are not now interfered with. They were the true bosses,—the very men we were looking for."

"The Misfortune of Being Rich Men's Sons"

"Is this all for the poor boy?"

"Every word. I trust that few, if any, of the readers of Success have the misfortune to be rich men's sons. They are heavily weighted in the race. A basketful of bonds is the heaviest basket a young man ever had to carry. He generally gets to staggering under it. The vast majority of rich men's sons are unable to resist the temptations to which wealth subjects them, and they sink to unworthy lives. It is not from this class that the poor beginner has rivalry to fear. The partner's sons will never trouble you much, but look out that some boys poorer, much poorer, than yourselves, whose parents cannot afford to give them any schooling, do not challenge you at the post and pass you at the grand stand. Look out for the boy who has to plunge into work direct from the common school, and begins by sweeping out the office. He is the probable dark horse that will take all the money and win all the applause."

Notes

1. "A Monarch of Metal Workers," *Success* 2 (3 June 1899): 453–54. On Andrew Carnegie. Reprinted as "Carnegie as a Metal Worker" in *How They Succeeded,* pp. 253–75; also as "A Poor Boy Who Once Borrowed Books Now Gives Away Libraries—Andrew Carnegie" in *Little Visits with Great Americans,* pp. 51–70. Andrew Carnegie (1835–1919).

2. An ancestor of Noah held to have lived 969 years.

3. *Triumphant Democracy* (New York, 1886).

Curious Shifts of the Poor[1]

Strange ways of relieving desperate poverty.—Last resources of New York's most pitiful medicants.

At the hour when Broadway assumes its most interesting aspect, a peculiar individual takes his stand at the corner of Twenty-sixth Street. It is the hour when the theatres are just beginning to receive their patrons. Fire signs, announcing the night's amusements, blaze on every hand. Cabs and carriages, their lamps gleaming like yellow eyes, patter by. Couples and parties of three and four are freely mingled in the common crowd which passes by in a thick stream, laughing and jesting. On Fifth Avenue are loungers, a few wealthy strollers, a gentleman in evening dress with a lady at his side, some clubmen, passing from one smoking room to another. Across the way the great hotels, the Hoffman House and the Fifth Avenue, show a hundred gleaming windows, their cafés and billiard rooms filled with a pleasure-loving throng. All about, the night has a feeling of pleasure and exhilaration, the curious enthusiasm of a great city, bent upon finding joy in a thousand different ways.

In the midst of this lightsome atmosphere a short, stocky-built soldier, in a great cape-overcoat and soft felt hat, takes his stand at the corner. For a while he is alone, gazing like any idler upon an ever-fascinating scene. A policeman passes, saluting him as Captain, in a friendly way. An urchin, who has seen him there before, stops and gazes. To all others he is nothing out of the ordinary save in dress, a stranger, whistling for his own amusement.

As the first half hour wanes, certain characters appear. Here and there in the passing crowd one may see now and then a loiterer, edging interestedly near. A slouchy figure crosses the opposite corner and glances furtively in his direction. Another comes down Fifth Avenue to the corner of Twenty-sixth Street, takes a general survey and hobbles off again. Two or three noticeable Bowery types edge along the Fifth Avenue side of Madison Square, but do not venture over.

170

The soldier in his cape-overcoat walks a line of ten feet at his corner, to and fro, whistling.

As nine o'clock approaches, some of the hubbub of the earlier hour passes. On Broadway the crowd is neither so thick nor so gay. There are fewer cabs passing. The atmosphere of the hotels is not so youthful. The air, too, is colder. On every hand move curious figures, watchers and peepers without an imaginary circle, which they are afraid to enter—dozens in all. Presently, with the arrival of a keener sense of cold, one figure comes forward. It crosses Broadway from out the shadow of Twenty-sixth Street, and, in a halting, circuitous way, arrives close to the waiting figure. There is something shamefaced, a diffident air about the movement, as if the intention were to conceal any idea of stopping until the very last moment. Then, suddenly, close to the soldier comes the halt. The Captain looks in recognition, but there is no especial greeting. The newcomer nods slightly, and murmurs something, like one who waits for gifts. The other simply motions toward the edge of the walk.

"Stand over there."

The spell is broken. Even while the soldier resumes his short, solemn walk, other figures shuffle forward. They do not so much as greet the leader, but join the one, shuffling and hitching and scraping their feet.

"Cold, isn't it?"

"I don't like winter."

"Looks as though it might snow."

The motley company has increased to ten. One or two know each other and converse. Others stand off a few feet, not wishing to be in the crowd, and yet not counted out. They are peevish, crusty, silent, eying nothing in particular, and moving their feet. The soldier, counting sufficient to begin, comes forward.

"Beds, eh, all of you?"

There is a general shuffle and murmur of approval.

"Well, line up here. I'll see what I can do. I haven't a cent myself."

They fall into a sort of broken, ragged line. One sees now some of the chief characteristics by contrast. There is a wooden leg in the line. Hats are all drooping, a collection that would ill become a second-hand Hester Street basement collection. Trousers are all warped and frayed at the bottom, and coats worn and faded. In the glare of the street lights, some of the faces look dry and chalky. Others are red with blotches, and puffed in the cheeks and under the eyes. One or two are raw-boned and remind one of railroad hands. A few spectators come near, drawn by the seemingly conferring group, then more and more, and quickly there is a pushing, gaping crowd. Some-one in the line begins to talk.

"Silence!" exclaims the Captain. "Now, then, gentlemen, these men are without beds. They have got to have some place to sleep to-night. They can't lie out in the street. I need twelve cents to put one to bed. Who will give it to me?"

No reply.

"Well, we'll have to wait here, boys, until someone does. Twelve cents isn't so very much for one man."

"Here is fifteen," exclaims a young man, who is peering forward with strained eyes. "It's all I can afford."

"All right; now I have fifteen. Step out of the line," and seizing the one at the end of the line nearest him by the shoulder, the Captain marches him off a little way and stands him up alone.

Coming back, he resumes his place before the little line and begins again.

"I have three cents here. These men must be put to bed somehow. There are," counting, "one, two, three, four, five, six, seven, eight, nine, ten, eleven, twelve men. Nine cents more will put the next man to bed, give him a good, comfortable bed for the night. I go right along and look after that myself. Who will give me nine cents?"

One of the watchers, this time a middle-aged man, hands in a five-cent piece.

"Good. Now I have eight cents. Four more will give this man a bed. Come, gentlemen, we are going very slow this evening. You all have good beds. How about these?"

"Here you are," remarked a bystander, putting a coin into his hand.

"That," says the Captain, looking at the coin, "pays for two beds for two men and leaves five for the next one. Who will give seven cents more?"

On the one hand the little line of those whose beds are secure is growing, but on the other the bedless waxes long. Silently the queer drift of poverty washes in, and they take their places at the foot of the line unnoticed. Ever and anon the Captain counts and announces the number remaining. Its growth neither dismays nor interests him. He does not even speak of it. His concern is wholly over the next man, and the securing of twelve cents. Strangers, gazing out of mere curios-ity, find their sympathies enlisted, and pay into the hands of the Captain dimes and quarters, as he states in a short, brusque, unaf-fected way, the predicament of the men.

In the line of men whose beds are secure, a relaxed air is apparent.

The strain of uncertainty being removed, there is moderate good feeling, and some leaning toward sociability. Those nearest one another begin to talk. Politics, religion, the state of the government, some newspaper sensations, and the more notorious facts of the world find mouth-pieces and auditors here. Vague and rambling are the discussions. Cracked and husky voices pronounce forcibly on odd things. There are squints and leers and dull ox-like stares from those who are too dull or too weary to converse.

Standing tells. In the course of time the earliest arrivals become weary and uneasy. There is a constant shifting from one foot to the other, a leaning out and looking back to see how many more must be provided for before the company can march away. Comments are made and crude wishes for the urging forward of things.

"Huh! There's a lot back there yet."

"Yes, must be over a hundred to-night."

"Look at the guy in the cab."

"Captain's a great fellow, ain't he?"

A cab has stopped. Some gentleman in evening dress reaches out a bill to the Captain, who takes it with simple thanks, and turns away to his line. There is a general craning of necks as the jewel in the broad white shirt-front sparkles and the cab moves off. Even the crowd gapes in awe.

"That fixes up nine men for the night," says the Captain, counting out as many of the line near him. "Line up over there. Now, then, there are only seven. I need twelve cents."

Money comes slow. In the course of time the crowd thins out to a meagre handful. Fifth Avenue, save for an occasional cab or foot-passenger, is bare. Broadway is thinly peopled with pedestrians. Only now and then a stranger passing notices the small group, hands out a coin and goes away, unheeding.

The Captain is stolid and determined. He talks on, very slowly, uttering the fewest words, and with a certain assurance, as though he could not fail.

"Come, I can't stay out here all night. These men are getting tired and cold. Someone give me four cents."

There comes a time when he says nothing at all. Money is handed him, and for each twelve cents he singles out a man and puts him in the other line. Then he walks up and down as before, looking at the ground.

The theatres let out. Fire signs disappear. A clock strikes eleven. Another half hour, and he is down to the last two men.

A lady in opera cape and rustling silk skirt comes down Fifth Avenue, supported by her escort. The latter glances at the line and comes over. There is a bill in his fingers.

"Here you are," he says.

"Thanks," says the Captain. "Now we have some for to-morrow night."

The last two are lined up. The soldier walks along, studying his line and counting.

"One hundred and thirty-seven," he exclaims, when he reaches the head.

"Now, boys, line up there. Steady now, we'll be off in a minute."

He places himself at the head and calls out, "Forward, march!" and away they go.

Across Fifth Avenue, through Madison Square, by the winding path, east on Twenty-third Street, and down Third Avenue trudges the long, serpentine company.

Below Tenth Street is a lodging house, and here the queer, ragamuffin line brings up, while the Captain enters in to arrange. In a few minutes the deal is consummated, and the line marches slowly in, each being provided with a key as the Captain looks on. When the last one has disappeared up the dingy stairway, he comes out, muffles his great coat closer in the cold air, pulls down his slouch brim, and tramps, a solitary, silent figure, into the night.

Such is the Captain's idea of his duty to his fellow man. He is a strange man, with a strange bias. Utter confidence in Providence, perfectly sure that he deals direct with God, he takes this means of fulfilling his own destiny.

*   *   *

Outside the door of what was once a row of red brick family dwellings, in Fifteenth Street, but what is now a mission or convent house of the Sisters of Mercy, hangs a plain wooden contribution box, on which is painted the statement that every noon a meal is given free to all those who apply and ask for aid. This simple announcement is modest in the extreme, covering, as it does, a charity so broad. Unless one were looking up this matter in particular, he could stand at Sixth Avenue and Fifteenth Street for days, around the noon hour, and never notice that, out of the vast crowd that surges along that busy thoroughfare, there turned out, every few seconds, some weather-beaten, heavy-footed specimen of humanity, gaunt in countenance, and dilapidated in the matter of clothes. The fact is true, however, and the colder the day the more apparent it becomes. Space and lack of culinary room compels an arrangement which permits of only twenty-five or thirty eating at one time, so that a line has to be formed outside, and an orderly entrance effected.

One such line formed on a January day last year. It was peculiarly cold. Already, at eleven in the morning, several shambled forward out of Sixth Avenue, their thin clothes flapping and fluttering in the wind, and leaned up against the iron fence. One came up from the west out of Seventh Avenue and stopped close to the door, nearer than all the others. Those who had been waiting before him, but farther away, now drew near, and by a certain stolidity of demeanor, no words being spoken, indicated that they were first. The newcomer looked sullenly along the line and then moved out, taking his place at the foot. When order had been restored, the animal feeling of opposition relaxed.

"Must be pretty near noon," ventured one.

"It is," said another; "I've been waitin' nearly an hour."

"Gee, but it's cold."

The line was growing rapidly. Those at the head evidently congratulated themselves upon not having long to wait. There was much jerking of heads and looking down the line.

"It don't matter much how near you get to the front, so long as you're in the first twenty-five. You all go in together," commented one of the first twenty-five.

"This here Single Tax is the thing. There ain't goin' to be no order till it comes," said another, discussing that broader topic.

At last the door opened and the motherly Sister looked out. Slowly the line moved up, and one by one thirty men passed in. Then she interposed a stout arm and the line halted with six men on the steps. In this position they waited. After a while one of the earliest to go in came out, and then another. Every time one came out the line moved up. And this continued until two o'clock, when the last hungry dependent crossed the threshold, and the door was closed.

* * *

It was a winter evening. Already, at four o'clock, the sombre hue of night was thickening the air. A heavy snow was falling—a fine, picking, whipping snow, borne forward by a swift wind in long, thin lines. The street was bedded with it, six inches of cold, soft carpet, churned brown by the crush of teams and the feet of men. Along the Bowery, men slouched through it with collars up and hats pulled over their ears.

Before a dirty four-story building gathered a crowd of men. It began with the approach of two or three, who hung about the closed wooden doors, and beat their feet to keep them warm. They made no effort to go in, but shifted ruefully about, digging their hands deep in their pockets, and leering at the crowd and the increasing lamps. There were old men with grizzled beards and sunken eyes; men who were comparatively young, but shrunken by disease; men who were middle-aged.

With the growth of the crowd about the door came a murmur. It was not a conversation, but a running comment directed at anyone in general. It contained oaths and slang phrases.

"I wisht they'd hurry up."

"Look at the copper watchin'."

"Maybe it ain't winter, nuther."

"I wisht I was with Otis."

Now a sharper lash of wind cut down, and they huddled closer. There was no anger, no threatening words. It was all sullen endurance, unlightened by either wit or good fellowship.

A carriage went jingling by with some reclining figure in it. One of the members nearest the door saw it.

"Look at the bloke ridin'."

"He ain't so cold."

"Eh! Eh! Eh!" yelled another, the carriage having long since passed out of hearing.

Little by little the night crept on. Along the walk a crowd turned out on its way home. Still the men hung around the door, unwavering.

"Ain't they ever goin' to open up?" queried a hoarse voice suggestively.

This seemed to renew general interest in the closed door, and many gazed in that direction. They looked at it as dumb brutes look, as dogs paw and whine and study the knob. They shifted and blinked and muttered, now a curse, now a comment. Still they waited, and still the snow whirled and cut them.

A glimmer appeared through the transom overhead, where someone was lighting the gas. It sent a thrill of possibility through the watcher. On the old hats and peaked shoulders snow was piling. It gathered in little heaps and curves, and no one brushed it off. In the center of the crowd the warmth and steam melted it, and water trickled off hat-rims and down noses which the owners could not reach to scratch. On the outer rim the piles remained unmelted. Those who could not get in the center lowered their heads to the weather and bent their forms.

At last the bars grated inside and the crowd pricked up its ears. There was someone who called, "Slow up there now!" and then the door opened. It was push and jam for a minute, with grim, beast silence to prove its quality, and then the crowd lessened. It melted inward like logs floating, and disappeared. There were wet hats and shoulders, a cold, shrunken, disgruntled mass, pouring in between bleak walls. It was just six o'clock, and there was supper in every hurrying pedestrian's face.

"Do you sell anything to eat here?" questioned one of the grizzled old carpet-slippers who opened the door.

"No; nothin' but beds."

The waiting throng had been housed.

* * *

For nearly a quarter of a century Fleischman, the caterer, has given a loaf of bread to anyone who will come for it to the rear door of his restaurant, on the corner of Broadway and Ninth Street, at midnight. Every night, during twenty-three years, about three hundred men have formed in line, and, at the appointed time, marched past the doorway, picked their loaf from a great box placed just outside, and vanished again into the night. From the beginning to the present time there has been little change in the character or number of these men. There are two or three figures that have grown familiar to those who have seen this little procession pass year after year. Two of them have missed scarcely a night in fifteen years. There are about forty, more or less, regular callers. The remainder of the line is formed of strangers every night.

The line is not allowed to form before eleven o'clock. At this hour, perhaps a single figure shambles around the corner and halts on the edge of the sidewalk. Other figures appear and fall in behind. They come almost entirely one at a time. Haste is seldom manifest in their approach. Figures appear from every direction, limping slowly, slouching stupidly, or standing with assumed or real indifference, until the end of the line is reached, when they take their places and wait.

Most of those in the line are over thirty. There is seldom one under twenty. A low murmur of conversation is heard, but for the most part the men stand in stupid, unbroken silence. Here and there are two or three talkative ones, and if you pass close enough you will hear every topic of the times discussed or referred to, except those which are supposed to interest the poor. Wretchedness, poverty, hunger and distress are never mentioned. The possibilities of a match between prize-ring favorites, the day's evidence in the latest murder trial, the chance of war in Africa,[2] the latest improvements in automobiles,[3] the prosperity or depression of some other portion of the world, or the mistakes of the Government, from Washington to the campaign in Manila.[4] These, or others like them, are the topics of whatever conversation is held. It is for the most part a rambling, disconnected conversation.

"Wait until Dreyfus[5] gets out of prison," said one to his little black-eyed neighbor one night, "and you'll see them guys fallin' on his neck."

"Maybe they will and maybe they won't," the other muttered. "You needn't think, just because you see dagoes selling violets on Broadway, that the spring is here."

The passing of a Broadway car awakens a vague idea of progress, and some one remarks: "They'll have them things running by liquid air before we know it."

"I've driv mule cars by here myself," replies another.

A few moments before twelve a great box of bread is pushed outside the door, and exactly on the hour a portly round-faced German takes his position by it, and calls "Ready." The whole line at once, like a well-drilled company of regulars, moves swiftly, in good marching time, diagonally across the sidewalk to the inner edge and pushes, with only the noise of tramping feet, past the box. Each man reaches for a loaf, and, breaking line, wanders off by himself. Most of them do not even glance at their bread, but put it indifferently under their coats or in their pockets.

In the great sea of men here are these little eddies of driftwood, a hundred nightly in Madison Square, 300 outside a bakery at midnight, crowds without the lodging-houses in stormy weather, and all this day after day. These are the poor in body and in spirit. The lack of houses and lands and fine clothing is nothing. Many have these and are equally wretched. The cause of misery lies elsewhere. The attitude of pity which the world thinks proper to hold toward poverty is misplaced—a result of the failure to see and to realize. Poverty of the worldly goods is not in itself pitiful. A sickly body, an ignorant mind, a narrow spirit, brutal impulses and perverted appetites are the pitiful things. The adding of material riches to one thus afflicted would not remove him from out the pitiful. On the other hand, there are so-called poor people in every community among its ornaments. There is no pity for them, but rather love and honor. They are rich in wisdom and influence.

The individuals composing this driftwood are no more miserable than others. Most of them would be far more uncomfortable if compelled to lead respectable lives. They cannot be benefited by money. There may be a class of poor for whom a little money judiciously expended would result in good, but these are the lifeless flotsam and jetsam of society without vitality to ever revive. Few among them would survive a month if they should come suddenly into the possession of a fortune.

Their parade before us should not appeal to our pity, but should awaken us to what we are—for society is no better than its poorest type. They expose what is present, though better concealed, everywhere. They are the few skeletons of the sunlight—types of these with which society's closets are full. Civilization, in spite of its rapid progress, is still in profound ignorance of the things essential to a healthy, happy and prosperous life. Ignorance and error are everywhere manifest in the miseries and sufferings of men. Wealth may create an illusion, or modify a ghastly appearance of ignorance and error, but it cannot change the effect. The result is as real in the mansions of Fifth Avenue as in the midnight throng outside a baker's door.

The livid-faced dyspeptic who rides from his club to his apartments and pauses on the way to hand his dollar to the Captain should awaken the same pity as the shivering applicant for a free bed whom his dollar aids—pity for the ignorance and error that cause the distress of the world.

Notes

1. "Curious Shifts of the Poor," *Demorest's* 36 (November 1899): 22–26. Reprinted in *Sister Carrie,* ed. Donald Pizer (New York: Norton, 1970), pp. 403–12; also in *American Thought and Writing: The 1890's,* pp. 288–97. Dreiser incorporated each of these scenes into Chapter 45, "Curious Shifts of the Poor," and Chapter 47, "The Way of the Beaten: A Harp in the Wind," of *Sister Carrie* (New York: Doubleday, Page and Co., 1900). Dreiser also republished the second scene as "The Men in the Storm" in *The Color of a Great City,* pp. 228–30. More recently reprinted in *Theodore Dreiser: A Selection of Uncollected Prose,* ed. Donald Pizer (Detroit: Wayne State University Press, 1977), pp. 131–40.

2. The South African War (1899–1902).

3. Dreiser himself wrote an article on the development of motor vehicles in the United States, "The Horseless Age," included in the second volume.

4. The campaign took place during the Spanish American War of 1898.

5. Alfred Dreyfus (1859–1935), French army officer.

A True Patriarch:

A Study from Life[1]

ILLUSTRATED BY W. J. GLACKENS.[2]

On the streets of a certain moderate-sized county seat in Missouri may be seen a true patriarch. Tall, white-haired, stout in body and mind, he roams among his neighbors, dispensing sympathy and goodness through the leisure of his day. One might take him to be the genial Walt Whitman, of whom he is the living counterpart, or see in the clear eye, high forehead, and thick, honorable white hair a marked similarity to Bryant[3] as he appeared in his later years. Man's allotted term on earth he has already seen, and yet he is still strong in the councils of his people and rich in the accumulated interests of a lifetime.

At the present time, he is most interesting for the eccentricities which years of stalwart independence have developed, but these are lovable peculiarities, and only severed from remarkable actions by the compelling power of time and his increasing infirmities. The loud, though pleasant voice, and strong, often fiery, declamatory manner, are remnants of the days when his fellow-citizens were wholly swayed by the magnificence of his orations. Charmingly simple in manner, he still represents with it that old courtesy which made every stranger his guest. When moved by righteous indignation, there crops out the daring and domineering insistence of one who has always followed the right and knows its power.

Even to-day, if there is any topic worthy of discussion, and his fellow-citizens are in danger of going wrong, he becomes a haranguing prophet in the community. Every gate hears him, for he stops on his rounds in front of each, and calling the inhabitant out, pours forth such a volume of fact and argument as would remove all doubt of what he, at least, considers right. All of this he invariably accompanies by a magnificence of gesture worthy of a great orator.

At such times his mind is wholly engrossed with these matters, and I have it from his daughter that he may be seen coming down his private lawn, and even the public streets, shaking his head, gesticulating, sometimes sweeping upward with his arms, as if addressing his fellow-citizens in assemblage.

"He had pushed his big hat well back upon his forehead," she said on one occasion, "and, forgetful of the bitter cold, had taken off his overcoat and carried it on his arm. Occasionally he would stop quite still, as if he were addressing a companion, and with sweeping gestures illustrate some idea or other. Then, planting his big cane forcibly with each step, as though to compel acceptance, he came forward and entered the house."

The same suggestion of mental concentration may be seen in everything that he does, and I have seen him leading a pet Jersey cow home for milking with the same dignity of bearing and forcefulness of manner with which he addressed his fellow-citizens at a public meeting. He has no sense of difference from or superiority over his fellow-men, and only the keenest sympathy with all things human. Every man is his brother, every human being honest. When a purse is lost, forty-nine out of every fifty men will return it without thought of reward, if you can believe him.

In the little town where he has lived so many years, he knows every living creature from cattle upward, and has all their interests at heart. The sick, the poor, the widows, and the orphans are his special care. Every Sunday afternoon for years it has been his custom to go the rounds of the indigent, frequently carrying a basket of his good wife's dinner. This he would distribute along with consolation and advice. Occasionally he would return home of a winter's day very much engrossed with a discovery of some important instance of distress.

"On these very occasions," said his daughter, "he would, as he nearly always does, talk to himself on the way, as if he were discussing politics. You could never tell what he was coming for.

"'Mother,' he would say, 'I've found such a poor family.' This was delivered in most dramatic style after he had indicated something important by throwing his overcoat on the bed and standing his cane in the corner. 'They have moved into the old saloon. You know how open that is. There's a man, and several children. The mother is dead. They were on their way to Kansas, but it got so cold they've stopped here until the winter is broken. They're without food; almost no clothing. Can't we find something for them?'

"With his own labor he would help mother seek out the odds and ends that could be spared, and so armed, would return, arguing by the way, as if an errand of mercy were the last thing he contemplated."

Always of a reverent turn of mind, he took considerable interest in religious ministration, though he steadily and persistently refused, in his later years, to go to church. He had St. James' formula to quote in self-defense, which insists that, "Pure religion and undefiled before God and the Father is this, To visit the fatherless and widows in their affliction, and to keep himself unspotted from the world." Often, when pressed too close, he would deliver this with kindly violence, and never did he fail to live it. One of the most touching anecdotes representative of this was related to me by his daughter, who said:

"Mr. Kent, a poor man of the town, was sick for months previous to his death, and my father used to go often, sometimes daily, to visit him. He would spend perhaps a few minutes, perhaps an hour with him, singing, praying, and ministering to his spiritual wants. The pastor of the church living so far away, and coming only once a month, this duty devolved upon some one, and my father did his share, and felt more than repaid for the time spent by the gratitude shown by the many poor people he aided in this way.

"Mr. Kent's favorite song was 'On Jordan's Stormy Banks I Stand.' This he would have him sing, and his clear voice seemed to impart its strength to the sick man, and he would be eased and comforted by it.

"Upon one occasion Mr. Kent expressed a desire to hear a certain song. My father was not very familiar with it, but anxious to grant his request, came home and asked me if I would get a friend of mine and go with him and sing the song for him.

"We entered the sick-room, he leading us by the hand. Mr. Kent's face at once brightened, and father said to him:

"'Mr. Kent, I told you this morning I couldn't sing the song you asked for, but these girls know it, and have come to sing it for you.'

"Then, waving his hand gently toward us, he said:

"'Sing, children.'

"We did, and when we had finished, he knelt and offered a prayer, not for the poor man's recovery, but that he might put his trust in the Lord and meet death without fear. I have never been more deeply impressed nor felt more confident in the presence of death, for the man died soon after, soothed into perfect peace."

On one occasion he was sitting with some friends in front of the Court House, talking and sunning himself, when a neighbor came running up in great excitement, calling:

"Mr. White, Mr. White, come, right quick. Mrs. Sadler wants you."

He explained that the woman in question was dying, and, being afraid she would strangle in her last moments, had asked the bystanders to run for him, her old acquaintance, in the efficacy of whose prayers she had great faith. The old patriarch was without a coat, but, unmindful of that, he hastened after, arriving warm, but mentally well composed, at the bedside.

"Mr. White," she exclaimed excitedly upon seeing him, "I want you to pray that I won't strangle. I'm not afraid to die, but I don't want to die that way. I want you to offer a prayer for me that I may be saved from that. I'm so afraid."

Seeing by the woman's manner that she was very much overwrought in the nerves, he used all his art to soothe her.

"Have no more fear, Mrs. Sadler, now," he exclaimed solemnly. "You won't strangle. I will ask the Lord for you, and this evil will not come upon you. You need not have any fear.

"Kneel down, you," he exclaimed, turning upon the assembled neighbors and relatives, while he pushed his white hair back from his forehead. "Let us pray that this woman be allowed to pass away in peace." And even with the rustle of kneeling that accompanied his words, he lifted up his coatless arms and began to pray.

By dint of phraseology and his profound faith, he succeeded in inducing a feeling of peace and quiet in all of his hearers, and the sick woman, listening, sank into a restful stupor, from which all agony of mind had wholly disappeared. When the physical atmosphere of the room had been thus reorganized, he ceased and retired to the yard in front of the house, where was a shade tree, and a bench beneath. Here he seated himself to wipe his moist brow and recover his composure. In a few moments a slight commotion in the sick chamber denoted that the end had come. Several neighbors came out, and one said, "Well, it is all over, Mr. White. She is dead."

"She didn't strangle, did she?" he exclaimed, with great assurance.

"No," said the other, "the Lord granted her request."

"I knew she wouldn't," he replied. "Prayer is always answered."

I heard of this some time after, and one day asked Mr. White, while sitting with him on his front porch, whether he thought the Lord had directly answered in that instance.

"Answered! Of course He answered," he replied in his customary loud and positive tone.

"Might it not have been merely the change of atmosphere which was introduced by your voice and strength? The quality of your own thoughts goes for something in such matters. Mind acts on mind."

"Certainly," he said, in a manner as agreeable as if it had always been a doctrine with him. "But, after all," he added, "what is *that*—my mind, your mind, the sound of voice. It's all the Lord anyhow, whatever you think."

The poor, the blind, the insane, and sufferers of all sorts are objects of his keenest sympathies. Evidence of it flashes out at the most unexpected moments—loud, rough exclamations, which, however, contain a note so tender and suggestive as to defy translation. Thus while we were hotly discussing politics one day, there came down the street, past his home, a queer, half-ragged individual, who gazed about in an aimless sort of way, peering queerly over fences, looking idly down the road, staring strangely overhead into the blue. It was apparent, in a moment, that the man was crazy, some demented creature, harmless enough to be allowed abroad. The old man broke a sentence short in order to point and shake his head emotionally.

"Look at that," he said, with a pathetic sweep of the arm. "There's a poor, demented creature, with no one to look after him. His brother is a hard-working saddler. His sister is dead." He paused a moment, and then added: "I don't know. No one to look after them. No one to be interested. It seems as if you can't do anything but leave them to the mercy of God," and he shook his head again. The warm argument he had been indulging in was completely forgotten. He lapsed into silence, and all communication for the time being was ended, while he rocked silently in his great chair and thought.

One day, in passing the local poor farm, he came upon a man beating a poor idiot with a whip. It was beside a wood-pile, and the demented one was crying. In a moment Mr. White had jumped out of his conveyance, leaped over the fence, and confronted the amazed attendant with an uplifted arm.

"Not another lick!" he fairly shouted. "What do you mean by striking an idiot?"

"Why," explained the attendant, "I want him to carry in the wood, and he won't do it."

"It is not his place to bring in the wood. He isn't put here for that. He's put here to be taken care of. I'll see about this."

The man endeavored to explain that some work must be done by the inmates, and that this one was refractory. The only way he had of making him understand was by whipping him.

"Not another word," the old man blustered, overawing the country hireling, who knew him well. "I'll see to this," and after scaring the man so badly that whips were thereafter carefully concealed, he proceeded to the county court house. Court was not in session, and only the clerk was present when he came tramping down the aisle, and stood before the latter with his right hand uplifted in the position of one about to make oath.

"Swear me," he said solemnly, and without further explanation. "I want you to take this testimony under oath."

The clerk knew well enough the remarkable characteristics of his guest, whose actions were only too often inexplicable from the ground point of policy and convention. Without ado he got out ink and paper, and Mr. White began.

"I saw," he said, "in the yard of the county farm, a poor, helpless idiot, put in that institution by this county to be cared for, being beaten with a cowhide by Mark Sheffels, who is an attendant there, because he did not understand enough to carry in wood, which the people are hired to do. Think of it," he went on quite forgetting he was speaking for dictation, and going off into a most scorching arraignment of the entire system in which such brutality could occur. The clerk, realizing his importance in the community, quietly followed in a deferential way, putting down such salient features as he had time to write. When he was through he ventured to lift his voice in protest.

"You know, Mr. White," he said, "Sheffels is a member of our party, and was appointed by us. Of course, now, it's too bad that this thing should have happened, and he ought to be dropped, but if you are going to make a public matter of it this way, it may hurt us in the election next month."

The old patriarch gazed at him almost without comprehension of so petty a view.

"What!" he exclaimed. "What's that got to do with it? Do you want the Democratic Party to starve the poor and beat the insane?"

The opposition was rather flattened by the reply, and left the old gentleman to storm out. He had purified the political atmosphere, as if by lightning, and within the month following the offending attendant was dropped.

Politics, however, have long known his influence in a very similar way. There was a time when he was the chief political figure in the county, and possessed the gift of oratory beyond all his fellow-citizens. Men came miles to hear him, and he took occasion to voice his views on every important issue. It was his custom to have printed, at his own expense, a few placards announcing his coming, which he himself would carry to the town selected and personally nail up. When the hour came, the crowd was never wanting.

Personally I never knew how towering his figure had stood in the past, until I drifted in upon a lone bachelor, who occupied a hut some fifteen miles from the patriarch's present home, and who is rather noted in the community for his love of seclusion and indifference to current events. He had not visited the nearest village in something like five years, and had not been to the moderate-sized county seat in ten. Naturally he treasured memories of his younger days and more varied activity.

"I don't know," he said to me one day, in discussing modern statesmen and political fame; "getting up in politics is a queer game. I can't understand it. Men that you'd think ought to get up don't seem to. It doesn't seem to be real greatness that helps 'em along."

"What makes you say that?" I asked.

"Well, there used to be a man over here at Danville that I always thought would get up, and yet he didn't. He was the finest orator I ever heard."

"Who was he?" I asked.

"Arch White," he said quietly. "He was really a great man. He was a good man. Why, many's the time I've driven fifteen miles to hear him. I used to like to go into Danville just for that reason. He used to be around there, and sometimes he'd talk a little. He could stir a fellow up."

"Oratory alone won't make a statesman," I ventured, more to draw him out than to object.

"Oh, I know," he answered, "but he was a good man. The plainest-spoken fellow I ever heard. He seemed to be able to tell us just what was the matter with us. I've seen two thousand people up at High Hill hollerin' over what he was saying until you could hear them for miles."

"Why didn't he get up, do you suppose?"

"I dunno," he answered. "Guess he was too honest. He was a mighty determined man, and one that would talk out in convention. Whenever they got to twisting things and doing what wasn't just honest, I suppose he'd kick out. Anyhow, he didn't get up, and I've always wondered at it."

In Danville one hears other stories wholly bearing out this latter opinion. Thus a long, enduring political quarrel was once generated by an incident more important for what it revealed of the patriarch than for its natural details.

A certain young man, well known to him, came to Danville one day, and either drank up or gambled away a certain sum of money intrusted to him by his aunt for disposition in an entirely different manner. He was not too drunk when the day was all over to realize that he was in a rather serious predicament, and so riding out of town, traveled a little way and then returned, complaining that he had been set upon by the wayside, beaten, and finally robbed. His clothes were in a fine state of dilapidation, and even his body bore marks which amply seconded his protestation. It was in the slush and rain of the dark village street that he was picked up by the county treasurer, who, knowing the generosity of White and the fact that his door was always open to those in distress, even as for his own children, took the young man by the arm, and accompanying him, led him to the patriarch's door, where he personally applied. In a few moments it was opened by this shaggy citizen in person, who held a lamb over his head and peered outward into the darkness.

"Mr. White," said the treasurer, "it's me. I've got young Squiers here, who needs your aid and attention. He's been beaten and robbed out here on the road."

"Who?" asked the patriarch, stepping out and holding the lamp down so as to get a good look into the newcomer's face.

"Billy Squiers," explained the treasurer. "Can you give him shelter?"

The old gentleman gave no heed after his one searching look.

"N. Morton," he exclaimed in his invariable strong declamatory style, "I'll not take this man into my house. I know him. He's a drunkard and a liar. No one has robbed him. This is all a pretense, and I want you to take him away from here. Put him in the hotel. I'll pay his expenses for the night, but he can't come in here."

The treasurer fell back amazed at this onslaught, but recovered sufficiently to declare that his friend was no Christian, and that true religion commanded otherwise. He even went so far as to quote the parable of the good Samaritan, who passed down by way of Jericho and rescued him who had fallen among thieves. The argument had long continued in the night and rain before the old patriarch finally waved them both away.

"Don't you quote Scripture to me," he declaimed defiantly, at the same time flourished the lighted lamp in an oratorical sweep. "I know my Bible. There's nothing in it requiring me to shield liars and drunkards."

Nevertheless, the youth was housed and fed at his expense, and the penalty of opposition generated by this argument was borne in silence for many a year.

The crowning quality of his mercies are their humor. Even he is not unaware, in retrospect, of the figure he made in some instances, and will tell under provocation of his peculiar attitude. Partially from himself, from those who saw it, and the judge presiding was the following characteristic anecdote gathered. In the community with him lived a certain man by the name of Moore, who in his day had been an expert tobacco picker, but had come by an injury to his hand, and so turned cobbler. Mr. White had known him from boyhood up, and had been a witness to his change of fortunes, from the time when he had earned as much as seventy-five cents a day to the hour when he took a cobbler's kit upon his back and began to eke out a livelihood for his old age by traveling about the countryside mending shoes. At the time under consideration, this ex-tobacco picker had degenerated into Uncle Bobby Moore, and had picked up a few charitably inclined friends, with whom he spent the more pleasant portion of the year from spring to fall. It was his custom to begin his annual pilgrimage with a visit of ten days to Mr. White, where he would sit and cobble shoes for all the members of the household. From there he would go to another acquaintance some ten miles farther on, when he would enjoy the early fruit which was ripening in delicious quantity. He would then visit a friendly farmer whose home was upon the Missouri River, where he did his annual fishing, and so on by slow stages, until at last he would reach a neighborhood rich in cider presses, where he would wind up the fall, and end his travel for the winter.

As he grew older, however, Uncle Bobby reached the place where even by this method he could not make enough to sustain him in comfort during the winter season, free as his food and lodging were. Not desiring to put himself upon any friend for more than a short visit, he finally applied to the patriarch.

"I come to you, Mr. White," he said, "because I don't think I can do for myself any longer. My hand hurts me a good deal. I want to know if you won't help me to get into the county farm."

He went further and explained that he only wanted shelter during the inclement months, and that in summer he preferred to be out, so that he might visit his friends and enjoy his declining years.

"Come right down here," said the old gentleman, seizing him by the arm and leading off toward the court house, where the judge governing such cases was then sitting.

A trial was holding when he arrived there, but no matter. Down the aisle he led his charge, calling as he came:

"Your Honor, I want you to hear this case."

Agape, the spectators paused to listen. The judge, an old and appreciative friend, turned a grave and tender eye upon this latest eccentricity.

"What is it, Mr. White?" he inquired.

"Your Honor," he returned in his most earnest and oratorical manner, "this man here is an old and honorable citizen of this county. He has been here nearly all the days of his life, and every day of that time he earned an honest living. These people here," he said, gazing about upon the interested spectators, "can witness whether or not he was one of the best tobacco pickers this county ever saw. Mayhew," he interrupted himself to call to a spectator on one of the benches, "you know whether this man always earned an honest living. Speak up. Tell the Court, did he?"

"Yes, Mr. White," said Mayhew quickly, "he did."

"Morrison," he called, turning in another direction, where an aged farmer sat, "what do you know of this man?"

Mr. Morrison was about to reply, when the Court interfered.

"We know, Mr. White, that he is an honest man. Now what would you have us do?"

"Your Honor," resumed the speaker, indifferently following his own oratorical bent, "this man has always earned an honest living until he injured his hand here in some way, and since then has been cobbling for a living. However, he is getting old now and he can't earn as much as he used to, and so I brought him here to have him assigned a place in the county infirmary. I want you to make out an order admitting him to that institution, so that I can take it and go there with him, and see that he is comfortably placed."

"All right, Mr. White," replied the judge, surveying the two figures in mid-aisle, "I will so order."

"But, your Honor," he went on, "there's an exception I want made in this case. Mr. Moore has a few friends that he likes to visit in the summer, and who like to have him visit them. I want him to have the privilege of coming out in the summer to see these people, and to see me."

"All right, Mr. White," replied the judge, "he shall have that privilege."

Satisfied in these particulars, the aged citizen led his charge away and went with him to the infirmary, where he explained the order of the court and then left him.

Things went very well for a certain time, and Uncle Bobby was thought to be well disposed of, when one day he came to his friend again. It seems that only recently he had been changed about in quarters and put into a room with a slightly demented individual, whose nocturnal wanderings greatly disturbed his very necessary sleep.

"I want to know if you won't have them put me by myself, Mr. White," he concluded.

Again the old patriarch led him before the Court, breaking in upon the general proceedings in order to get the judge's immediate attention.

"Your Honor," he began without any apology, "this man here, Mr. Moore, has been comfortably housed by your order, and he's deeply grateful for it, but he's an old man, your Honor, and above all things needs his rest. Now of late they have quartered him with a poor, demented sufferer, who walks a good deal in his sleep, and it wears upon him. I've come here with him to ask you to allow him a room by himself, where he will be alone and rest undisturbed."

"Very well, Mr. White," said the Court, "it shall be as you request."

Without replying, the old gentleman turned and led the supplicant away.

Everything went peacefully now for a number of years until finally Uncle Bobby, growing rather feeble with age, came to Mr. White, and asked his old friend to promise him one thing.

"What is it?" said Mr. White.

By way of reply he described an old oak tree which grew in the yard of a Baptist church some miles from Danville, and said:

"I want you to promise that when I am dead you will see that I am buried under that tree."

The old fellow used great secrecy in his request, and begged to be assured that, wherever he happened to be when he died, Mr. White would come and get his body and carry it to the old oak.

The patriarch promised, and a few years went by, and then suddenly one day he learned that Uncle Bobby was dead.

"Where is his body?" he asked.

"Why, they buried it under the old white oak," was the answer, "at Mt. Horeb Church."

"What!" he exclaimed, "who told them to bury him there?"

"Why, *he* did," said the friend.

The patriarch was too astounded, however, to think of anything save his lost privilege of mercy.

"The confounded villain," he exclaimed pathetically. "He led me to believe that I was the only one he told. I was to have looked after his burial alone."

Notes

1. "A True Patriarch: A Study from Life," *McClure's* 18 (December 1901): 136–44. Reprinted as "A True Patriarch" with many stylistic alterations in *Twelve Men,* pp. 187–205. On Arch Herndon White, Dreiser's father-in-law, whom he fictionalized as Samuel Howdershell in "Rella," one of the portraits in *A Gallery of Women.*

2. William J. Glackens (1870–1938), though regarded as an American realist painter like Sloan and Luks, preferred to portray parks with exuberant people, or scenes of fashionable life in the shops and restaurants of New York.

3. William Cullen Bryant, Dreiser's favorite American poet. See his article, "The Home of William Cullen Bryant," included in this collection.

A Cripple Whose Energy Gives Inspiration[1]

"There is no excellence without great labor"

Noank is a small, grass-grown fishing town on the southeastern coast of Connecticut,—a little collection of pretty white cottages with green vines and ample shade trees. Years ago it was more important than it is to-day, for then vessels were fitted out there for long cruises into the Arctic Ocean, after whales, and for more certain if less profitable labor off Fisher's Island, where mackerel and cod were to be found in abundance. Thousands of dollars were in those days made annually by men who ventured to sea in ships. But the whaling business died out. Mackerel and cod were caught in decreasing quantities. Finally, Noank became rather slow and unimportant, in its fishing ventures, and was compelled to confine itself to the trapping of lobsters. On this industry, and the rising importance of its one ship-building yard, it has existed for years, the drag of great cumulative enterprises in other places in no way disturbing it.

Docks and wharves are now silent. The weatherbeaten buildings which front the water's edge harbor a few old sailors and fishermen, engaged upon drowsy and only slightly profitable labors. Further up the hillside, two grocery stores, a barber shop, a dry goods store and a meat market stand near the public school and the post office. Back of these are lanes lined with white cottages,—lovely, flower-scented pathways where families seem to dwell in perfect quiet.

A friend of mine and myself were sitting on the lawn surrounding the local Baptist church, one morning, discussing the possibilities of life and development in so small and silent a place, when a trivial incident turned the argument to the necessity of doing something to promote the organization and intelligence of the world. A woman appeared upon the side porch of one of the nearby houses and began

193

to knock the nails out of a box, which she was trying to break up for kindling. While she was doing this, she called two or three times and soon a boy, of twelve years came out and took from her the labor of breaking up the kindling. Then she went away and a sixteen-year-old girl came out of the house and sat down. Presently, the older woman returned, leaned against a post, and began criticising the work of the boy. The local meat-market clerk came up and rested a while. Finally a man, the husband, possibly, came around from the rear of the house, and then there were four people idling about the spot where one boy was indifferently laboring.

"There is a good illustration," said my companion. "Five people are trifling away a half-hour of a fine morning, and the whole world is waiting for deliverance from a thousand difficulties."

"Yes, indeed, there is endless labor to be done. Yet, if you should go to these people and ask them why they don't do something, they would tell you that there isn't anything to do in Noank."

"'Tell you,'—they have told me. The boy in the meat market told me, only yesterday, that there is no chance for anyone in Noank."

"I saw a lot of signs which tell much the same story; one in front of the post office, another in front of the public school, and one in the local fire house, reading, 'No loafing here.'"

"Yes," replied my companion, "there seems to be a great complaint on the part of the few merchants against those who think there is nothing to do. At least they try to warn them off their premises by signs."

While we were still pursuing this thought, a thickset, undersized cripple, of perhaps eighteen or nineteen years of age, came briskly down the lane which bordered the outer edge of the churchyard, and hurried up to the back entrance of the fire house next door. At first glance, he was rather commonplace-looking in his worn, baggy trousers; but a quick, sharp glance thrown our way, and a short return to his own thoughts, whatever they were, served to hold conjecture in abeyance. He went briskly to the door, unlocked it, entered, and threw open the windows. Soon he began moving the chairs about, and a few minutes later he was seen carefully sweeping the office of the fire house.

"There's the caretaker of that institution," said my companion.

"Yes, you'll usually find one boy, in a village of this sort, who works."

"It's curious that there shouldn't be more than one."

"It is curious that there aren't more great financiers than there are. There are hundreds of millions of people, but very few of them are doing anything in particular."

We talked on, paying no more attention to the young cripple, who finally came out, closed the door of the building, and hurried down the quiet street.

A day or two later, I was going up the main street from the railroad station, when I met the boy, hobbling energetically along, trundling a wheelbarrow in front of him. The barrow was full of mail sacks, and he was wheeling the load—which was considerable in the hot July sun,—as if it were nothing in particular. I nodded to him and he smiled. I turned, and, going after him, reached the station in time to see him meet a train. There were a half-dozen mail sacks to be taken off and put on, which he did so expeditiously that his crippled hip and foot seemed hardly an impediment. When the train had gone and his wheelbarrow was loaded and being pushed up the hill, toward the post office, I noticed that he was perspiring profusely.

In passing the local schoolhouse, one afternoon, I saw the doors and windows open, and, on espying the young cripple through one of the side windows, I went back and called to him.

"Do you take care of the school building, too?" I inquired.

"Yes, sir," he replied, smiling, "I'm the janitor in winter. I just open it once in a while to let in the fresh air and see that things are in order."

"You carry the mail in Noank, too, don't you?"

"Yes, sir."

"I saw you in the fire house the other morning."

"Yes, I take care of that."

"Anything else?"

"No, nothing in particular. I deliver papers, mornings and evenings."

"What time do you get up?"

"Oh, about six o'clock."

I did not ask about his income, though it occurred to me to do so at the time. But one day, happening to visit the neighboring city, I saw the same boy hobbling rapidly toward the principal wharf, his body fairly weighted with parcels of all sorts. He went down to the dock just in time to catch the local boat for Noank, and seemed in very high spirits. The captain and the crew of the little steamer seemed to know him well; and, after he had deposited his packages in the forward cabin, he came out and began an animated conversation with the former.

"How's marketing to-day?" asked the captain.

"Fair."

"Get all you went for?"

"Pretty nearly."

He talked seriously with his friend about some local matter; and, when he was through and alone, I ventured to say to him:—

"This is one of your occupations you didn't tell me about."

"No," he replied, greeting me pleasantly; "I forgot this. I run errands for people there occasionally."

"Private families?"

"Oh, everybody. They all know me. I get anything for anybody that can't come."

"Have you many other things to do?"

"No others,—that is,—nothing regular. I do odd jobs whenever I can get them."

"I should like to know how much you make out of all your labors," I said.

"Oh, I don't make so very much,—not in the summer time, anyhow. It's better in winter."

"How's that?"

"Well, I am janitor of the school in winter, and that doesn't pay anything during the summer months."

"I saw you working there, though."

"Oh, I take care of it just the same," he replied.

"How much do you get a month for your janitor work?"

"Forty dollars."

"How much does your post office work pay you?"

"Fourteen."

"A week?"

"A month."

"Then you have the fire house to take care of."

"Yes, I get ten dollars a month for that."

"What do you get for your errand-running?"

"Oh, I do that largely as a favor. Sometimes people pay me something, sometimes they don't."

"But you expend railroad fare on it."

"Oh, they pay me enough to bring me a little out of it,—five dollars a month, sometimes."

"What do you earn by selling newspapers?"

"Well, I make about as much out of that, possibly."

He looked at me and smiled, as I began to figure up his income. "Seventy-five dollars a month!" I exclaimed. "That's pretty good for Noank."

"Yes, but you see I don't make that in summer. I only make about thirty a month until school opens," he said.

"I know," I said; "but, even so, that makes a yearly average of sixty dollars or thereabouts."

"Yes, about that," he said, shrewdly.

"That ought to put you in the way of making a fair income some day," I said.

"I have not seen my way to anything yet," he replied.

I thought of this energy and its curious ramification in a village seemingly so unpromising as Noank.

One afternoon, a company of boys, lounging in the shade of a sailmaker's loft, arrested my attention. They were of about the same age as the crippled mail carrier. All of them were sound in wind and limb. On meeting one and another of these idlers from time to time thereafter, I made it a point to get into conversation with them, and to find out, if possible, what their attitude to their life and surroundings was. One of them, a lounger in the shop of a local sailboat-maker, looked exceedingly disgusted when I asked him what sort of a village Noank is.

"'Tain't much of anything, that anybody could ever find out," he said.

"What do the boys do here when they grow up and want to earn a little money now and then?"

"They don't do anything, unless they get away from this place," he replied.

"That young fellow who carries the mail seems to be making a pretty good living out of it."

"He may," was the reply. "There ain't anybody else that does." Suddenly he brightened and added, "People favor him."

"Why?"

"Well, he's got a game leg."

I smiled at the thought of this being looked upon as an advantage instead of a disadvantage.

"Most people would look upon that as being something against him," I replied.

"Well, they don't around here," he answered.

"How do you expect to get a start?" I asked.

"Oh, I'll get out of here one of these days," he replied.

"Where do you think you'll go,—to New London?"

"I don't know," he said. "I'll go somewhere, though, pretty soon."

Another boy rowed me over to Mystic Island, after I had induced him to by finding a boat free of charge and paying him a quarter.

"Well," I said, "what sort of a town is Noank for a boy to get along in?"

"There ain't anything to do here," he replied.

"Isn't there a chance to get something to do in the shipyards?"

"No," he said, "they don't hire anything but Canucks from up in Canada, who, when they get a dollar and a quarter a day, imagine they're in heaven."

"How much do you think they ought to get?" I asked.

"They ought'n't to get anything,—them fellows. If they didn't come down here, wages would be a lot higher than they are. It's them that's keeping the people around here, that would work, out of jobs."

"Couldn't you go in with them and earn more, if you should deserve it?"

"I wouldn't want to work among them fellows," he replied.

While we were talking, a lobster-trapping vessel went by, and that put me in mind of the endless quantity of free fishing there is in the sea. Anyone can go out into the waters of the bay about there and set a trap or pot for lobsters. Blackfish, porgies, mackerel and cod are still caught in such a helpful order of rotation that no one ever needs to complain of a day in the year when he cannot fish. Blue crabs, round clams, eels and other seafood are plentiful, and may be readily sold in the local market. Lobsters bring ten cents a pound, and codfish four. Blue crabs sell for two cents apiece, and clams at twenty cents a mess, or pailful. Lobster pots can be bought, ready to set, for a dollar each. A boat could be rented for as little as one dollar and twenty-five cents a week.

"Why don't you try fishing?" I asked. "There ought to be a little money in trapping for lobsters, I should think."

"There is, if you have a big yacht," he said. "There ain't any money in trying for them right around here."

"How about clam-digging?" I inquired.

"There's a bay up there where there's a lot of them," he returned, quickly,—"round clams."

"Why don't you try for them?"

"Well, you could," he said, "but you couldn't get a steady market for them. They're only bought here once in a while."

"Did you ever try to get work on one of the fishing boats?"

"No, they don't pay nothing."

His obvious weariness with local conditions reminded me of the mail carrier, whom I mentioned.

"Yes," he said, "people give him things 'cause he's a cripple."

I received this explanation from several others who could see no opportunities in the prevailing conditions; and, finally, I decided to go to the cripple and ask him how he got his start, and what his intentions as to his future were. Coming out of the post office one day, I encountered him.

"They tell me," I said, "that you have picked up all you have to do in Noank from favoritism. Is that so?"

"I don't know what you mean," he replied. "Is it this work I'm doing? Is that what you mean?"

"Yes," I said, "somebody told me that it was given to you because people wanted to be kind to you."

"Maybe they did," he said, cheerfully; "I don't know. I know I have it to do all right."

"Who got you the job in the post office?" I inquired.

"I did."

"How did you get it?"

"I heard that the man who had it before me was going to resign, and I went and asked for it."

"Was it given to you just on your asking?"

"Well," he said, diffidently, "I offered to do it for a little less than I knew they had been paying the other man."

"How did you get the school janitorship?"

"I applied to the school board."

"Did you go, yourself?"

"Yes, sir."

"Did you get anyone to help you?"

"Well, I went to men who knew me, and told them I'd like to have it."

"What about the fire-house work?"

"That was offered to me."

"After you had these other positions?"

"Yes, sir."

"How did you get the newspaper route?"

"Well, I built that up, myself. There wasn't anyone delivering newspapers here, and so I decided to try to get a few customers if I could."

"And how about the parcel-carrying you do?"

"I did that work just as a favor, in the beginning. I didn't expect anyone to pay me for that."

"Well," I said, "what are you going to do with your money, anyhow?"

"I don't have so very much, after I pay all my expenses. Living is expensive nowadays."

"Expenses?"

"Yes; I live with my family."

I learned, afterwards, that, with his father, who really earned less than the boy, he supported his mother, two sisters, and a younger brother, contributing freely to their maintenance.

"Do you expect to stay in Noank forever?"

"Only until I can get something to do."

"Have you fixed your mind on anything better you would like to do? What is your ambition?"

"Well, I've thought something of the news and book business."

"Where?—In Boston?"

"No, sir, you don't catch me going to Boston."

"What's the matter with Boston?"

"It isn't business-like enough for me."

"You've been there, have you?"

"Yes, sir."

"How about New York?"

"Well, I wouldn't mind going there, if I could. A person might build up a good business there, if he had a chance."

"How about New London?"

"That's a good town," he said; and, with that keen appreciation of opportunities which makes a successful business man, he began, in answer to my questions, to dilate in a particular way upon several of its advantages. He knew about all the great manufactories there. He knew its successful men, and of its industries that were likely to develop.

"How do you know all this?" I asked.

"I've looked about, some, down there," he replied, sagely.

"What do you think of the opportunities of a boy anywhere?" I inquired.

"O, he can always pick up a little something," he replied. "It isn't always that you can get a start in a town, but you can pick up something."

"Have you any idea what you are going to drift into eventually?"

"I haven't," he said. "What I'm trying to do is to save a little money, just now. When I get that, I don't know what I'll do."

"You won't let it get away from you?"

"I don't know," he replied. "You never can tell,"—but he looked as if he knew better.

I left him, and he went busily about his affairs. During the remainder of my stay, it was always as it had been. Everybody seemed to like him. He was the typical village product of energy.

One day, I said to the leading grocer of the village, a man of considerable energy and commercial ability:—

"What do you suppose will ever become of that cripple that carries the mail? He seems to be a very bright young fellow."

"Oh, he'll get along," he replied. "He's the best boy in town. You can rely on him. He's perfectly honest."

"It's too bad he's so crippled."

"That won't make any difference with him. Everybody knows him. I hear that the general passenger agent of this division is going to make a place for him next year. He's seen him a good many times taking the mail on and off, and I guess he likes him. Other people have spoken to me about him. He'll get along."

"It pays to be energetic, doesn't it?"

"Indeed it does. If a lot more of the boys about here would hustle around a little more, they'd do better. As it is, we've got to put up signs to keep them off our doorsteps. Yes, Harry's a good boy," he concluded. "He's perfectly honest."

Note

1. "A Cripple Whose Energy Gives Inspiration," *Success* 5 (February 1902): 72–73.

PART THREE

ART AND ARTISTS

Henry Mosler,
A Painter for the People[1]

From childhood our human nature asks for a story. No other way of teaching finds so many learners; no class of literature finds so many readers. Stories are what the human ear loves to hear, and stories, too, written in color on canvas are what the human eye loves to look upon. It may be that they are not the highest form of literature or art, but no one will dispute that the delightfully single-moral story, or story-painting, is the most helpful to the masses.

It is the painter of *genre* subjects who preaches to ten thousand, and before whose picture in the great galleries of the world the crowd is gathered. It is he who goes out into the by-ways where the common people dwell and there sees what is simply merry and what pitiful beyond all solace. It is he who with color and brush pictures that point of the story which explains all that has gone before, and suggests all that will surely follow. It doesn't matter much how poor the coloring may be. It isn't vital to the tale, that it should be the measure of accuracy in detail. It is enough that it tells the sweet, sad story and makes you pause in recognition—greeting a scene which you have gazed upon before.

The world has heard a long while, and a great deal of Henry Mosler. His is one of those lives that interest because it has been filled with such energy and broad human sympathy, as we imagine all lives ought to be filled. His pictures have attracted no end of attention, because from somewhere he early caught the power of expressing in color the earthly scenes which appealed to him most. No, he wasn't born with the power to sit down and paint a great picture such as his "Prodigal's Return," but simply with a desire to picture things. That desire led him on until he came in contact with the world, and then it nerved him to fight on, overcoming as best he could, until at last struggle had strengthened his arm, and cleared his mind of illusions and false impressions, and he was ready to paint. As Heine has it, the artist is ever the child in the fable whose tears are pearls. Ah! the world, that cruel stepmother, beats the poor child the harder to make him shed more pearls.

In 1850 Henry Mosler, Sr., a poor lithographer's assistant, worked in one of the small New York shops of what was then an infant industry. He didn't prosper rapidly and the trade wasn't flourishing in any very gratifying manner, and so when little Henry came and the duty of caring for him and providing for his future devolved upon him, he decided that it would be better to go West and allow the boy to grow up with the country. Accordingly he made a journey into what was then the far country of Cincinnati, and finding that he might use his lithographic knowledge in a small business way there, he came back, had the little household effects packed, and traveled by stage to Syracuse, where the Erie branch of the old Ohio canal passed, and where passengers were taken on the canal boats for Cincinnati. Little Henry was not too young to notice, and still remembers the stretch of forest that crowded close to the mule path, and the long days in which the boat glided slowly after the long-eared motive power, which trotted ahead in the distance, accompanied by a philosophic driver, whose whistling was as incessant as it was off the key.

In Cincinnati Mosler *père* started a small lithographic business, and, as soon as he was old enough, young Henry was taught to sketch useful, if not ornamental, labels upon stone. Exhibiting peculiar efficiency at this task, he was permitted to aspire towards the glorious art of wood engraving, in which field, in those days, lay immensely wider chances of success and fame. Not long after he was apprenticed to a wood-engraver, one A. M. Grosvenor, whose name was yet to resound with the fame of arctic exploration. This amiable scientist and student soon discovered that the forte of his pupil lay in drawing, and encouraged him to persevere, becoming at once a teacher as well as master.

About this time a further impulse was added, for the youth in the course of the growth of his head and the wear and tear which time ruthlessly inflicts on youthful head-gear, came in contact with an old hatter, who eked out a moderate existence by the sale of divers and sundry tiles and slouches, as well as by the painting of signs, labels, and small pictures. The better to do this, he had set up an easel in the back of his shop, where he devoted the hours between the appearance of customers (and they were not numerous) to his artistic labors. Into the mysteries of this inner temple young Mosler was gradually initiated, the more so as he had a true taste for art as then existent in signs, and was not a mere youthful Philistine come to scoff.

The old hatter possessed a palette and various foils of color and brushes, and here, for such service in sign-decorating as he could lend, young Mosler was allowed to experiment with colors and their values. This aroused his interest to a nervous degree, and many were the signs and labels which issued from the temple—the hatter's artistic fame increasing apace with the surrounding public.

"The good things of life are not to be had singly," says Lamb, "but come to us with a mixture; like a schoolboy's holiday, with a task affixed to the tail of it." Lithography did not pay so well, and the family decided to try another move, courting fortune under new conditions. It was in 1856 that the family removed to Richmond, Ind., where the student, fresh from the teachings of the wood engraver and the art temple of the hatter, started on his own account as an engraver of wood. At the same time he began to sketch from nature without a teacher. It came to the ears of the village gossips that the new youth in town could paint, and that he had been seen in different places in the outskirts of the village sketching. This was proof positive that he could paint, and so the village volunteer fire department decided to honor him with a commission. They needed a banner wherewith to dramtically lead their heavy onslaught on all fires, and accordingly he was waited upon and formally given the order. The result was a marvel of flamboyant color—a banner such as any self-respecting fire would run from on sight. My word for it, or you can see the banner yourself, still proudly preserved, if you ever visit Richmond.

After a while Mosler pined for Cincinnati and returned, where he managed while working at his trade to enter the studio of James H. Beard, an artist of the time. It was while working under Beard that Fort Sumter[2] was bombarded, and the War of the Rebellion began. Soon thereafter Major Anderson, fresh from the glory of Fort Sumter, was tendered a reception in Cincinnati, and young Mosler saw him throughout the festivities incident to his passage through the place. One of those "ten strike" ideas came along—he would sketch the scenes of the reception and send them to *Harper's Weekly,* then foremost in the pictorial illustration of the war. They were good sketches, dramatic and interesting, and the editor of *Harper's* grabbed at the chance of having a good artist on the western battle-ground. No expensive man to hire, no outfit to buy, no passage money! Mr. Mosler was commissioned to get anything in the war line, and he started for Louisville, where there was trouble, and there made sketches of it.

In a little while he met Sherman,[3] who gave the mere youth a scant reception, and later he saw war—lots of it, and became aide-de-camp to General R. W. Johnson. There were Mumfordsville, Perryville, Shiloh, Pittsburg Landing—battles where all the rattle and crash of arms tested his powers of drawing, and gave him plenty of opportunity to make money. He stayed with it until he had enough money to pay for an art education abroad, and then in 1863 threw up his commission and came to New York *en route* to Europe. When his employers saw him they were amazed, for they thought they had been paying a sedate, middle-aged man—not a boy.

In Europe he studied two years at Düsseldorf, the centre of German thoroughness and sentiment, and later spent one year under Hebert in Paris. Then he came back to America with a profound distaste for *chic* and for fragmentary, aimless sketching. He settled down to paint, and "the great picture" every young artist dreams of appeared in 1866. He called it "The Lost Cause"—a Confederate soldier returning home after the war only to find his log cabin vacant and dilapidated, the roof fallen in, the casements wide and bare, and over all green vines and flowers and the smiling summer skies.

The picture became popular, retained its popularity, and was sold, whereupon, in 1869, the artist got married. He also took a studio in the old Dodworth building on Fifth Avenue. His fame was beginning to be noised about, carriages began to stop in front of his door, and orders for portraits were not infrequent, and he painted them— alternating between New York and Cincinnati—until he had hoarded enough money to make another try at Europe and another dash at the lamp of Parisian fame.

It was in 1874 that he started for Munich with his wife and lately arrived baby, and in Munich he remained for three years, studying, took his first medal from the Royal Academy there, and then descended on Paris.

There hangs in the Luxembourg National Gallery in Paris a painting called "Le Retour." It represents the characteristic Breton interior, with the huge carved bed or *lit clos,* and the great old fireplace. In the bed lies the body of an old Breton mother, the bed clothes drawn about her face, the blessed candles burning solemnly at either side of her head. At the bedside are two people who have come together, the prodigal returned, too late, and the village father who administered the last sad rites to the sleeper within. Before the bed, in deepest contrition, kneels the wanderer, who had expected a different welcome. The little green sprig with which he had bedecked his hat in anticipation of the joy of reunion lies fallen upon the floor. The bundle of trivial presents remains pitifully unopened. Anguish speaks in every curve of the body, the sunken head, buried in hands that hide the drip of tears. And beside stands the solemn figure of the priest, a monument to the uselessness of sobs and tears and the language of consolation.

This picture was sent to the Salon once. It had been the desire of the painter of it to exhibit a picture in the Salon, but great pictures take a long while to paint, and frames are expensive. However, he began, worked long and lived economically, and finally sent it, when he had barely enough money to purchase a suitable frame. On the day of the opening of the Salon, he repaired, with many misgivings, to the exhibition building, losing himself modestly in the throng of artists, literary men, and dilettanti who make interesting that occasion. He had some small hope as he went along of finding his picture in one of the many rooms, in some corner, perhaps, or high up on the walls, but as apartment after apartment revealed only the great canvases of others, his heart sank, and at last, after all but the Hall of Honor had been searched, he turned quite desolate with the conviction that his picture had been rejected.

Though his interest in the exhibition had waned with his disappointment, he still followed the crowd through the great door into this room, and on toward the chief object of interest, a picture hidden from view by the throng about it. It was not an easy matter, but eventually he came near enough, and stood motionless before his masterwork, hung nobly in the place of honor.

It was Henry Mosler who stood there before his "Le Retour" on the wall, although it seemed too good to be true that he, almost unknown in the great art world of Paris, should, out of thousands of artists, have his picture hung in the Hall of Honor, and *on the line.* It was a fact, however, and better still, the painting was bought by the French Government for the Luxembourg Gallery—the very first one by an American artist to achieve that distinction. The journey from Richmond, Ind., to Paris had been completed.

Far up on the twelfth floor of the famous Carnegie Music Hall in New York, where the air is pure and the light clear, the visitor will be interested as he finds one of the great studios of the city—one of the inner tabernacles whence issues great artistic force, to go abroad over the land. Six years ago Carnegie Music Hall was set apart for high artistic service, and from the evening when the tones of the first "Overture, Leonora No. 3" of Beethoven filled the great music hall, the series of orchestral and choral performances has gone on, increasing and accumulating, until the very walls seem saturated with lovely sound. Naturally the new temple of music became the center of activities having to do with music and art, and to-day the structure is a veritable hive, wherein dwell a host of the successful in music, art, and literature.

In a suite of three broadly lighted rooms are the studios of the now distinguished Henry Mosler, Chevalier of the Legion of Honor, Officer of the French Academy, Associate of the American National Academy of Design, and possessor of a dozen medals. How he came here, to such wealth and distinction, since the memorable day at the Salon, is a long story, and almost too loaded with Gradgrind facts to be interesting. Within the spacious apartments there are many properties appropriate to the studio of so distinguished a man. Rare vessels made of hammered copper adorn the walls and shelves. Ceramic wares from Rome, a quaintly carved closet bed from Brittany, such as the Breton mother might have lain in at the prodigal's return, a Breton cradle, and a host of other antiques, sufficient in number to stock a respectable museum of aesthetics, are to be seen. There are splendid specimens of carved woodwork, and especially two wondrously carved Byzantine chests of 1660 and 1668, which doubtless served as armories in some ecclesiastical household of the time. On many easels the unusual number of finished productions attract the eye, showing the prosaic industry that has gone hand in hand with talent to achieve distinction.

The occupant is a stout, thick-set, neatly dressed American, exceedingly genial of countenance, and utterly free of mannerisms. Hair, eye-brows, and mustache are slightly gray, the eyes deep-set and the face free of those wrinkles of care that so often mark the man who has fought the good fight. He has that warm wholesomeness of temperament that expresses itself in a solid handshake and a witty story. It is always a good day with him, and the young student may learn the value of industry when he ascertains how early in the day the master is at his easel. He works thoroughly and long, like an old world student, devoting himself to a great patronage of the wealthy who come for portraits. It is the means of making money which later permits him to devote time and energy to the greater master subjects, which he paints without much hope of reward for them.

In this studio Mr. Mosler may be seen almost any day painting with untiring regularity. With him will be found his son, Gustave Henry, and his daughter, Edith, both of whom have entered the artistic field, and there have shown that talent is often very truly inherited. He is still in the prime of years; his home is one of the largest of the country places in the Catskills, and his great pictures are safely housed in the museums and mansions of the world.

Honor after honor has been heaped upon him, and there are few countries that are not proud in the possession of one of his pictures. His paintings of Breton life and manners would illustrate a volume on that subject, and his pictures of American scenes and incidents touch some of the deepest chords of the human heart. He is an artist not of to-day alone, but for such time as oil and canvas last, for his pictures are truths taken from life, and as such must always interest those who are interested in life.

A partial list of his most distinguished paintings now exhibited in various parts of the world, in addition to the ones given here and the charming Red Riding-Hood on the cover of this number of *Demorest's,* includes: The Lost Cause, 1869; Return of the Prodigal, 1879; The Spinning Girl, 1880; The Purchase of the Wedding Gown, 1880; The Return of the Fisherwoman, 1881; The Night After the Battle, 1881; The Discussion of the Marriage Contract, 1882; The Wedding Morn, 1883; The Last Sacrament, 1884; The Village Clock-Maker, 1884; The Approaching Storm, 1885; Abandoned, 1886; The Visit of the Marquise, 1887; The White Captive, 1887; The Harvest Dance, 1888; The Last Moments, 1889; The Husking Bee, 1890; Good Counsel, 1891; The Milking Hour, 1892; The Wedding Feast, 1892; The Chimney Corner, 1893; The Brittany Legend, 1894; A Normandy Garden, 1894; The Village Tinker, 1895; Mending the Net, 1895.

Notes

1. "Henry Mosler, a Painter for the People," *Demorest's* 34 (February 1898): 67–69. Henry Mosler (1841–1920).
2. The scene of the engagement marking the beginning of the Civil War, located at entrance to Charleston Harbor, South Carolina.
3. William Tecumseh Sherman (1820–1891), American general.
4. Smart elegance and sophistication.

The Art of MacMonnies and Morgan[1]

That familiarity breeds respect whenever the subject is worthy is as true as that it breeds contempt when opposite, and it is some inkling of this truth that has caused many critics of Frederick W. MacMonnies' work to assert that the action of the Board of Commissioners of the Boston Public Library, in voting to reject the now famous "Bacchante and Child," may lead the public to an appreciative estimation of the sculptor's genius. It cannot be quite pleasant to one of Mr. MacMonnies' mould of mind to acquire fame in such a manner, and yet the discussion of the morality of his Bacchante has made him more celebrated than the merits or demerits of his work ever could. Thus the purists, in not being able to distinguish between art and life, and looking upon a bronze Bacchante as a brazen young woman, have done for the talented sculptor what years of conscientious toil could scarcely have done—secured for him general public consideration. Fortunately the merit of his work can be depended upon to do the rest.

That the Bacchante is one of Mr. MacMonnies' best things so far has been said before this. It is one which any sculptor would not hesitate to acknowledge. The figure is one of the most wonderfully executed pieces of statuary in modern art. The pose upon one foot is most remarkable. But few attempts to get such an effect have been made in the whole history of art; you could count them all on the fingers of one hand. It is surely needless to insist again that the sculptor's motive has plainly been to represent the beauty of a sudden and spontaneous movement, and not to glorify either inebriety or wantonness. The dancing Bacchante is a well-known subject in classic art, and it should scarcely be necessary to tell any one that bodily action can hardly be shown draped. Certain necessary conventions (to say nothing of the Northern climate) require that in actual life we shall usually go clothed; but these conventions and conditions of climate have never been considered necessary to bronze or stone.

Your true artist groans when he thinks how the modern costume

212

deforms and belies the appearance of the wearer. Clothes, *per se,* are not things of beauty. The only art or beauty they possess is that which is suggested by the concealed form, which shines through, as it were. All that clothes do is to distort the form, and few artists will consent to detract from their sculptures of stone and bronze, no matter who may wail to the contrary.

Spirited and graceful line has always had an attraction for Mac-Monnies. One of his first essays, the little "Pan and Rohallion," illustrates his tendency to fasten on the beauty of a momentary pose. Although the boy is standing, and piping away all unconscious of the effort he is making to maintaining his balance, every muscle is adjusted to keep his position on the globular support, and we are made to feel the rhythmical movement that must accompany the strain. This is true of others of MacMonnies' carvings—a constant effort to make some fleeting harmony of form and movement permanent. At times this insistence on movement has interfered with the intended effect of a figure. The statue of Nathan Hale in City Hall Square is an example. This fine, ideal carving of the young patriot, so young, so proud, so determined, is one of the few notable public ornaments of New York; and yet, in spite of our sympathy, we find that the contrast between the activity of the youthful hero and the restraint to which he is supposed to be subjected is too much—is a sculptural misconception. The figure is too elate, too buoyant with pride and scorn. But, after all, only a MacMonnies could make it so.

In the much larger and more important group, his great fountain in the Court of Honor of the Administration Building at the Chicago Exhibition, MacMonnies showed that he could bring many figures into concerted action. Though somewhat lacking in simplicity, this work was nevertheless a splendid product of the Franco-American imagination. Its composition was fine from every point of view, and all that was especially good in it was original. The general idea of a marine triumph which this embodied is, of course, as old as the Romans, and one could guess without struggling where the sculptor got hints for his tritons and nymphs and sea-horses. But no one before had got the same or even similar effects with those well-known ingredients. His love of graceful line worked itself out in that instance, as did his splendid decorative instinct. That the work was not preserved and made permanent is one of the many regrettable things in connection with the disappearance of all that made the great World's Fair.

In the smaller sculpture piece, his "Boy with Heron," the sense of action, lightness, gayety, and grace of pose and line is most emphatic. If there is anything in bronze or stone that will illustrate what this fine

MacMonnies's statue of Nathan Hale. Courtesy of Art Commission of the City of New York

sense of health, buoyancy—the spring upward of the soul—may be, it is this sprightly bit of bronze. It is everything that activity and a boy's sense of triumph and possession could be. It is finely decorative, and the latter quality may be spoken of in connection with the statue of Shakespeare, by the same sculptor, which graces the new Congressional Library.

Frederick MacMonnies, according to the records, was born in 1863, and is now, consequently, thirty-four years old. His first studies were made under the direction of the New York sculptor, St. Gaudens,[2] whom he assisted in some of his most important works, getting thus, from the start, a practical education in the technical part of the sculptor's art. This has been of great service to him and partly accounts for his rapid advance. In 1885, having already made much progress in his studies, he entered the École des Beaux-Arts in Paris, and three years later set up a studio of his own. In his earlier work the influence of both St. Gaudens and his second teacher, Falguière,[3] is easily traceable. But the personality which is visible even in his first work has asserted itself more and more, until now his productions are entirely original. This progress has not been even. It has been marked at times by extraordinary efforts, not all of them successful. For instance, in his statue of Diana he spent a year endeavoring to follow Falguière's footsteps, and yet surpass him at some point. The result showed a work not at all his best, and finding that progress was impossible in that direction, he turned to Nature, choosing a new path for himself. It may be added that Diana only secured him an honorable mention at the Salon, while the year after, with a portrait of Mr. Stranahan, he gained a second medal!

The work upon the Chicago fountain, which established his reputation as a decorative sculptor in America, was the next work of importance. His Bacchante, which is perhaps the crowning work of his career so far, marking the full development of his style, was begun in 1894. The more recent work for the bronze doors of the new Congressional Library, and the statue of Fame not long since unveiled at West Point, are distinctly separated from his early work of the sort. He has reached an understanding of his art, his possibilities, and evidently, his limitations. Following now in the wake of Nature, he is not liable to further err.

In general it may be said that in the treatment of the figure he keeps close to the model and expends his fancy upon the drapery and accessories. His work at times shows that he has developed a taste for the refinement of the old Greeks and Romans, as shown in the bronzes from Pompeii.

Mr. and Mrs. MacMonnies spent the past summer at Guiverney, in France, where they have a picturesque house with a charming garden. Marcelle, the famous Parisian model, posed for him, and it is not unlikely that he has something of much merit already prepared for the coming winter exhibition at Paris.

From the easel of William Morgan have come many pictures of homely interest and beauty. He is one of a few painters who have touched upon the home-life, the very modest home-life, where mother and children are clearly in the foreground. For some reason his brush has run to that subject now for quite a number of years, and, in a way, he has become identified with the young mother and the ruddy infant—the ragged, light-hearted, happy boy of ten—and indeed all that pertains to the earlier and more youthful days of the young family.

Morgan's father was a London tradesman who had laid up a modest fortune, and with it a desire that his son should follow his bent without restraint. Consequently, at the age of fourteen he was sent to Paris where he came under the eye of Couture,[4] the eminent French teacher of thirty years ago. Under Couture he was supposed to study, but it was the sights and sounds of Paris that gave him the most food for reflection, and his pure technical study languished. But he acquired the thing that art stands for, its ideal, and came into an appreciative understanding of the inner beauty of art.

He clung to his studio work, however, and made spasmodic efforts at copying plaster casts and great paintings, but soon wearied, and, not desiring to return to England, a disappointment to his father, shipped as a sailor for three years. Tiring of the sea, he finally brought up in New York, penniless and almost professionless. He managed, however, to secure employment as a draughtsman, and half-decided to abandon painting, but within three years he was again turning to brush and canvas for his living.

He had a world of self-reliance. While struggling to paint pictures that would sell, he was an independent student. "I never saw a man paint," he says. "I did a very little studying at the Academy of Design, and nothing of any consequence. More often I thought out my subject, hired my models, and pitched in, just copying the figures and forcing myself to make the painted expressions conform to my idea. It isn't an easy thing to do, and I have often wished that I had given more time to study when I had the opportunity of the schools, but I did well enough to live."

This kind of self-reliance made his marriage in 1868 a subject of public interest to New York, for the parents of the girl of his choice were rich while he was without means. Lack of money did not deter him, however, and he planned and carried out an elopement into New Jersey, where the marriage was duly solemnized. This done, they returned and never were forgiven—an incident that may not be art, but was decidedly Morganesque, as other events have proved.

Notes

1. "The Art of MacMonnies and Morgan," *Metropolitan* 7 (February 1898): 143–51. On Frederick William MacMonnies (1863–1937) and William Morgan (1826–1900).

2. Augustus Saint-Gaudens (1848–1907), Irish-born sculptor in America, was considered the artistic heir to Quincy Ward's realism. See Dreiser's article, "The Foremost of American Suclptors, J. Q. A. Ward," included in this collection.

3. Jean Alexandre Joseph Falguière (1831–1900), French sculptor and painter, specialized in female mythological subjects in bronze.

4. Thomas Couture (1815–1879), Belgian painter of historical subjects.

Benjamin Eggleston, Painter[1]

Out of the West seem to come the young men with strong, if not new ideas, and the forceful manner in which they do what they undertake to do soon attracts attention to them, large as the metropolis is. I have heard it said that no one could imagine an Edison hidden in the great host of people who swarm, an indefinite mass, in our public ways. No more can one imagine an equally distinctive character in any field, long lost to public view. Distinctive, characterful, energetic men are not so numerous after all, and for the talented there is always a place.

This thought is especially suggested by the rise of Benjamin Eggleston, a young painter of an idealistic turn, whose pictures have attracted more and more attention during the past few years. At the last exhibition of the American Academy of Design one of his pictures, "Dreamy Summer," commanded the good favor of the hanging committee, and was given an especially conspicuous position in the south gallery, where it attracted a host of admirers. It was talked of also as a fine example of what some artists consider the chief merit of painting—exquisite coloring. Idea is one thing, they will tell you, form is another, purpose is a third, but coloring, good coloring is above all the first, the most to be desired. In point of coloring this picture was indeed beautiful, and this fact was soon generally realized (to Mr. Eggleston's advantage), for no sooner was the exhibition closed than the picture was bid in by the Boston Art Club, at the highest price thus far paid him for any of his work.

While on the present subject it may be said that this is the bone of contention in art, this store set by color. A great many painters hold to it that the great painter is the great colorist, and then turn right around and lavish rare praise on men whose great charm is not color at all, but spiritualized idea. How many have I heard glory in the paintings of G. F. Watts,[2] works in which the idea is everything, and then admit, in conclusion, that "he doesn't know anything about color at all." Similarly I have heard artists who are master colorists themselves, whose paintings are splendid examples of charm in form, strengthened by a fine taste in color, dwell with the most deep-souled admiration upon the work of Rossetti,[3] whose spiritual ideas are almost everything. Such ideas as he did not express in paintings, Rossetti put in the form of sonnets and verses, which will give him eternal fame as a poet. On the other hand, such ideas as he did not express in the shape of poems he put forth in paintings, and there is in the Royal Academy in London an entire room set apart for these paintings of his—a room to himself. Yet Rossetti was not a great colorist by any means. A dozen of his contemporaries did vastly more charming color work, but there can be no question of his standing as a painter. This always seemed to me to prove that an idea might be so fine, so beautiful and ethereal, that if the color work were almost bad and the drawing almost mediocre, the picture would still be a great picture, and the painter of it a great painter. It certainly is so with Watts, and he is not the only one.

It is by no means my intention to disparage the work of Eggleston on the ideal side. Although so far his pictures have usually contained but one figure, and that of a woman, he is not devoid of idea or purpose. These women he paints now are the most beautiful things he finds on which to lavish his color schemes. There are other ideas in store, ideas which if ever worked out with the same faithfulness to detail and the same beauty of color, will astonish the natives in more ways than one. For he contemplates pictures in which poetic idea will predominate, and some really appealing idea be set forth with all the charm of manner at his command. Such work Byam Shaw[4] has done for England, and there is no valid reason why America should not have a Shaw.

This sense of color, so strong in Mr. Eggleston, coupled with his strong, graceful drawing and poetic ideas, has placed his work in the first rank of American art. Black and white reproductions of his work give no idea of this, its chief charm, which must be seen to be appreciated. Too often it is greatly the other way, and photographic reproductions of pictures give indication of something truly beautiful, when if the original were introduced, its defects of color and massing of shadows would destroy the charm entirely. For this reason it is almost impossible to obtain an opinion, favorable or otherwise, from any artist, who has nothing but the photograph of a painting to judge by. "My boy," I have heard them say again and again, "you never can tell. This photograph shows a beautiful idea, but if I were shown the original the whole handling of the color scheme might be so wretched that all its charm would be gone."

In the present instance the chief charm would be added. No one, I dare say, has a finer feeling for the beauty of textures of various kinds than Mr. Eggleston. The curtain, rugs, laces, brocades and other surfaces which appear in his pictures are reproduced in a manner calculated to deceive the eye into the belief that here and there the real material has been introduced. The genuineness of his flesh tints are gratifying to the eye, and his conception of what constitutes ease and beauty, and grace of posture, is pleasing in the extreme. All his pictures thus far have been illustrative of luxurious grace and beauty in women, so much so, that they are almost unAmerican or perhaps even Oriental in touch, but as pictures they are none the less meritorious.

How this peculiar sense of beauty has come to develop itself along these lines and learned so pleasing a mode of expression is another of the mysteries of life. The painter has never studied abroad. All his days from the cradle up were spent in such places as Red Wing, St. Paul, Dayton and other northwestern and middle-states cities. The detail of his struggles to attain ability and recognition in his chosen field would make excellent material for that Samuel Smiles type of people, who delight to write concerning self-help. His father, who was a soldier in the civil war, had taken a soldier's homestead in Redwood County, Minnesota, where young Eggleston lived until he was seventeen, working on his father's farm in summer and attending the high school at Marshall in the winter. He gave, he has told me, every leisure moment to art in some form, having had from boyhood a taste and talent for painting. At that time his parents recognized his ability, but being poor, were unable to give him the proper schooling, so he determined to work his own way upward in the profession, and leaving the farm, at the age of seventeen, he went to Red Wing, Minn., where his uncle was living, and by painting portraits and teaching, supported himself and saved about $150.

With this he went to Minneapolis and entered the art school, which had just been opened, under the direction of Douglas Volk. There he remained a year, when he was obliged to give up his studies, but secured the position of staff artist on the Minneapolis "Tribune."

The memory of this time is now very pleasing to Mr. Eggleston, although he was dissatisfied with it then. Far as it was from his hope of painting, it was training of a fair kind, as all tasks connected with daily journalism must be. All sorts of conditions of men and events came up for illustration, and his pen was never idle. He has a collection of these drawings which is large enough to stagger the average onlooker. It was practice in drawing all the time, and as he made it a point never to shirk his work, the exercise of his pen was advantageous and kept fresh for him such knowledge as he had gained from Volk. It gave him an opportunity to try his hand on small artistic subjects, and some of these are not half bad, even in the light of his present standing.

For two years he worked steadily with his pen, keeping on with brush work at odd times, until his health forced him to give up the work, when he removed to Geneva, Ohio, where his parents had betaken themselves. Recovering his health, he came East in the fall of 1889, and settled in Brooklyn, where he made notable acquaintances and painted a number of portraits. In 1891 he contributed to the Academy of Design two pictures, "The Model" and "The Cast Vender," which were favorably commented upon and subsequently sold.

In 1895 he went abroad for a year, when he exhibited at the Paris Salon. On his return he again took up his residence in Brooklyn, where he has remained since, and where he is building at present a handsome studio, in order to better prosecute his artistic plans.

Mr. Eggleston is quite a young man, having just turned thirty, and has the energy and physique to carry out his ideals. He is an admirer of the English school of painters, particularly Millais,[5] whose classic subjects and exquisite coloring are his delight. If anything may be predicted of any painter, his art is turning to the Grecian and allegorical style, where the imagination can have wider range, unhampered by the prosaic garb of the moderns. He is already ranked among the idealists, though not incapable of realistic or detailed work. Perhaps it would be better to say that he has the gift of imparting to subjects realistically treated the poetry of his own nature, thus lifting them far above the level of "faithful transcripts" of nature and life.

Concerning his own work, he is not at all opposed to talking, although modestly preferring to discuss method rather than accomplishment. "What I have painted thus far," he said to me, "is not really a fair showing, because all I have done has been worked out under the most trying conditions. A strong criticism may be honestly brought to bear upon the paintings of a man who is well equipped with all the facilities that make for good painting. Once a man is thoroughly equipped, after the manner of a successful artist, he should do good work. But with the artist, who is not thus equipped, it narrows down to the best work which can be done under adverse conditions.

"You will understand better what I mean when I mention a picture by Abbey.[6] Being rich, well furnished with a great studio, an immense wardrobe of historical costumes, and able to hire not one but a dozen or two score models, and clothe them according to his subject in hand—such a man can arrange a spectacle for himself and paint it. There is no question of his doing it well, but he has the advantage over another man of equal talent, who may not have the studio, the costumes or the models to paint from.

"My pictures have all been single figure pictures because I had neither the place, the costumes, nor the models for more elaborate studies. Every artist goes through such a trial in the beginning. So far as my experience goes, I find that the man who can paint a moderate sized picture or a limited subject well, can paint a larger and more extended subject better. I am speaking of beginners now, and not of those men who began ostentatiously and narrowed down in the end to single figures. Such men have found their limitations, and can only do small things well."

If any of the thousands of newspaper artists could see him lovingly going over a large scrap-book filled with newspaper sketches of "old settlers" and "prominent citizens" of the time of his journalistic work, it might stir hope within them anew. They are not better drawings of fires and newly arrived actors, of captured criminals and runaway maidens than are to be found any day in our morning papers. As he says, "most anyone can learn to draw accurately and satisfactorily." It is breaking away and capturing the art of color for your ideas that involves the struggle.

If I were a newspaper artist with painter's ambitions I should retire and consider that.

Notes

1. "Benjamin Eggleston, Painter," *Ainslee's* 1 (April 1898): 41–47. On Benjamin Osro Eggleston (1867–1937).

2. George Frederic Watts (1817–1904), English painter and sculptor.

3. Dante Gabriel Rossetti (1828–1882), English painter and poet.

4. Byam John Shaw (1872–1919), English genre painter and illustrator.

5. Sir John Everett Millais (1829–1896), English painter.

6. Edwin Austin Abbey (1852–1911), one of America's most popular illustrators, delighted the public with his historical and literary subjects.

A Great American Caricaturist[1]

It is no longer a question whether illustration and caricature art have a great deal to do with the tide of affairs. If it were there would be no such bidding among great journals for such men as Davenport, Bush[2] and the few others who have fame as caricaturists. The former was offered his own price, practically, for but two cartoons a week, by a great Ohio daily, during Mr. Hanna's recent senatorial struggle.[3] An equally interesting bid was made for him by a syndicate of newspapers. Mr. Bush, of New York, has also been blessed with large offers for his services, so that caricatures may at least be said to be valuable to newspapers.

In truth pictures impress, much more effectively than words, a sentiment, an idea or a truth. A caricature, again, may be well defined as the skeleton of a character, and a caricaturist is one who takes an X-ray glance at the impressive bearing of a great public character, and then draws for you the skeleton of it—the miserable threads of ambition, greed, and other qualities by which too often, it is strung together. Take, for instance, the case of Mr. Hanna. The Presidential manager is by no means the person one meeting him casually might imagine, or mayhap that Mr. Hanna would like to be thought; Davenport, the subject of the present sketch, looking beyond the glad, joyous handshaking surface, pretends to see the fat, dollar-marked, short-term senator with whom everyone is familiar. However we view the Ohio senator, individually, no one will deny the stinging sneer which leers in these pictures of the man. The lines of Davenport's pen crack like swishing whips on the backs of the naked.

A glance at the accompanying caricatures shows what Mr. Davenport's pen does for well-known public characters. Under his glance there deports that dignity and impressiveness which report of their public deeds would suggest. During several campaigns now, Mr. Davenport has drawn constantly, and the sarcasm of his pen has excited the admiration of even those who adhere to the men he so graphically flails. His caricatures of Hanna, McKinley, Reed[4] and Croker[5] are perhaps better known by now than the circulated photos of these men. The mind of anyone with a spark of humor in his soul will not soon forget these wonderful delineations. They have not served to enwrap our public men in a roseate cloud of glory. Rather they have stripped many a national idol of his finery and published him to the world as exceedingly human indeed.

This peculiar genius is a product of the remote West. He was born on an Oregon farm, and while his talents and instincts in the way of caricature are his by inheritance, he had in the general sense no training in this field. He attended no academy of design, and no art league has conventionalized his ideas or weakened his vigorous methods. Yet he has studied all his life. One of his distinguishing traits is a love for animals. He had a personal acquaintance with every domesticated creature on his father's farm before he was four years old, and at three his only playthings were lead pencils and white paper. He spent hours reproducing the farm animals in their various moods. None of these early scribblings have been preserved, and the barn whose sides he embellished with drawings of fighting chickens and cavorting swine has been torn down. Therefore no monument of his talent in its archaic condition is to be seen. From his early days he devoted time to "making pictures" which relatives thought might better be employed in work or study. His school teachers rebuked him and in return he caricatured them. Then, too, his love for animals in its indirect results loaded him with many undesirable associates. His tendencies were toward the thorough-bred in all kinds of stock. He eschewed sleep to witness unholy cockfights, and he has "heeled and gaffed" the victors in many warm mains. At the age of 16 he had ridden more than one race horse that went to the post "a long shot" and emerged "a winner."

His race course and cockpit companions made Davenport an object of local regret, and by his relatives he was regarded with suspicion. The measure of iniquity seemed to overflow when he joined a passing circus. His case was regarded as one of hopeless retrogression. A long line of preachers, lawyers and college men were in different branches of his ancestors, and yet Homer Calvin was of free will and intent, a "deckhand" in a menagerie!

His circus experience came to pass through strained relations between him and his school teacher. The district had procured an ideal master. He conducted county teachers' institutes in summer, grafted appletrees in the spring, and taught in winter.

Davenport senior was a school director and had great hopes of his

son's educational future under such a meritorious tutor. The master
had no appreciation of art as then set for by the youthful caricaturist.
He forbade its practice in the school room. This soured the scholar.
One day a party of visitors happening in the teacher called the class in
physical geography. The unwilling Davenport was a member.

"Homer," asked the teacher, "when does the new day begin?"

Here Homer was divided in opinion as to whether it was an idle jest
the teacher was working off or a deep laid attack upon his liberties.

"It begins where the night leaves off," he replied, "and lemme tell
you I don't aim to waste my time answering any more of your fool
questions."

He abandoned academic pursuits at that juncture and the same
night departed through a bedroom window to join the circus. He had
won the love of the superintendent of the show, when it exhibited in
his home town, by the boundless energy with which he catered to the
elephant's appetite. It was with the circus that Davenport gained that
intimate knowledge of wild animals, that makes some of his drawings
in which they are included so mirth-provoking.

This life he followed for some time. His reason for leaving it is a bit
of a caricature humor worth repeating. It came out in a conversation I
had with him, where he began with:

"Did you ever oil an elephant?"

The great cartoonist was putting a cornice in the pachyderm wherewith it is a part of his business to symbolize the Republican party. I
remarked on the excellence of the likeness, but denied experience as
an oiler.

"I should be able to draw an elephant all right," he continued. "I
was assistant managing editor of one for six months. And you never
oiled one? I did, or tried to, and that's why I quit the circus. I was
getting along all right with Bonaparte—that was our elephant's
name—and we had become quite gossipy. One day our boss came to—
he was something of a drinker—and said to me: 'It is coming on
spring, Homer, and I guess you'd better begin to oil Napoleon.'

"He gave me a barrel of linseed oil and a broom for a starter and I
went to work. Just before the elephant's hip is a big hollow. You may
have noticed it. I never got by that. That hollow spot soaked up oil like
it was a sponge. I worked three weeks on Bonaparte's hip and used up
five barrels of oil. It was like a rain in a thirsty desert. It made no show
whatever and five minutes after I'd deluged the elephant, the hollow
in his hip would be as dry as a country road. I got discouraged. I
couldn't soften up Bonaparte's hip and so I hunted up the boss. He
was fairly sober and I told him I intended quitting.

" 'What for?' he asked. 'You and Bonaparte hit it off all right, don't you?'

" 'Yes,' I said, 'but I ain't equipped properly for trade. I can white-wash a barn,' I told him, 'with any boy in Oregon, but I can't get the hang of oiling an elephant. I'm discouraged, and I'm going to leave.' "

After he had abandoned the circus to its fate he attached himself to the destinies of a threshing machine. Then he served a term in the cab of a locomotive; his great ambition in youth was to become an eingeer, and he nearly realized it. All the time he drew. His father finally persuaded him to leave the railway and enter a preparatory school, with a view to taking a college course. Still he made pictures. One day a friend with a newspaper acquaintance bestowed one of Davenport's efforts on an editor. From this point the finish was seen. In a week Davenport was on the art staff at a salary of $7.

To-day Mr. Davenport is but thirty years old and his cartoons are known wherever a newspaper is printed in the English language. His salary is the largest received by any newspaper artist in America. No matter what may be our political or personal persuasion, one cannot examine the products of Davenport's pen and not find them keen and laughable, unless one is content to acknowledge oneself ungifted with a sense of humor. Speaker Reed, whom the artist's scalpellike pen has handled none too gently, told Davenport that while his pictures are not extremely flattering they are very funny.

Yet there is at times a something greater than fun expressed in the swift, eager strokes and dashing curves which tell their story so well. Davenport's representation of Uncle Sam is one of his most character-istic and pleasing creations. The type of our dear old land has such a vigor and health of limb, such a shrewd, generous expression of eye. Every caricaturist of the country draws the figure and that very often. Perhaps Davenport's of them all is the most enduring and most de-lightful. One never tires looking at it. The drawing which pictures Uncle Sam hailing a toast to the Queen of England at the time of her jubilee, is undoubtedly one of the most graceful and dignified car-toons we have ever produced.

Personally he is a very gentle sort of individual, not at all irascible in temper and somewhat mild in his estimate of men. He has humor, too, of the Jerome K. Jerome order, exaggerative, but delightful. He is tall, fair, healthy and rawboned, and very obliging in his disposition. Those who knew Eugene Field,[6] the western poet, would perhaps recall him in looking at Mr. Davenport. One would suspect that he would draw roughly, for like all Westerners he has no taste for luxury, and rather pities those creatures who are so refined and re-refined that they lack vitality enough to digest a plain meal. He admires strong, plain men, and wouldn't do much to injure the reputation of one.

"I have convictions," Mr. Davenport once said to me, "and I wouldn't deride a man, unless I felt that there was cause for it."

Besides this honesty he has wit and a humor that is irresistible. Once when I asked him for data on which to base a sketch of him, he opened a drawer in his desk, from where he lifted some forty folios of manuscript, saying, "I've got it right here. I hope my father is willing to stand for all there is in that literary production," he added. "I read it and discovered what had hitherto escaped my notice, my father is a novelist. This romance purports to be a sketch of my bounding career. A press association running short of half hour chats with the nieces of notable women desired a series of personal recollections from the progenitors of cartoonists. This is my father's response. It reads like a dream. I'm glad my father thinks so well of me, but I have felt obliged to suppress its publication. There is a novelette that will never know the press, but you can rely on the statistics you will find. When he left the figures, he simply let his ideals wreck his judgment. If I were to let that go to print I would die in a year trying to live up to it," and with that he calmly handed it over to me.

I have heard Davenport described as being "as good as Nast."[7] As a political cartoonist he is worth many Nasts. His work possesses human interest, shows a humorous but thorough acquaintance with his fellow man that has never appeared in Nast's. Nast was great because he was unique. In his day he had no competition. He was the only cartoonist, and had a week to produce each picture. No daily newspaper in the country owned an engraving plant when Nast was making his name; there were no newspaper artists. To-day every newspaper makes its own engravings and each one has an art staff. Where Nast had no rivals Davenport has a thousand. He has conquered with the aid of his personal merits only. It is a long trip from the straw carrier of a threshing machine to Davenport's abiding place, but he has made the journey in eight years.

Notes

1. "A Great American Caricaturist," *Ainslee's* 1 (May 1898): 336–41. On Homer Calvin Davenport (1867–1912).

2. Charles Green Bush (1842–1909), American dessinateur and caricaturist.

3. Mark [Marcus Alonzo] Hanna (1837–1904), American businessman and politician, tried to promote big business.

4. Thomas Brackett Reed (1839–1902), one-term Speaker of the House of Representatives.

5. See note 9 to "The Real Choate," included in this volume, p. 157.

6. See note 4 to "Edmund Clarence Stedman at Home," included in this volume, p. 90.

7. Thomas Nast (1840–1902), German-born cartoonist in America.

The Sculpture of Fernando Miranda[1]

Sculpture we may safely assert is an honest kind of art, partaking in a measure of the simplicity and candor which seems to dwell with those who toil with their hands. Certainly there is no more pleasing sight than to see a man of ideas and fine sentiments, one educated in the lore of the world of characters, events and places, slowly building with his hands out of clay a material representation of the thing that is with him but a dream. There is in his case none of the clap-trap environment that goes with so many other professions. No decorations, no railings, no affectations or ceremonies—simply a few needful stands and implements, a few models of form and character, a few barrels of clay, and the genius who can fashion his ideas out of earth with his fingers has all he needs.

A man who achieves distinction in such a field is necessarily an honest man. It is quite impossible to be otherwise and be great. Such height of aspiration does it take, such feeling for accuracy, such appreciation for the salient points of greatness in men, that one must feel and know them before the fingers can fashion and the eye acknowledge that the representation is true to the original. To do as much means that one must feel and know great characteristics, and before one can really feel and know one must in an humble way *be* these things, and therein lies the honesty of sculpture.

Without other word on that score it is pleasant to know that the work of Fernando Miranda has the quality of genuineness in it, a quality that has brought him good repute as an American sculptor. Essentially a man of fine ideas and feeling, he has the admirable power of giving his ideas and his knowledge exquisite expression in the material of the potter. Although foreign-born, he has grasped the principles and qualities of the American people, for which our great men have stood, and in fashioning them in clay he has made them shine with all that can stand forth in the body, of what is really spiritual and above the material. This ability has raised his statues of distinguished men into public favor. Indeed, his choice as president of the American Sculpture Society vouches for the respect and esteem in which his American sentiments and ability are held. I should say, before going farther, however, that Mr. Miranda is an American only by naturalization. At this time when we are involved in such serious difficulties with Spain, it is almost dangerous to avow that he is a Spaniard by birth, yet such is the case. He is a native of Valencia, Spain, and was still a resident of that country at the time of the Philadelphia Centennial, when he removed to the United States and became a citizen. Indeed, he was a pupil of the sculptor Piquer,[2] at the court of Queen Isabella II, and by King Alfonso XII, he was created Commendador of the Royal Order of Isabella. He is also a Spanish Knight, having been created such by the Spanish court in 1890, in acknowledgment of his early services in Spain, and as a token of good will. But nevertheless, Mr. Miranda holds himself an American. At the present day the city of Newark is about the task of erecting a statue of General Washington by Mr. Miranda, in one of its public squares. Indeed he has various portraits, busts and statues of our eminent men scattered throughout the country, but the funds of our towns and inland cities invariably limit the importance of these so that they are deserving of little more than a mention here.

Some months since when it became known that Mr. MacMonnies's statue of "The Bacchante"[3] was not to be replaced in the Boston Library courtyard, whence, as every one knows, it was removed because of the manner in which the spirit of the statue clashed with the solemnity of the architecture of the library, Mr. Miranda submitted to the library officials a suggestion for a statue which seemed more appropriate than the one displaced. The statue was to represent the "Spirit of Research." The suggestion was approved, and the work was completed, and will eventually be placed in the library courtyard. This work is a fine example of the idealism in Mr. Miranda's work. It represents the Spirit of Research as a female figure, veiled, to signify that knowledge is hidden from human eyes by a veil of ignorance and difficulty, which must first be brushed aside before clearness of vision is attained. The left hand of the figure is represented as putting aside this veil.

Further suggestion of research is given in the pose of the figure, which is completely draped, is easy and graceful, and yet is indicative of power. One foot rests on an ancient Athenian ruin, and the other has just stepped on the death case of an Egyptian mummy, from which the head of the dead has been crowded out as the foot of knowledge crushes the concealing case. The whole is indicative of the trend of modern research, back through Grecian and Egyptian civilization to the earliest forms of life. On the arm of the figure rests a tablet, on which the secrets dug from the buried past are to be inscribed, and in the right hand is the lamp of knowledge, as well as the stylus with which the writing will be done.

There is this in Mr. Miranda's allegory: It is simple and yet dignified, high and still apparent. It is true of his decorative panel "Slumber," where with the veil of night half concealing her face, Nature sleeps. And indeed it is true of all of his numerous decorations in the homes of leisure class who have made use of his art.

But if his public monuments of importance are only few in number, the amount of his sculptural compositions held by private individuals makes ample compensation. These consist of decorative panels and separate allegorical figures which are cast in bronze and held by those who love sculptural ornamentation in the home. A few years ago all American sculptors depended on their public commissions for a livelihood, but the rise of American bronze-casting industries has so cheapened the cost of artistic casting that a sculptor can now design a sculptured piece and have it cast at so reasonable a figure that this branch of his art has become profitable. He can obtain replicas of his work at such nominal rates that the average well-to-do Americans can buy them, and in this way hundreds of duplicates of a single figure cast in bronze can be obtained and sold, netting the sculptor a very satisfactory sum all told. Mr. Miranda, as well as others of our native sculptors, now devote themselves more than ever to the doing of small figures of ideal subjects in bronze. Both the sculptor and the collector benefit by this fact, for the artist may now find stimulus to his genius for invention, and be freed from sole dependence upon the portrait busts, the doing of which cannot always be agreeable to the imaginative workman, while the collector can obtain a representative collection of distinguished artists without expending enormous sums for large works. Among Mr. Miranda's later efforts are several that are reproduced herewith, namely, his "Head of Christ," and "Slumber." His design for a new dollar is also not very old, being an answer to a government call for an appropriate design for a new American dollar. Mr. Miranda has combined originality with artistic ability. It represents Columbia seated on a throne composed of the products of the land, while her footstool is an anvil with its accompanying hammer and ore. In one hand she holds the torch of light, while the other rests on a shield, which is washed by the ocean waves. In reverse is an eagle with outspread wings overshadowing the United States, bearing in its talons both the olive branch of peace and the arrows of war. The design is wholly meritorious, and may supersede the one common to our present dollar.

Slightly distinguished from his work as a sculptor is his work as president of the American Sculpture Society. In that capacity the sculptor holds forth as a censor of American art, and one who seeks for the people as a whole the highest representation in bronze and stone. In this capacity Mr. Miranda has been in many a public argument, not only with other artists, but with the newspapers, public organizations which contemplate the erection of monuments, down to evangelists like Moody,[4] who sweepingly condemn the art of a nation as a corrupting influence. On the latter subject Mr. Miranda's reply to Mr. Moody, through the press, will bear repetition, not only for its sound sense and the fact that it was uttered by him in his official capacity and in answer to so noted a character as Evangelist Moody, but because of its importance as a refutation of future assertions of a similar character. He said in substance:

"Would it not be outrageous to condemn every country that perpetuated its history by monuments, when the monuments represent not only the history of, but the human race itself, both in spirit and body? That is just what Mr. Moody is doing in his condemnation of works of art. The human form in its natural beauty is God's greatest work, and consequently, any one who attempts to preclude with excessive zeal all nude works of art is misled by narrow conceptions of what is noble and good in the universe. My son, who is now thirteen years of age, is just as familiar with the human form in the nude as I am myself. I do not keep him out of my studio. He comes here at all times and is being educated to see nothing immodest in a nude figure of man or woman."

In like manner Mr. Miranda has fought all tax on art, and indeed anything and everything that had aught in it detrimental to the best interests of American sculpture.

At present his studio is at the headquarters of the American Sculpture Society in West Tenth Street, where the works of that body are kept. As a consequence it is much more commodious than that of most sculptors, and certainly more rich in works of art. As a rule, however, the sculptor is in a world of his own, strange and unconnected with the other professions of the world. Garbed like a whitewasher in canvas coat, apron and overalls, he is not an unpoetical figure as he moves about in the forest of his own creation, bringing form and beauty out of shapeless clay. His walls hold dusty shelves peopled with antiques and the pseudo-classic studies of his youth.

Around him stand colossal figures that seem alive and thinking, even when most unfinished, or half-hidden in damp clothes. Indeed, his nimble fingers seem to be releasing a soul and body from imprisonment, and not merely building clumsy clay into a statue.

It is a room of solemnities and solitude as a rule where the artist truly communes with himself and works out the best that is in him. In such a place where an earnest man works there is ever an air of distinction and individuality. This is true of most studies, and certainly of Mr. Miranda's, for he is not only a hard and conscientious worker, but a man of high ideals and unvarying aim.

Notes

1. "The Sculpture of Fernando Miranda," *Ainslee's* 2 (September 1898): 113–18.
2. José Piquer, II (born 1832), Spanish sculptor.
3. See Dreiser's article, "The Art of MacMonnies and Morgan," included in this collection.
4. Dwight Lyman Moody (1837–1899), American evangelist.

The Making of
Stained-Glass Windows[1]

A recent exhibition of American colored glass in Berlin has won extensive praise from those in Europe who are interested in the most beautiful of the industrial arts. It is not putting it too strongly to say that the results of American invention and skill have been a revelation when it has been freely admitted that the opalescent glass is far superior to the famous Roman ware, which it has been the aim of the foreign artist and artisan to equal ever since the revival of interest in this material. Beyond this it is hardly necessary to do more than enunciate a principle upon which American decorative art has been developed, and that is that the results must express entirely new ideas. In the making of picture windows the European artist has sought, first of all, to reproduce the work of the Middle Ages, very beautiful as it is, but the American, with a lack of respect for tradition which, after all, generally proves commendable in the long run, understands beyond everything else that the medieval artist would have done better if he had only known how. Therefore, with a more perfect acquaintance with the properties of his material, the American artist has, by abandoning the old system in several respects, as we shall see later on, produced results so splendid, and so thoroughly in accordance with modern scientific knowledge, that his work is bound to be universally adopted for its better meeting the demands of the day. In doing this, he has returned fundamentally to the principle of the very earliest recorded attempt at using colored glass for filling window openings—made by Singhalese artists about 306 B.C.—the combination of small gemlike pieces of glass, having all the brilliancy and depth of color that are found in precious stones—the true "mosaic principle."

But before using these differentiating terms, the reader must be sure of the vernacular. We speak of "mosaic," "stained" and "painted" glass. In mosaic glass the design is brought out by the use of shaped fragments of colored glass, bound together by strips of doubly

Selecting the plating

grooved lead; in stained glass a permanent transparent color effect is secured by the action of heat on certain metallic oxides applied to the surface as pigments, while in painted glass the colors are produced by enamels fused to the surface by means of heat.

Painted glass was one of the artistic glories of the Middle Ages. There is but little of it left now. The dawn of the modern world, through the Renaissance of Grecian and Roman art and literature, in Italy, which spread instantly over civilized Europe, put a sudden end to the development of medieval ideas. For over three hundred years, until the Romantic revival, early in the present century, everything that stood for Gothic art was ugly, it was wrong, it was all that "out of style" and "bad taste" imply. And against what could resentment created by the sight of monuments that could not be suppressed or hidden better be directed than a painted window?

We now understand what distinguishes the three kinds of glass used in window-making. It frequently happens, and in the older examples of ecclesiastical design it is nearly always the case, that all are combined in one window. American artists have abandoned the use of paint and stain, since they are not only less durable but also less brilliant than homogeneous colored glass. There is a decided tendency to rely entirely upon the mosaic treatment, and to limit the use of paint to the representation of the human figure.

The superiority of American glass windows lies in several points, greatest of which is that their makers have succeeded in producing every variety of glass. To accomplish all that has been done so far, glass has been made in all the colors of the spectrum and has undergone a thousand different transformations. The shapes have been not less varied than the colors. The so-called "jewels," or pieces of richly colored glass cut with facets after the manner of precious stones, have added immensely to the brilliancy of modern designs, and have been particularly effective when introduced in the setting or framework of a picture window. They are imported for the most part from Germany, but the greater part of the flat glass used is made in the immediate neighborhood of New York, under the direct supervision of the art-workers who utilize it. As many as five hundred color combinations are carried in stock by the glass factories.

In the manufacture of this glass for windows, the material employed is much the same as in ordinary sheet and plate glass—a double silicate of lime and soda, the coloring being due to the addition of metallic oxides which are soluble in the fused glass. The materials needed for the basis are, as before, sand, limestone and alkali. They are mixed in the proper proportions—that is to say, about thirty parts of lime and forty of soda to every hundred parts of sand, and are fused in fire-clay crucibles in the ordinary glass furnace. The coloring matter is added at different stages of the process, according to the nature of the material.

The mineral world has been pretty thoroughly ransacked to obtain the needed colors, and additions to the list are constantly being made as the result of further investigation. The violet shades are generally produced from manganese or from very small quantities of cobalt. The deep blues, indigos, purple-blues and normal blues are had from varying portions of cobalt. Peacock-blue comes from copper, and the finest greens are got from copper and chromium. The dull sea-water tint comes from ferrous oxide. The oxide of copper gives an emerald-green.

The yellows come from a variety of sources. The sesquioxide of uranium gives a fine fluorescent yellow; the oxide of lead a pale yellow, and the oxide of silver applied as a pigment to the surface of glass a permanent yellow stain. The higher oxide of iron gives an orange color, but as it has a strong tendency to become reduced, it is necessary during the manipulation of the glass to keep some oxidizing agent present, such as oxide of manganese.

In the reds a number of excellent shades are readily obtainable. Manganese furnishes a variety of pinkish reds; copper, in its lower oxide, the fine blood-red of Bohemian glass, and gold the deepest and most brilliant of all reds, that of the well-known ruby glass.

This list, however, is but a fragment. It bears to the complete array of color at the command of the glass-worker about the same relation that an inventory of crude pigments would bear to the fine distinctions of an artist's color-box. It is intended only to suggest the mineral basis of many others. The fine gradations of color, and the rich tones, are difficult to obtain. In many cases it has taken much experiment. The magnificent window designed by Mr. John La Farge,[2] which now faces the chancel in Trinity Church, Boston, owes the brilliancy of its peacock hues to the combination of some seventeen ingredients.

The superiority of American art-work in glass, however, is largely due to the introduction of the opalescent glass,[3] which is now winning such admiration abroad. The colors are readily obtained from any one of a half-dozen minerals.

So much for the glass; the building of the window is more interesting yet.

The artist or designer, having chosen his motive, proceeds to work it out roughly on paper. He keeps in mind, of course, the truth that the function of colored glass is to modify and not to impede the light. Therefore his scheme of color is studied with great care in its relation to the ever-varying light to be transmitted through the glass, the harmony of color with color, and so on. On the other hand, the lines in his drawings of figures are so planned that they profile against the background, as if they were intended for low relief, and his leads are so arranged as to assist the drawing, to emphasize the outline and to deepen the shadows. He also plans to avoid the use of leads altogether when they might diminish the translucent qualities or brilliancy of the glass.

His sketch is at first little more than a suggestion, a small colored sheet a few inches long. If this is judged to contain the proper spirit and feeling of the proposed window, a larger and more clearly outlined sketch is made, and if this prove satisfactory it becomes the nucleus of a window. The next step is to enlarge this to a size which will be a distinct and perfect guide to the artisan who builds the window from it.

The enlargement of the colored sketch to its full size is usually done by women. Upon the walls of the workshop are tacked large sheets of heavy manila paper, and upon these are drawn all outlines and shades of the design very distinctly. As much of the enlargement as possible is done mechanically, but there always remains much free-hand work requiring genuine artistic feeling. Indeed, throughout the entire process, artists, true both in feeling and technic, are needed even in the most mechanical portions. When the enlargement is finished, the cartoon is divided up by heavy black lines so disposed as to represent the doubly grooved lead which will hold the fragments of colored glass together.

Sketch and cartoon are now taken to the storeroom, and appropriate glass for the window is selected and laid aside. This may mean almost a restocking of the room if the appropriate material is not to be found there. As the accidental element, in spite of all the skill on the part of the glass-worker, is necessarily large, it sometimes happens that a ton of glass must be searched over to find a few pounds of just the right sort. In some cases several months pass before the right tints are selected.

The draftsman now makes two sets of copies of the cartoon, by means of carbon transfer paper. One of these is kept as a guide for the artist who leads the bits of glass together; the other is divided into patterns, the divisions following the places of the doubly grooved lead lines.

In making the artist's copies, of which there are two, the draftsman uses his stylus where he thinks the pieces of glass should be separated. For instance, he finds a spot of rich blue. He runs the point around the edge of this single color. When he has thus marked out every separate color and all the lines of the figure, he takes off the cartoon and underneath is the manila sheet marked for the exact number of pieces of glass of which the window will be composed. These separate pieces are all numbered on the paper, and then the two sheets are separated.

One of these sheets is cut into patterns by a three-bladed scissors, which follows all the lines made by the stylus. If an ordinary pair of shears were used, the lines would be accurately cut, but there would be no space left between the pieces for the lead which is used to hold them together. The three-bladed scissors not only cuts along the lines, but cuts out a piece an eighth of an inch broad where the line is, and therefore each piece of paper gives the exact size of its corresponding bit of glass.

The other artist's copy, all properly marked and numbered, is kept for reference in putting the window together.

The manila cartoon, which shows the doubly grooved lead lines, is now laid under a sheet of ordinary window-glass. The black lines are then traced upon the pane, and the "glass easel," as it is called, is stood up before a window, and all the pieces of the cartoon that was cut up are fastened upon it, in the order in which they belong, by means of bits of soft wax. When this is done, it will be seen that the pieces of paper separated from each other by an eighth of an inch represent the pieces of glass to be used.

The glass for the window has already been picked out according to the original color sketch, and now comes the most important part of the mechanical process. The glazier must remove each of the numbered slips of paper pasted on the glass easel, and replace it with glass of the color which the colored cartoon at his elbow indicates. The wax that holds the slip of paper on the easel will also hold the piece of glass when it is found and cut to the proper size.

The glazier then, with the artist standing by, with the cartoon and color scheme before him, removes one of the pieces of paper (or templates, as they are called), and passes a sheet of glass of the approximate color over the clear space. This is done until a sheet of glass is found which corresponds with the color sought. Sometimes a dozen or more sheets must be tried before the right piece is found. The sheet finally selected is cut to the size of the template and put in its place. This process is repeated until every piece of paper on the easel has been removed and replaced by glass of the same size and the proper color.

The colored sketch and the enlarged cartoon are always kept in sight, so that the completed window may always be in mind. The workmen who select and cut the glass have acquired a surprising skill in adapting its accidental variations to the needed expression of the thought. In mosaic glass of purely geometrical design, the requirements of color harmony alone need attention, but in the picture window, in addition to this, a very appreciative eye is needed to seize upon just the right combination to bring out the draperies and the background and the sky. It is frequently impossible to secure the desired effect with one thickness of glass and the glass is then doubled. This practice gives both better drawing and deeper color. In the matter of draperies, particularly, this principle is used with telling effect. In one of the windows here shown, the draperies of the figures were executed in white opalescent glass, and the dainty shades desired—pale green, pink and yellow—secured by placing back of this fragments of plain glass of the proper color. The effect could scarcely be more delicate, yet the color tones are full and strong.

In another window, the design of Mrs. Cox,[4] the rich purple draperies of a seated figure were first executed in a vivid blue. This was backed with ruby glass, and the result is a magnificent purple, as much finer than the artist's paper color as the sunshine is better than gaslight.

Coming to the flesh portions of the picture, the designer again takes a hand in the work. The portions are cut from white opalescent glass and mounted in rough frames before a window. Nearly all other light is cut off. In this way the artist can see his work under precisely the conditions of the window's final disposal, and can paint to correspondingly good advantage. The colors are put on rather heavily, to allow for firing, and for the distance at which the faces will commonly be seen. In many cases the paint is put on solidly and then picked off with a sharp instrument, giving much the effect of etching.

The painting is done in small sections, as it is necessary to fire the glass, which is done from two to four times. Each firing requires about an hour and a half, and six hours is allowed for the kiln to cool down. Before the last firing, the flesh portions are taken to the figure room and given place in the otherwise completed picture. In this way the artist can judge just what must be done to bring them into perfect harmony with the general color scheme.

When finally the window stands completed on the glass easel, the fragments of colored glass are removed one by one and placed in a tray, which is carried to the workbench of the glazier, where the pattern to guide the leading has been spread out. A piece of glass is laid in its proper place as marked on the design. This forms a starting point to which piece after piece is added, until the whole window is put together, the pieces being fastened together with narrow lines of lead.

The strip of lead used has lateral grooves to receive the edge of the glass, while the anterior and posterior surfaces are smooth. As the metal is soft and flexible, the glazier has no trouble in bending it around the glass, no matter what the outline may be. Nails are used to hold the outer edge firm. When all pieces have been set in the lead grooves, the joints are soldered together on both sides of the window, and at the same time tinned in order to protect them from rust and decay.

In the American school of picture-window makers, the subject of leads has been studied with great attention, with the result that there has been a noteworthy improvement in the method of leading. Leads are now made that will bend laterally but in no other direction, and these are used where the window is exposed to strong winds; also, strong and broad leads are made in forms which give them the appearance of being much smaller; others are made like hair-lines, and yet are strong.

There is another point of contrast between the American artist in glass and the European, and it is this: The former seeks for perfect color effects, paying very little attention to form, as long as he reaches his chromatic aim. For this he has been found fault with by some few foreign critics, "men accustomed," as a recent writer puts it, "to the crude color of Bavarian, Belgian and French modern glass, or to the sad, ineffectual glass of England, and not capable of understanding our advance."

Americans do have faults, however, and the great one hitherto has been their disregard of the relationship of their windows to architectural surroundings; and, again, through their clear knowledge that the true value of glass as a decorative material is dependent upon its color, the combination of the same, the prismatic play of light, and the niceties in light and shade, they have been led to give too much attention to this and have too often been careless in their drawing.

Such faults are certainly not unconquerable, and have been overlooked rather than created in the evolution of this art along the original lines that have been mentioned.

With this evolution there has gone a marked increase in public interest and appreciation. The outlook for the minor arts in this country is most hopeful, and the subject is one on which there is much to be said to our young men and young women. It ought to be possible to repeat the success of the Berlin exhibition, which was mentioned at the beginning of this article, in other lines of artistic design and construction than that of the glazier, whose strides have been astonishingly rapid.

Those who have helped most to bring about this high state of development are still alive, and so laboring at their art that it is safe to say that the glazier has returned to his workshop to adorn the world, or its architectural side, as it has never been adorned before. He has come back to adorn not only the church, but the municipal edifice and the home. Moreover, he has come back to stay, for it is comforting to reflect that our esthetic development has reached a point where whatever has beauty and utility, no matter of what style of art or of what age, is free from revulsions of taste and sentiment.

Notes

1. "The Making of Stained-Glass Windows," *Cosmopolitan* 26 (January 1899): 243–52.

2. John La Farge (1835–1910), born into a family of French émigrés in America, studied art in Paris. The interior decoration of the Trinity Church made La Farge the most famous interior designer and mural painter in America.

3. Refers to the famous "opaline," one of the new kinds of stained glass developed by La Farge.

4. Dreiser wrote an article, "Work of Mrs. Kenyon Cox," *Cosmopolitan* 24 (March 1899): 477–80.

He Became Famous in a Day[1]

Paul Weyland Bartlett, the American Sculptor whose Artistic Creations, the Labor of Many Months, Excited Surprise and Admiration in Paris

Paul Weyland Bartlett is a very young man, very full of enthusiasm, and has not done all that he will do; but he is one whose work takes rank over many others, in that it is sincere and painstaking and beautiful. He is a young man to whose work you would not deny sincere praise, and yet from whom it would be wise to withhold the final word, because he has not done all he can do. All that can be said is that here is a talented man. His ideas are poetic, and his representations of them are skillful. He is worth studying.

Mr. Bartlett only recently came back from Europe, where he spent many successful years; he has a studio in —st Twentieth Street, where he is now doing some interesting work. The particular thing at the present time is an equestrian statue of General Hooker, which is all finished save some of the decorative work on the large circular base upon which it is to stand. The entrance to this base he had decided to ornament with a design of eagles, and had gone to the expense and trouble of purchasing a large, bald-headed eagle, from which to work as a model. The crusty captive from aerial heights did not favor the idea at all, and sullenly moped in his great cage, which occupied one end of the studio. His demeanor did not deter the artist in the least, however, who sat before the cage day after day, studying the characteristics of the splendid fowl, and making models of him in clay. Finally, after nearly a month of observation and study, the designs of suitable eagles were completed, and the captive was sent out to the artist's country place, to rest and recuperate.

Success Won by Toilsome Efforts

That is an instance of the care and pains taken to make sculpture, in a sense, a living thing. The clay eagle must be, in all things, like the

Paul Weyland Bartlett, "The Bear Tamer." Courtesy of the Corcoran Gallery of Art, Gift of Mrs. Paul Weyland Bartlett

living,—must suggest the spark of life, even though it be but an ornament to a wall enclosing a monument.

Few sculptors are more patient. I remember knocking at Mr. Bartlett's studio door one wintry evening when it was almost dark. There was no light inside; but, stumbling through the gloom, I found the young artist still hard at work. His eyes had become used to the shadow, and he had not noticed that the day, for his work at least, was done.

Mr. Bartlett came to distinguish himself very rapidly in Paris, but it was only after the most toilsome effort. Anyone who exhibits at the Salon does so along with hundreds of others, and however admirable a piece of sculpture may be, it is very apt to rest unnoticed among the vast collection of clays, marbles, and bronzes shown at each exhibition. Mr. Bartlett realized this. His work might be good, but what of it. Paris is filled with artists of talent. If he exhibited one large piece, he courted failure, however undeserved. Consequently, he studied to avoid this. He would not exhibit one, but would display hundreds of pieces of sculpture. Ah! but the Salon does not admit more than two pieces of sculpture by one artist. It was different with small bronzes. If each piece of sculpture were no bigger than his hand, or, at most, his two hands, he could put a hundred in a glass case or two, and the cases would be admitted and exhibited. This he knew. At once he decided to take advantage of it. It meant ever so much more work, for it is nearly as difficult to model a small design in clay as it is a large one, but he would gain in attention and criticism. Therefore, work was nothing. He toiled devotedly until he had made over a hundred models,—perfect, inspiring designs of historic characters,—animals, insects; in short, a small museum of sculptured curiosities. These he decided to send, but he was not yet satisfied.

He Cast His Own Work in Bronze

He knew from long years of apprenticeship in a bronze-casting foundry how to cast in bronze. The expense of careful work of this kind is considerable, and as he was not wealthy, he could not think of paying for having his splendid collection so cast. Still, he wanted to exhibit bronzes, and therefore decided to cast his work himself. He secured the privilege from the founder with whom he had been apprenticed of working in the shops. With his own hands he made the molds for his statuettes, and cast them in bronze, firing them in such a way as to give them all the rare hues shown in the finest examples of bronzes handed down from the Greek and Roman period. These he displayed in his case, and had it admitted to the Salon. Then he awaited the verdict. The vitrine or case containing his exquisite bronzes was the talk of the exhibition. Hundreds stopped to admire the number of delicate and perfect representations and the beautiful coloring. Parisian artists examined and questioned and gesticulated before the case. This set the critics to examining, and they made the artist celebrated. Mr. Bartlett found himself famous in a day, the papers said; but he knew better. After years of preparation, and months and months of particular and painstaking toil, recognition had come to him. It was a great effort.

For the Congressional Library

Mr. Bartlett had done good work before this. Indeed, he had considerable standing as a sculptor, but it had not crystallized into that thing called fame, until this bright idea was carried out. He went to Paris when a child. His father wisely sent him from America, where he was surrounded by things commercial, to Paris, where he could make his home, learn to love the old masters, grow up with the sense of the beautiful, and have other gods than money. He worked quietly for many years, and then, in 1889, exhibited some "Dancing Indians" and "Dancing Bears," which won for him a gold medal, and brought him into notice. He revisited the United States then, and had virtually decided to stay, when he found, after he had accepted some American contracts, that he could work better in Europe. He therefore determined to fill his American orders in a Parisian studio.

One order was from the United States government, for three statues for the new Congressional Library,—one of Galileo, one of Columbus, and the third of Michelangelo. These statues were made in Paris, but the young sculptor respected American sentiment in the matter; and so, in 1897, he shipped a plaster-cast of Columbus to New York, to be cast in bronze, although it could have been much more cheaply cast on the other side. It was the first ever shipped across the Atlantic to be cast in America.

The third statue of the series, Michelangelo, was also modeled in Paris and shipped to this country, where it is now being cast. Of these two, the first brought to Mr. Bartlett much favorable comment and praise. The Columbus is a colossal figure, with power expressed in every line of the face and every fold of the cloak. It is one of the most commanding works produced in late years. The statue of Michelangelo has not yet been given to the public for criticism, but has been seen by a number of American sculptors. Several of these, including J. Q. A. Ward,[2] the president of the New York Sculpture Society, called one morning at the foundry to look at the model. When they entered the room, the beauty and power of the work took their fancy, and the entire company exclaimed, simultaneously, "Bravo," and "Well done." Mr. Bartlett was not present at the time to hear it, but he was duly informed and congratulated.

Other Examples of Bartlett's Work

At present, Mr. Bartlett is in New York, and has decided to stay in America. He has taken a large studio and accepted several American contracts, which he purposes to execute here. No one has a greater knowledge of bronze and bronze-casting than this young man, and he has the advantage of being a tireless worker. He steers clear of specialties, that dangerous rock on which so much talent has foundered, and is as brilliant in his execution of a "Torso of a Girl," or of a "Dead Lion," as he is in his historical figures. His poetical organization and delicate touch are also exemplified in a door of a mausoleum, which he recently completed, and which now stands in Woodlawn Cemetery, wherein the ethereal form of a woman stands surrounded by poppies and leaves. He has also done a figure of a man bent with grief, which is particularly fine. The muscles on the back and arms stand out with all the force of some great passionate grief that overpowers him.

Mr. Bartlett is only thirty-five years of age, but his talent is mature, and of all the younger sculptors, certainly no one has exhibited more evidence of genius.

The Real and the Ideal in Sculpture

The true sculptor may readily say with the true poet: "I captain an army of shining and generous dreams." His privilege it is, along with the painter and the writer, to work out his ideas in such form that they shall inspire men with their beauty and their meaning. It is his privilege to help the world to a better and more beautiful life, and well the true sculptor understands all this.

His business is not with the casting of the bronze or with this or that party who desires such and such a statue for such and such a place and time. He has to do with himself and his ideals solely,—with how he may best purify his heart, and strengthen and make sure his arm; so that, when that internal speaking which men call inspiration comes, his mind may be bright and quick to interpret what it says, and his hands ready and capable to build up, out of clay, a material representation of that internal thought which was awakened in him.

You will hear of sculptors, from time to time, who are doing this work for such and such a park, or this decoration of such and such a building, and it would seem, on the mere external statement of the case, that the man who does the most of such things, is the greatest sculptor. This is really as it should be, but it is not always true. Sometimes the greatest of them do things in clay and marble that are so fine in sentiment, so beautiful in form, that they are too good for the average use of men. They will not suit a public highway or park, and look out of place in a public institution. A sculptor who makes such works of art must languish in penury if he does not chance upon a wealthy lover of the beautiful who will be his patron, and look to it that he does not want while he employs his time in this, to him, unprofitable task, as the world of business takes it,—not unprofitable in reality, however, but the very best of profit for his own mind and heart, and of incalculable advantage and profit to the world.

All sculptors are not alike, however. Some have most high ideals, which they combine with great physical strength and much energy and business sense. It is a rare composition, but when you do find it in an individual, you may be sure that he is either already distinguished or destined shortly to be, and that he will obtain much of what the world has to give its heroes in the way of honor and emoluments while he lives.

You will frequently find a man who, while these things come to him, cares very little for them. He will prove to be a man who is happiest in those old comfortable clothes in which he works. The studio, in the silent light of which he gathers and forms his clay, and slowly models out his ideas, will be much the most comfortable place in the world for him, and amid that silent company of the creatures of his brain, he will work away the years, but little heeding what the world may say, and having his keenest pleasure in the thought that his work is good. In such devotion to art, a true artist finds his ideal life.

Notes

1. "He Became Famous in a Day," *Success* 2 (28 January 1899): 143–44. On Paul Weyland Bartlett. Reprinted as "Artistic Fame in a Day—after Long Years of Preparation" in *Talks with Great Workers,* pp. 221–24. Paul Weyland Bartlett (1865–1925).

2. See Dreiser's article, "The Foremost of American Sculptors, J. Q. A. Ward," included in this collection.

A Master of Photography[1]

Alfred Stieglitz Has Proven That a Great Photograph
Is Worth Years of Labor to Make

There is one man among the master photographers who so towers
above his followers that there is no longer any dispute as to his leadership. His name is Alfred Stieglitz, and it has become very widely
known. His work is so esteemed the world over among those who love
art in photographs, and who love to study and emulate superior and
original methods, that it has come to have a high market value. Single
prints from his negatives sell at prices ranging from fifty to one hundred dollars. A large card-mounted edition of twelve photogravures
of his pictures having been issued, it was in demand at premium at
once, selling for fifteen dollars per copy. Several of the largest pub-
lishing houses have offered him cash bonuses of no trivial proportions to write a book on photography, or issue a large volume of his
pictures in half-tone; but he is too sincere an artist to put himself
forward until the time and his own work are riper for the results he
aims to achieve.

Patience in Art

It would be difficult to tell whether his pictures are so superior to
those of others. Art is an elusive thing. It must be seen. He waited in
the rain for hours to get a picture that would express the sweep and
vigor of a stormy day. He did not snap his camera right and left. In
the end, patience prevailed. A moment came when a sweep of gray
drops was so evident as to be photographable, and he photographed
them. Other photographers had tried before. Others had taken
scores of negatives, all dim and lifeless. He, with a little two-by-four
detective camera, saw his opportunity and made it avail, and "A Rainy

Alfred Stieglitz, "Self Portrait, 1910." Courtesy of Dorothy Norman

Alfred Stieglitz, "The Incoming Boat, Katwyk, 1894." Courtesy of Dorothy Norman

Day in Fifth Avenue" became one of the most generally admired of his many pictures.

Similarly, he was the first to make night pictures,—a thing never before thought possible in photography. He planted his camera in the public ways and stood beside it for hours. He did it time and time again, making a series of pictures which attracted no end of attention.

It is not all patience, however. There is a fine feeling which guides his decision. He would not photograph an imperfect picture. He is keen and quick to discover what is wanting, to take out and put in. So when you see one of his pictures, you will discover that it "looks more like a painting." There will be that selection of subject, that delicacy of treatment, and that charm of situation and sentiment which all rare paintings have. Only color will be missing, and this, in fact, will be compensated for by the clear, crowning reality of the thing.

It was in Berlin that Mr. Stieglitz first studied photography. There,

Alfred Stieglitz, "Two Towers, New York, 1893–94." Courtesy of Dorothy Norman

in 1885, he was studying mechanical engineering at the Polytechnic School, when Dr. Vogel, of the photo-chemical laboratory, persuaded the young man that a course of theoretical photography would be of great value in his profession. Mr. Stieglitz took up the work and followed it closely, only to become convinced that it was a worthy field in itself, and suitable to his ambition. In 1887, two years after he entered a picture, "A Good Story," in a contest which the London "Amateur Photographer" arranged, winning a silver medal. More, the merit of the picture called forth a letter of praise and encouragement from the judge of award, Dr. P. H. Emmerson, one of the best amateur photographers in England.

This was merely a beginning. In the twelve years which have elapsed since then, he gathered honors rapidly, until now he possesses one hundred medals, bronze, silver and gold, and a number of certificates of acceptance from institutions which are most conservative. The latter he values most, because they represent a severer test, and, consequently, greater appreciation.

Mr. Stieglitz came to his native city, New York, in 1888, but did not stay long. He went back to Europe for two years, where he made some remarkable studies, and then returned to New York for good. He began by endeavoring to settle down in business, not as a mechanical engineer,—for he had abandoned that,—but in trade. He could not endure it, however, and returned to the study of photography, which has since proved so valuable to him.

It was during the years following Mr. Stieglitz's return to America that his best work was done. He attracted attention by constantly securing an artistic photograph of something never before attempted. He introduced new and simpler methods. At the same time, he proved that a great photograph is worth years of labor to make. One instance is particularly well known in photographic art circles. It was the making of the picture, "The L in a Storm." The picture was made with a little three by four detective camera. It was a blinding snow scene, made at a moment when the elements were most clearly picturesque. He made a print of it which was striking enough, and which, with most photographers, would have ended the matter. Not so with him. Small as the plate was, it contained much that was unessential and weakened the composition. Accordingly, all this was cut out and an enlarged transparency made of the part which was to be kept,— about half of the original. In the development of this, and the still further enlarged negative, much care had to be taken and many plates used. The contrast had to be reduced, parts held back, and others brought forward. In fact, everything had to be done which could, by purely photographic methods, tend to convey the impression produced by the original scene. Often, months of work are devoted to such a picture; not constant, of course, but six or eight hours a week. In this case, the photograph was taken four or five years ago, and only completed a few months since. It had grown to an eleven-by-fourteen print, a gem of art. It was not so very much different from the early copies, and yet just sufficient to make the last pure art. The range of tone had been modified so as to make the falling snow more prominent, and a couple of girders in the foreground had been removed. There was no retouching, for that is something which no pictorial worker will countenance, but only a few changes accomplished by purely photographic and honorable means and methods.

His Achievements and His Tasks

But Mr. Stieglitz's work is greater than his reputation, and to him is due much of the prominence which artistic photography has gained. About two years ago, there were two large but practically dead clubs in New York, one of which boasted Mr. Stieglitz as a member. Neither was successful until he took the lead and united the two in the Camera Club.[2] Immediately, the combination of talent and numbers prospered. The membership increased to over three hundred, and the entrance fee and annual dues were doubled. An eight-thousand-dollar photographic plant was installed, free to all members. "Camera Notes" was founded, and, in little more than a year, the club had become one of the wealthiest organizations of the sort in the country.

Mr. Stieglitz has organized exhibits which have brought out talent the land over. He has set himself three tasks, which, if accomplished, will bring recognition to photography as an art of the first importance.

The first of these is to elevate the standard of pictorial photography in America. The second, to establish an annual exhibition, of a much higher order than anything yet known, giving no awards, but only a certificate of acceptance, which shall be, in itself, a treasure; third, to establish a National Academy of Photography. That Mr. Stieglitz will succeed no one doubts who understands his marvelous ability.

Notes

1. "A Master of Photography," *Success* 2 (10 June 1899): 471. On Alfred Stieglitz. Reprinted as "Years of Labor to Make of Photography a Fine Art" in *Talks with Great Workers,* pp. 235–39. Alfred Stieglitz (1864–1946).

2. Dreiser was so much interested in photography as a new discipline of art that he wrote a long well-detailed article, "The Camera Club of New York," *Ainslee's* 4 (October 1899): 324–35.

The Foremost of American Sculptors[1]

There is no more picturesque figure in the world of American art to-day than J. Q. A. Ward. If anyone may be said to stand for the spirit of sculpture, it is he. Rich in experience and wide in fame, he stands, one might say, preeminent in his field. Not that his work may be declared better than that of any other American sculptor, or that he outshines them all in his intellectual and moral qualities. So much could not be unreservedly said, but only that a combination of service, years, and liberality has placed him so conspicuously and deservedly in the public favor as to be counted first.

In the Greater New York of to-day there are 12 noted examples of his art. He has decorated its squares, streets, and parks. The statues of Washington in Wall Street, of Greeley in Printing House Square and its replica in Greeley Square, of Horace Roebling in Madison Square, are by him. In Central Park are his statues of Shakespeare, the Indian and His Dog, a New England Pilgrim, and an ideal figure representative of the Seventh Regiment. In Brooklyn are two of his most celebrated characterizations, General Grant and Henry Ward Beecher;[2] and elsewhere in the greater city are statues of Commodore Perry, William E. Dodge, William H. Fogg, and Engineer Halls.

At Hartford, Conn., the roof of the capitol carries six figures in marble (repeated once, forming 12 figures in all) by him which represent Art, Science, Music, Poetry, Commerce, and Agriculture. In the park of the same capitol stands Israel Putnam[3] in bronze—rebel uniform and high boots, a most imposing figure. At Burlington, Vt., stands Mr. Ward's heroic bronze figure of Lafayette.[4] At Newburyport, Mass., there is a heroic standing statue of Washington, and at Charleston, S. C., a colossal bust of Gilmore Sumner.[5]

The national capital has two important monuments by Ward: one, at the foot of Capitol Hill, is a portrait figure of General Garfield; the other is that of Gen. George H. Thomas. Elsewhere, as at Columbus, Ohio, Spartansburg, Va., and Gettysburg, are statues of Dr. Lincoln Goodale, Gen. Daniel Morgan, and Gen. John Reynolds.

Mr. Ward is a man who has always possessed a genial social spirit. Unlike most of his profession, he has mingled freely with the world

John Quincy Adams Ward, "Henry Ward Beecher." Courtesy of the Metropolitan Museum of Art, Rogers Fund, 1917.

outside his chosen sphere. Literature, politics, and sociology have interested and broadened him. He early became the friend and companion of broad and influential men in other spheres. By the strength of his own character and the sincerity of his belief he made them to understand art. Thru his impression on them he gave the whole subject a dignity—the American phase of it.

Moreover, there is scarcely a sculptor of note to-day in this country who is not indebted to him for some liberal service rendered at a time when it was most essential. He has distributed patronage with the liberality of a prince, and when his own great reputation brought him the majority of public contracts he generously turned them over impartially to one after another of the deserving young men in his field until all were helped and satisfied.

Ward came to New York, out of Ohio, a raw, uneducated youth. He had been born and raised at Urbana.[6] There were no art interests there. He saw nothing in his infancy or youth calculated to awaken an

"Indian Hunter." Courtesy of the New-York Historical Society

artistic instinct, and yet, he says, the artistic desire was always with him.

"I can not remember the time when I did not want to express myself in form. During my first year at school, which was my sixth in age, I had got so far with my natural instinct as to fashion rude figures out of mud. So strong and satisfying was this taste in me that I had much rather sit down by the creek-bed trying to make the head of a man than go a-fishing. On Saturdays I would work all day long on my hobby. I had a little crevice in a mill-dam where I hid my tools and things before I went home.

"If my memory serves me rightly, I forgot to go to school one morning, I was so interested in some clay effigies I was making. My father found out what I was doing and hunted me up—or down. I recall looking up from my labor and finding him gazing over my shoulder at what I was doing. I was considerably frightened, and yet, in the face of the worst, was pleased that he should see what I considered some remarkable things by me. He displayed lenient consideration for my taste and my achievement, but reminded me, in his kind, stern way, that I must not waste my time.

"After all, I think he was rather proud of my remarkable diversion, altho he was not the sort of father who would ever have said so in my presence. He was a quiet, reserved Presbyterian, and said little at any time. Still he must have talked of the matter, for altho I said nothing, the fact that I molded heads and figures out of clay got around our little town. People came down to our house at the end of the village 'to see the queer things Mr. Ward's boy had been making.' That flattered me considerably, and I remember my first touch of vanity displayed itself in my taking exception to their intrusion, and declaring that they were not finished and that I wanted no judgment passed on them until they were."

In this little town of Urbana Mr. Ward dwelt uninterruptedly until he came to New York. He never looked upon a piece of real sculpture until he was sixteen years of age. His parents were not aware that this youthful propensity to model meant anything. That he should follow this bent year after year with ever-increasing enthusiasm proves the doctrine of innate tendencies. All he really needed was the sight of perfect work to set him upon the trail of perfection himself. This came one day when he visited Cincinnati. It was at the time that the Greek Slave of Hiram Powers[7] was in the zenith of its fame. It was being exhibited in the cities of America as the marvel of the age, and young Ward was taken to see it. He says that he was delighted with the privilege. The work was for him a divine, far-off accomplishment. It seemed a marvel of perfection, the last gracious suggestion of inspired fingers.

"Oh," he said, "if I could only do something like that!"

Powers was in Cincinnati at the time, but the boy was too diffident to seek an interview with him. He went back to his little, plain Ohio town filled with a sense of its narrowness and limitation. It was small and blank and unappreciative. He desired more than anything else to leave it and to go where the great pieces of sculpture were. He thought of New York and of studios, and dreamed of splendid pieces of his own being exhibited there and glorified as this one was; and then he returned with a partially awakened sense of his many artistic deficiencies to his mud-modeling.

Ward says that for years after seeing this first figure it seemed to him that the great sculptor must be a man born with such a keen appreciation of the beautiful and such a ready sense of accuracy that he set before him a piece of marble, and with hammer and chisel fancy caused the "chips to fly" until a beautiful form had been brought forth. He could not conceive of slowness or pondering. His own meager progress seemed all out of order.

"I was sure that beautiful work was not done that way, and that my poor slow-modeled clay images were but an evidence of my dulness. I felt a deep, bitter resentment in my heart because my fingers were slow and my sense of accuracy uncertain. That made me think of abandoning the struggle and taking up any chance business opportunity that offered, and often in my heart I gave up with an agonizing sense of separation and loss my dreamed-of career and turned to home affairs—as I thought for good. It was never to be that way, however."

One reason for it not being so was the understanding and good will of the ambitious boy's older sister, who resided with her husband in Brooklyn. She occasionally visited her parents in Urbana and was constantly informed of the tendency and progress of her younger brother. One of her visits occurred shortly after Ward had seen the Greek Slave. He was all enthusiasm in his description of the masterpiece, and she entered into his delight. After conversing with him for days and finding his heart was wholly enlisted, she proposed that he be allowed to follow an artistic career. Their parents did not object, and finally it was agreed that the boy should return with her. Accordingly he came, and thru friends H. K. Browne was induced to take him into his studio. The details of his entrance into the art world are best told by himself:

"Browne's studio was in Brooklyn. On the appointed morning I started out to begin my apprenticeship with him. I had the idea that talented sculptors hewed out their beautiful compositions rapidly and without preparation. I chose to go alone to the studio and without any introduction. When I got there some statuary was being moved out and the door was open. I walked in unheeded. The great place was barn-like, but full of the bits of figure-work that I had long craved to see. No one seemed to be or to have been hewing anything. A few barrels of clay were in one corner, some revolving stands in another. A young man, stretched prone upon the floor, was diligently studying an anatomical chart. As I waited and gazed about the truth dawned upon me. There was no invariable need of hewing and making the chips fly. Artists modeled as I had tried to do. A great load lifted from me instantly, and I faced the master of the place with a light heart."

Ward was always an active worker under his master, and gained his esteem to such an extent that he became his favorite. He shunned no difficulties and took no credit. Toward the last years of his apprenticeship Browne began the equestrian statue of Washington which now stands in Union Square, and called Ward to work with him. The apprentice toiled harder than the master and gave the work a strong smack of his genius. When it was modeled and cast in bronze, the workmen began to set it up, but soon fell out over some question of trade privileges, and struck. When the sculptor stood appalled at the delay the apprentice threw off his coat, and, seizing some tools, said he would finish placing it. No objection was offered, and like a workman he entered the body of the statue and hammered and filed away, bolting and riveting the work until in three days it was done.

Browne was so pleased with his pupil's work that he refused to take the full credit of the labor, and so to-day those who examine the statue see both Browne and Ward's names inscribed as the sculptors.

A good light is thrown on the young sculptor, as he was then, by some comment that his teacher made publicly, years later, when the pupil was famous:

"Ward," he said, "is a sculptor of great originality, accuracy, and power. He was seven years in my studio, closely applied to study, devoted to severe routine work—the discipline of which is the basis and stepping-stone to great achievement. When he left me he did not comprehend his powers, nor anticipate their result. I did not perceive his gifts fully until one day he placed before me a little model of the Indian and Dog. I remember well that on occasion of converse with other and less laboriously drilled art students Ward would speak impatiently on the lack of knowledge on their part, not seeing that such observation as a result of comparison of acquirements was due to his superior knowledge, rather than to their lack of it. Once, when he was most impatient, I reminded him of the old German music-master who had with great severity confined a pupil possessing rare talent to routine lesson and study practise exclusively. After three years the pupil, unconscious of the power this practise had brought but also prevented him from proving, heard a more advanced pupil playing a truly difficult piece.

" 'Will I ever be able to play that?' he asked.

" 'Surely,' said his teacher, 'you can play that now. You are the best performer on your instrument in harmony.' After that Ward was content to practise and not originate in my service, and the value of his training has been exemplified."

This piece of sculpture, the Indian and His Dog, to which Browne refers was the very earliest of Mr. Ward's ideal compositions, and has lived in greatest public favor. The composition of it occupied the odd moments of several years.

During its early days it enjoyed quite as much public comment as Powers's Greek Slave, which Ward as a boy had so much admired. The sculptor preserves to-day a large bundle of scrap-books filled with laudatory notices, and, besides, has a closet whose shelves are completely filled with sere and rumpled clippings.

In spite of the great success of Ward's first attempt, his work was not to be in the sculpturing of ideal subjects. I once asked him why American sculptors gave so much attention to portrait sculpture and so little to ideal work.

"Because the demand is so," he answered. "It goes back to the time of the civil war. Before that war what American sculpture there was was ideal in character. There were Indians and hunters and so on in great abundance. Every man with a pretension to artistic taste must needs have a stock of them in his home. They were carved without much regard to art. If they had a general resemblance to what they attempted to represent, that was sufficient. But with the outbreak of the war all this kind of statuary was thrown away or stowed in lumber-rooms. All attention was fastened upon the front of war. The nation's heroes filled the nation's eye, as they do again to-day. Heroes will again be the chief subject of sculpture for the next ten years."

Mr. Ward's first portrait statue was that of Commodore Oliver H. Perry. August Belmont, who was a great admirer of the naval hero, had seen the Indian Hunter and His Dog and was greatly struck with it. He sought the sculptor, who was just then beginning his career, and asked what his "figures were" for a statue of Perry. Ward named them.

Belmont accepted,—"and," says Ward, "after that I was never without a commission."

The period in which he was never without a commission endured until 1885, when he cut it short himself by refusing to take any more. "No, I have had my share," was his kindly response to every request. "I have acquired all the money and all the distinction I care for. Give it to the younger men. It would be an injustice to them for me to take it."

During all this time his fame had been spreading rapidly. The price of his labor rose from as low as a thousand dollars for a statue up to one hundred thousand. He was taken to be the finest expression of American art, and what he said dominated the opinion of the public in an almost arbitrary fashion.

What Ward did in organizing the National Sculptors' Society is understood and appreciated fully by none but artists themselves. His labor in breaking down the barriers of jealousy and misunderstanding among sculptors is quite a story in itself. He was rewarded with the presidency of this distinguished body, which he has held uninterruptedly ever since.

To-day he lives the life of the retired artist. He still maintains one of the handsomest and best-equipped studios in the world, where he spends most of his time. He does not put himself to any stress of labor, however, but merely works there according to his fancy, doing the things of his fancy. That he has ceased accepting commissions for himself is no sign that he has ceased producing works of art. Indeed, it is under the new dispensation of his time that he has returned to the unbroken contemplation of the ideal.

Concerning the interest of the American people in sculpture he once said to me:

"I believe that our people are naturally rather more artistic than any other branch of the so-called Anglo-Saxon or North people. They have a native skill and certain other qualities essential to the make-up of a sculptor to a remarkable degree. They have vigorous thought, wholesome sentiment, and good imaginative or inventive qualities.

"Thus far our art has been rather crude and along one line, as in the case of war heroes, but we are doing better. We have now art organizations fully able to give us the best expert judgment on questions of art. There can be no verdict so good. The opinions of one artist may go wrong, but those of an association of artists are scarcely apt to be erroneous.

"We have, as yet, no distinctive school of American art in either sculpture or painting. It takes centuries to found a distinct school. As to the progress of sculpture here, tho, it is good. It is not so much, perhaps, what we have already achieved as what we are ready to achieve. For the first time in our history we are putting up a public building that is decorated in a worthy style. I refer to the new public library in Washington."

Notes

1. "The Foremost of American Sculptors," *New Voice* 16 (17 June 1899): 4–5, 13. On John Quincy Adams Ward (1830–1910).
2. Henry Ward Beecher (1813–1887), American clergyman.
3. Israel Putnam (1718–1790), American Revolutionary general.
4. Marquis de Lafayette (1757–1834), French general and statesman.
5. Unidentified.
6. Located thirty-five miles west of Columbus. Ward is buried in the Oak Dale Cemetery beneath a copy of his famous statue, *The Indian Hunter.*
7. Hiram Powers (1805–1873), whose *The Greek Slave,* the first of his figures to be carved in marble, made his reputation as America's Michelangelo.

C. C. Curran[1]

Those individuals who find it a pleasure to go the rounds of our American galleries and art exhibits, making themselves wise in the merits or demerits of the various artists, have encountered, from time to time, during the past few years, some paintings by C. C. Curran. These, for certain qualities of innocent charm and sweet out-of-door freshness, arrest the attention. Their subject-matter is most simple at times; they are seldom interwoven with any secret allusion or suggestion, and as seldom with any seriousness of mien, and yet they are poetic in feeling, skillful in execution and rich in color. One could never say of any one of them, "Here is a powerful picture." The subject-matter does not answer to that term. They are too delicate, too fanciful, too—

> "Rich in the simple
> worship of a day"

—to be enjoyed by any save the lovers of Nature's most idyllic phases.

Mr. Curran is a young Ohioan who has been in New York since 1883, with the exception of a trip or two to Europe, and who in that time, has gradually been extended honorable recognition as a painter. He is spoken of as a Kentuckian, now and then, from the fact that he happened to be born while his parents were spending a few weeks' vacation in the old State.

Those who know him personally would be able to pick out examples of Mr. Curran's work, in any general exhibit, for qualities redolent of two worlds. These scenes which he paints are at once Ohio and Paris combined. They are things out of the woodland of the old Buckeye State, lightened by a refinement and delicacy of technique gathered by admiring study of the best French masters. Mr. Curran frankly says that Dagnan Bouveret[2] is his master, the one painter who has influenced him greatly. Anyone who has seen Bouveret's work can trace the similarity of spirit, at least. Yet, quite easily, the initiated can see that there is a personality back of the sentiments and beauties which Mr. Curran's pictures express. Only a warm feeling for color and tones, for sunlight and moonlight and the fleeting shams and fancies of a day, could move an artist to paint the "Spirits of the Flowers." That picture, with its soft, white roses and whiter maidens, yields such a breath of dew and delight as only the poets translate for us out of romance. It is Grecian in conception and value. All of Curran's paintings have something of this quality. They seek out a lightness and brightness in life, noted of all men, yet seldom compounded effectively in a painting. One picture in particular comes back at the present moment as having quite essentially the touch of our own day and yet nothing passing in it, nothing that a hundred years will make stale or out of date. It is that of a few children playing by the waterside. It does not matter that they are children dressed after the fancy and dictation of a modern mother; this only gives it a to-day-ishness that will please those who rejoice in a latter-day atmosphere. It has real permanence in the spirit of childish play out-of-doors, that it gives; the feeling of young blood rejoicing to the extent of shouts, and laughter, and tears in sunshine, and earth and water. There is something of the spirit that Stevenson voices in his "Child's Garden of Verses,"[3] and particularly in the lines:

> "I called the little pool a sea;
> The little hills were big to me,
>   For I am very small.
> I made a boat, I made a town,
> I searched the caverns up and down
>   And named them one and all."

Indeed, if one may venture so much praise without first qualifying his technique, it may be said that all of Mr. Curran's pictures are Stevensonian in spirit. They represent that interest in those little sylvan combinations of nature which so pleased Stevenson. In his "Inland Voyage," the latter never fails to dilate upon the appearance of the maidens seen from his canoe, as he skirted inland gardens and country walks.

He was forever expecting to come suddenly—

> "By meadows where at afternoon
> The growing maidens troop in June
> To loose their girdles on the grass";
> "To light with unfamiliar face
> On chaste Diana's bathing place."

He was never more delighted than when observing boys and girls racing in joyous games. Glimpses of children digging in the earth, sailing their boats or playing on the greensward, awakened such a responsive poetic echo as has never been seen in verse before. He compounded his essays and his rustic volumes of these things. While they are not great; not anything of what the common conception of what a great piece of literature ought to be—"mighty weapon to further the aim of man"—yet they are delicious, aesthetic contributions to the beauty of life, ivory carvings in prose, and worthy the tender solicitude of every lover of things so dainty.

This is not to say, however, that Curran's pictures are such delicious pieces of painting as Mr. Stevenson's compositions are literature. The latter's place is fixed; his fame is too great. Curran is yet youthful in his labor and innocent of fame in its broadest sense. He is still studying to perfect his interpretation of the spirituality of certain things actual and commonplace.

There is fair possibility of his gaining high place in American Art. He is young, serious and free from the vice of over-production. Some of his pictures are worthy of the term beautiful in its cleanest sense. Even in the poorer pictures there is evident straining after poetic expression—an effort to put down, in colors, those rich sidelights of life's glimpses of beauty that lead us on to joy.

This summer Mr. Curran has a studio at Stroudsburg, Pa.,[4] a region rich in mountain vistas and rugged scenery. With him are his wife and his five-year-old boy, to whom he is devoted. The former is a lady of much culture whose interest in art and literature is great. Her critical opinion is both clear and unbiased, and she is said, by those who know her, to be that balance in her husband's life which is always on the side of ideality, and yet sanity, in things which he does.

Mr. Curran's New York studio is in Sixty-first Street. He is a member of the Salmagundi[5] and Athletic clubs and an officer in both. Like Bruce Crane and several of the younger artists, he takes interest in art organization and frequently serves on committees of admission and display at the various art bodies. He is well liked personally, being good-natured and with an eye for character.

A fact that he comments upon with amusement, is in connection with the prevailing impression that he is a Kentuckian. The chief recognition resulting from this distinction, he says, has come from various charity-fund committees, which, seeing his name mentioned, in connection with numerous Art exhibits throughout the country, have ventured to address him in behalf of their respective causes. Not a rich man himself, these appeals have their humorous side, illustrating, as they do, the wide gap between a man's reputation and his

"A Breezy Day." Courtesy of Pennsylvania Academy of Fine Arts, Gilpin Trust Fund

actual financial standing. Altogether Mr. Curran is one of the most promising of the younger figures in American Art.

As to his work, perhaps fault might be found with some of the minor qualities of his pictures. Where the spirit of Art is so gentle and so keenly imbued with the delicacy and feeling of our constantly renewing green world, even much, were it so, could be forgiven. His work has purity of subject and feeling, and poetry of conception. For the expression of the serener phases of life, little more is required.

Notes

1. "C. C. Curran," *Truth* 18 (September 1899): 227–31. Charles C. Curran (1861–1942).

2. Pascal Adolphe Jean Dagnan-Bouveret (1852–1929), French painter.

3. Robert Louis Stevenson (1850–1894), author of *Treasure Island*, addressed *A Child's Garden of Verses* (1885), his first volume of poems, to young children.

4. Located forty miles southeast of Scranton.

5. The most prestigious artists' club in New York, of which Dreiser became a member in 1897.

The Color of To-day[1]

Life's little ironies are not always manifest. We hear of its tragedies like far-distant sounds, but the reality does not work itself out before our very eyes. Therefore, the real incidents which I am about to relate have value if for nothing more than their simplicity and the color of to-day which they involve.

I first called upon W. L. S——, Jr., in the winter of 1895. I had known of him before only by reputation, or, what is nearer the truth, by seeing his name in one of the great Sunday papers, attached to several drawings of the most lively interest. These drawings depicted night scenes in the city of New York, and appeared as colored supplements, ten by twenty-six inches. They represented the spectacular scenes which the citizen and the stranger most delight in—Madison Square in a drizzle; the Bowery lighted by a thousand lamps and crowded with "L" and surface cars; Sixth Avenue looking north from Fourteenth Street.

I was an editor[2] at the time and on the lookout for interesting illustrations of this sort, and when a little later I was in need of a colored supplement for the Christmas number I decided to call upon S——. I knew absolutely nothing about the world of art save what I had gathered from books and current literary comment of all sorts, and was, therefore, in a mood to behold something exceedingly ornate and bizarre in the atmosphere with which I should find my illustrator surrounded.

I was not disappointed. I was greeted by a small, wiry, lean-looking individual arrayed in a bicycle suit, whose countenance could be best described as wearing a perpetual look of astonishment. He had one eye which fixed you with a strange, unmoving solemnity, owing to the fact that it was glass. His skin was anything but fair, and might be termed sallow. He wore a close, sharp-pointed Vandyke beard, and his gold-bridge glasses sat at almost right angles upon his nose. His forehead was high, his good eye alert, his hair sandy-colored and tousled, and his whole manner indicated thought, feeling, remarkable nervous energy, and, above all, a rasping and jovial sort of egotism which rather pleased me than not.

I noticed no more than this on my first visit, owing to the fact that I was very much overawed and greatly concerned about the price which he would charge me, not knowing what rate he might wish to exact, and being desirous of coming away at least unabashed by his magnificence and independence.

"What's it for?" he asked, when I suggested a drawing.

I informed him.

"You say you want it for a double-page centre?"

"Yes."

"Well, I'll do it for a hundred and fifty dollars."

I was taken considerably aback, as I had not contemplated paying more than a hundred.

"I get that from all the magazines," he added, seeing my hesitation, "wherever a supplement is intended."

"I don't think I could pay more than a hundred," I said, after a few moments' consideration.

"You couldn't?" he said, sharply, as if about to reprove me.

I shook my head.

"Well," he said, "let's see a copy of your publication."

The chief value of this conversation was that it taught me that the man's manner was no indication of his mood. I had thought he was impatient and indifferent, but I saw now that it was more, or rather less, than that. He was simply excitable, somewhat like the French, and meant only to be businesslike. The upshot of it all was that he agreed to do it for one hundred, and asked me very solemnly to say nothing about it.

I may say here that I came upon S—— in the full blush of his fancies and ambitions, and just when he was upon the verge of their realization. He was not yet successful. A hundred dollars was a very fair price indeed. His powers, however, had reached that stage where they could soon command their full value.

I could see at once that the man was ambitious. He was bubbling over with the enthusiasm of youth and an intense desire for recognition. He knew he had talent. The knowledge of it gave him an air and an independence of manner which might have been irritating to some. Besides, he was slightly affected, argue to the contrary as he would, and was altogether full of his own hopes and ambitions.

The matter of painting this picture necessitated my presence on several occasions, and during this time I got better acquainted with him. Certain ideas and desires which we held in common drew us toward each other, and I soon began to see that he was somewhat of a remarkable individual. He talked with the greatest ease upon a score of subjects—literature, art, politics, music, the drama, and history. He seemed to have read the latest novels; to have seen many of the current plays; to have talked with important people. A recent Governor—then a Commissioner—often came to his studio to talk and play chess with him. A very able architect, more private in character, was his bosom friend. He had artist associates galore, many of whom had studios in the same building or the immediate vicinity. He had acquaintances in other walks of life—literary and business men, all of whom seemed to enjoy his company, and who were very fond of calling and spending an hour in his studio.

I had only called the second time, and was going away, when he showed me a steamship he had constructed with his own hands—a fair-sized model, which was complete in every detail, even to the imitation stokers in the boiler-room, and which would run by the hour if supplied with oil and water. This model illustrated his skill in mechanical construction, which I soon learned was great. He was a member of several engineering societies, and devoted some of his carefully organized days in studying and keeping up with the problems in mechanics.

"Oh, that's nothing," he observed when I marvelled at the size and perfection of the model. "I'll show you something else, if you have time some day, which may amuse you."

I begged him to give me an idea of what it was, and he then explained that he had constructed several model war-ships,[3] and that it was his pleasure to take them out and fight them on a pond somewhere out on Long Island.

"We'll go out some day," he said when I showed appropriate interest, "and have them fight each other. You'll see how it's done."

I waited for this outing some time, and then finally mentioned it.

"We'll go to-morrow," he said. "Can you be around here by ten o'clock?"

Ten the next morning saw me promptly at the studio, and five minutes later we were off.

When we arrived at Long Island City we went to the first convenient arm of the sea and undid the precious fighters, which he much delighted in.

After studying the contour of the little inlet for a few moments, he took some measurements with a tapeline, stuck up two twigs in two places for guide-posts, and proceeded to load and get up steam in his warships. Afterwards he set the rudders, and then took them to the water-side and floated them at the points where he had placed the twigs.

These few details done, he again studied the situation carefully, headed the vessels to the fraction of an inch toward a certain point on the opposite shore, and began testing the steam.

"When I say ready, you push this lever here," he said, indicating a little brass handle fastened to the stern-post. "Don't let her move an inch until you do that. You'll see some tall firing."

He hastened to the other side, where his own boat was anchored, and began an excited examination. He was like a school-boy with a fine toy.

At a word, I moved the lever as requested, and the two vessels began steaming out toward one another. Their weight and speed were such that the light wind blowing affected them not in the least, and their prows struck with an audible crack. This threw them side by side, steaming head on together. At the same time it operated to set in motion their guns, which fired broadsides in such rapid succession as to give a suggestion of rapid revolver practice. Quite a smoke rose, and when it rolled away one of the vessels was already nearly under water, and the other was keeling with the inflow of water from the port side. S——lost no time, but throwing off his coat, jumped in and swam to the rescue.

Throughout this entire incident his manner was that of an enthusiastic boy who had something exceedingly novel. He did not laugh. In all our acquaintance I never once heard him give a sound, hearty laugh. His delight did not express itself in that way. It showed only in an excess of sharp movements, short verbal expressions, gleams of the eye.

I saw from this the man's delight in the engineering of the world, and humored him in it. He was most pleased to think that any one should feel so, and would thereafter be at the greatest pains to show all that he had under way in the mechanical line, and schemes he had for enjoying himself in this work in the future. It seemed rather a recreation for him than anything else. Like him, I could not help delighting in the perfect toys which he created, but the intricate details and slow process of manufacture were brain-racking. For not only would he draw the engine in all its parts, but he would buy the raw material and cast and drill and polish each separate part.

One of the things which impressed me deeply upon my second visit was the sight of a fine passenger engine, a duplicate of the great 999 of the New York Central, which stood on brass rails laid along an old library shelf that had probably belonged to the previous occupant of the studio. This engine was a splendid object to look upon—strong, heavy, silent-running, with the fineness and grace of a perfect sewing-machine. It was duly trimmed with brass and nickel, after the manner of the great "flyers," and seemed so sturdy and powerful that one could not restrain the desire to see it run.

"How do you like that?" S—— exclaimed when he saw me looking at it.

"It's splendid." I said.

"See how she runs," he exclaimed, moving it up and down. "No noise about that."

He fairly caressed the mechanism with his hand, and went off into a most careful analysis of its qualities.

"I could build that engine," he exclaimed at last, enthusiastically, "if I were down in the Baldwin company's place. I could make her break the record."

"I haven't the slightest doubt in the world," I answered.

This engine was a source of great expense to him, as well as the chief point in a fine scheme. He had made brass rails for it, sufficient to extend about the four sides of the studio—something like seventy feet. He had made passenger-cars of the most handsome order, with all the equipments of brakes, vestibules, Pintsch gas, and so on, and had labelled it "The Great Pullman Line." One day, when we were quite friendly, he brought from his home all the rails, in a carpet-bag, and gave an exhibition of his engine's speed, attaching the cars and getting up sufficient steam to cause the engine to race about the room at a rate which was exciting, to say the least. He had an arrangement by which it would pick up water and stop automatically. It was on this occasion that he confided what he called his great biograph scheme.

"I propose to let the people see the photographic representation of an actual wreck—engine, cars, people, all tumbled down together after a collision, and no imitation, either—the actual thing."

"How do you propose to do it?" I asked.

"Well, that's the thing," he said, banteringly. "Now, how do you suppose I'd do it?"

"Hire a railroad to have a wreck and kill a few people," I suggested.

"Well, I've got a better thing than that. A railroad couldn't plan anything more real than mine will be."

I urged him to tell me if he valued my sanity and not cause me to puzzle any longer.

"This is it," he exclaimed, suddenly. "You see how realistic this engine is, don't you?"

I acknowledged that I did.

"Well," he confided. "I'm building another just like it—it's costing me three hundred dollars, and the passenger-cars will cost as much more. Now I'm going to fix up some scenery on my roof—a gorge, a line of wood, a river, and a bridge. I'm going to make the water tumble over big rocks just above the bridge and run underneath it. Then I'm going to lay this track around these rocks, through the woods, across the bridge, and off into the woods again.

"I'm going to put on the two trains and time them so they'll meet on the bridge. Just when they come into view where they can see each other, a post on the side of the track will strike the cabs in such a way as to throw the firemen out on the steps just as if they were going to jump. When the engines take the bridge they'll explode caps that will set fire to oil and powder and burn it up."

"Then what?" I asked.

"Well, I've got it planned automatically so that you will see people jumping out of the cars and tumbling down on the rocks, the flames spring up and taking to the cars, and all that. Don't you believe it?" he added, as I smiled at the idea. "Look here," and he produced a model of one of the occupants of the cars. He labored for an hour to show all the intricate details, until I was bound to admit the practicability and novelty of the idea. Then he explained that instantaneous photography was to be applied at such close range that the picture would appear life size. The actuality of the occurrence would do the rest.

Incredulity still lingered with me for a time, but when I saw the second train growing, the figures and apparatus gradually being modelled, and the correspondence and conferences going on between the artist and several companies which wished to gain control of the idea, I was perfectly sure that it would some day come to pass.

As I have stated, when I first met S—— he had not realized any of his dreams. It was just at that moment when the tide was about to turn. He surprised me by the assurance, born of his wonderful ability, with which he went about all things.

"I've got an order from the *Ladies' Home Journal,*" he said to me one day. "They came to me."

"Good," I said. "What is it?"

"Somebody's writing up the terminal facilities of New York."

He had before him an Academy board, on which was sketched in, in wash, a midnight express striking out across the Jersey meadows, with sparks blazing from the smoke-stack and dim lights burning in the sleepers. It was a vivid thing, strong with all the strength of an engine, and rich in the go and enthusiasm which adhere to such actual affairs.

"I want to make a good thing of this," he said. "It may do me some good."

A little later he got his first order from Harper's. He could not disguise that he was pleased, much as he tried to carry it off with an air. It was some time before the Spanish War broke out, and the sketches he was to do related to the navy.

He labored at this order with the most tireless enthusiasm. Marine construction was his delight anyhow, and he spent hours and days making studies about the great vessels, getting not only the atmosphere, but the mechanical detail. When he did the pictures they represented all that he felt.

"You know those drawings?" he said, the day after he delivered them.

"Yes."

"I set a good stiff price on them and demanded my drawings back when they were through."

"Did you get them?"

"Yep. It will give them more respect for what I'm trying to do," he said.

Not long after he illustrated one of Kipling's stories.

He was in high feather at this, but grim and repressed with all. One could see by the nervous movements of his wiry body that he was delighted over it.

Not long after Kipling came to his studio. It was by special arrangement, but S—— received him as if he were nothing out of the ordinary. They talked over the galley proofs, and the author went away.

"It's coming my way now," he said, when he could no longer conceal his feelings. "I want to do something good on this."

Through all this rise from obscurity to recognition, he lived with his friends and interested himself in the mechanics I have described. His drawing, his engine-building, his literary studies, and recreations were all mixed, jumbled, plunging pell-mell, as it were, on to distinction. In the first six months of his studio life he had learned to fence, and often dropped his brush to put on the mask and assume the foils with one of his companions.

As our friendship increased, I found how many were the man's accomplishments and how wide his range of sympathies. He was an expert bicyclist, as well as a trick rider, and used a camera in a way to make an amateur envious. He could sing, having a fine tenor voice, which I heard the very day I learned that he could sing. It so happened that I owed him an outing at the theatre, and invited him to come with me that evening.

"Can't do it," he replied.

"All right," I said.

"I'm part of an entertainment to-night or I would," he added, apologetically.

"What do you do?" I inquired.

"Sing."

"Get out!" I said.

"So be it," he answered. "Come up this evening."

To this I finally agreed, and was surprised to observe the ease with which he rendered his solo. He had an exquisitely clear and powerful voice, and received a long round of applause, which he refused to acknowledge by singing again.

The influence of success is easily observable in a man of so volatile a nature. It seems to me that I could have told by his manner, day by day, the washing in of the separate ripples of the inrolling tide of success. He was all alive, all fanciful, and the tale of his conquests was told in his eye. Sometime in the second year of our acquaintanceship I called at his studio in response to a card which he had stuck under my office door. It was his habit of drawing an outline head of himself—something almost bordering upon a caricature—and writing underneath it "I called," together with any word he might have to say. This day he was in his usual high good spirits, and rallied me upon having an office which was only a blind. He had a roundabout way of getting to talk about his personal affairs, and I soon saw that he had something very interesting to himself to communicate. At last he said.

"I'm thinking of going to Europe next summer."

"Is that so?" I replied. "For pleasure?"

"Well, partly."

"What's up outside of that?" I asked.

"I'm going to represent the American Architectural League at the international convention."

"I didn't know you were an architect," I said.

"Well, I'm not," he answered, "professionally, I've studied it pretty thoroughly."

"Well, you seem to be coming up, Louis," I remarked.

"I'm doing all right," he answered.

He went on working at his easel as if his fate depended upon what he was doing. He had the fortunate quality of being able to work and converse most entertainingly at the same time. He seemed to enjoy company under such circumstances.

"You didn't know I was a baron, did you?" he finally observed.

"No," I answered, thinking he was exercising his fancy for the moment. "Where do you keep your baronial lands, my lord?"

"In Germany, kind sir," he replied, banteringly.

Then in his customary excitable mood he dropped his brushes and stood up.

"You don't believe me, do you?" he exclaimed, looking over his drooping glasses.

"Why, certainly I believe it if you are serious. Are you truly a baron?"

"It was this way," he said: "My grandfather was a baron. My father was the youngest of two brothers. His brother got the title and what was left of the estate. That he managed to go through with, and then he died. Now, no one has bothered about the title—"

"And you're going back to claim it?"

"Exactly."

I took it all lightly at first, but in time I began to perceive that it was a serious ambition. He truly wanted to be Baron S——, and add to himself the lustre of his ancestors.

With all this, the man was not an aristocrat in his feelings. He had the liveliest sympathies for republican theories and institutions—only he considered his life a thing apart. He had a fine mind, philosophically and logically considered. He could reason upon all things, from the latest mathematical theorem to Christian Science. Naturally, being so much of an individualist, he was drifting toward a firm belief in the latter, and was never weary of discussing the power of mind—its wondrous ramifications and influences. Also, he was a student of the English school of philosophy, and loved to get up mathematical and mechanical demonstrations of certain philosophic truths. Thus he worked out by means of a polygon, whose sides were of unequal lengths, a theory of friendship which is too intricate to explain here.

From now on I watched his career with the liveliest interest. He was a charming and a warm friend, and never neglected for a moment the niceties and duties which such a relationship demands. I heard from him frequently in many and various ways, dined with him regularly every Wednesday, and rejoiced with him in his triumphs, now more and more frequent. He went to Europe and spent the season which he had contemplated. He did the illustrations for a fine fast express story which one of the magazines published, and came back flushed and ready to try hard for a membership in the American Water-Color Society.

I shall never forget his anxiety to get in that notable body. He worked hard and long on several pictures which should not only be hung on the line, but enlist sufficient interest among the artists to gain him a vote of admission. He mentioned it frequently and bored me with his eyes to see what I would think of him.

"Go ahead," I said; "you have more right to membership than many another I know. Try hard."

He painted not one, but four pictures, and sent them all. They were very interesting after their kind, two being scenes from the great terminal yards of the railroad, two others landscapes under misty or rainy conditions. Three of these pictures were passed and two of them hung on the line. The third was *skyed,* but he was admitted to membership.

I was delighted for his sake, for I could see, when he gave me the intelligence, that it was a matter which had keyed up his whole nervous system.

Not long after this we were walking up Broadway, one drizzly autumn evening, on our way to the theatre. Life, ambition, and our future were the *small* subjects under discussion. The street, as usual, was crowded. On every hand blazed the fire signs. The yellow light was beautifully reflected in the wet sidewalks and gray cobblestones shiny with water.

When we reached Greeley Square, that brilliant and almost sputtering spectacle of light and merriment, S—— took me by the arm.

"Come over here," he said. "I want you to look at it from here."

He took me to a point where, by the intersection of the lines of the converging streets, one could not only see Greeley Square, but a large part of Herald Square, with its huge theatrical sign of fire and its measure of store lights and lamps of vehicles. It was, of course, an inspiring scene. The broad, converging walks were alive with people. A perfect jam of vehicles marked the spot where the horse and cable cars intersected. Overhead was the elevated station, its lights augmented every few minutes by long trains of brightly lighted cars filled with truly metropolitan crowds.

"Do you see the quality of that? Look at the blend of the lights and shadows in there under the L."

I looked and gazed in silent admiration.

"See, right here before us—that pool of water there—do you get that? Now, that isn't silver-colored, as it's usually represented. It's a prism. Don't you see the hundred points of light?"

I acknowledged the variety of color, which I had scarcely observed before.

"You may think one would skip that in viewing a great scene, but the artist mustn't. He must get that all, whether you notice or not. It gives feeling, even when you don't see it."

I acknowledged the value of this ideal.

"It's a great spectacle," he said. "It's got more flesh and blood in it than people usually think for."

"Why don't you paint it?" I asked.

He turned on me as if he had been waiting for the suggestion.

"That's something I want to tell you," he said. "I am. I've sketched it a half-dozen times already. I haven't got it yet. But I'm going to."

I heard more of these dreams, intensifying all the while, until the recent war broke out.[4] Then he was off in a great rush of war work. I scarcely saw him for six weeks, owing to some travels of my own, but I saw his name. One day in Broadway I stopped to see why a large crowd was gathered about a window in the Hoffman House. It was one of S——'s drawings of our harbor defences, done as if the artist had been sitting at the bottom of the sea. The fishes, the green water, the hull of a massive war-ship—all were there—and about, the grim torpedoes. This put it into my head to go about and see him. He was as tense and strenuous as ever. The glittering treasure at the end of the rainbow was more than ever in his eye. His body was almost sore from travelling.

"I am in it now," he said, referring to the war movement. "I am going to Tampa."

"Be gone long?" I asked.

"Not this first time. I'll only be down there three weeks."

"I'll see you then."

"Supposing we make it certain," he said. "What do you say to dining together this coming Sunday three weeks?"

I went away, wishing him a fine trip, and feeling that his dreams must now soon begin to come true. He was growing in reputation. Some war pictures, such as he could do, would set people talking. Then he would paint his prize pictures, finish his wreck scheme, become a baron, and be great.

Three weeks later I knocked at his studio door. It was a fine spring-like day, even though winter was still in control. I expected confidently to hear his quick, cheery step inside. Not a sound in reply. I knocked harder, but still received no answer. Then I went to the other doors about. He might be with his friends, but they were not in. I went away, thinking that his war duties had interfered—that he had not returned.

Nevertheless, there was something depressing about that portion of the building in which his studio was located. I felt as if it should not be, and decided to call again. Monday it was the same, and Tuesday.

That same evening I was sitting in the library of the Salmagundi Club,[5] when a well-known artist addressed me.

"You knew S——, didn't you?" he said.

"Yes; what of it?"

"You knew he was dead, didn't you?"

"What?" I said.

"Yes, he died of fever, this morning."

I looked at him without speaking for a moment.

"Too bad," he said. "Such a clever boy, Louis was. Awfully clever. I feel sorry for his father."[6]

It did not take long to verify his statement. His name was in the perfunctory death lists of the papers the next morning. No other notice of any sort. Only a half-dozen seemed to know that he had ever lived.

And yet it seemed to me that a great tragedy had happened—he was so ambitious, so full of plans. His dreams were so likely of fulfilment.

I saw the little grave afterward and the empty studio. His desks revealed several inventions and many plans of useful things. But these came to nothing. There was no one to continue the work.

It seemed to me at the time as if a beautiful lamp, enlightening a splendid scene, had been suddenly puffed out; as if a hundred bubbles of iridescent hues had been shattered by a breath. We toil so much, we dream so richly, we hasten so fast, and, lo! the green door is opened. We are through it, and its grassy surface has sealed us from the world, forever, before we have ceased running.

Notes

1. "The Color of To-day," *Harper's Weekly* 45 (14 December 1901): 1272–73. On William Louis Sonntag, Jr. (1870–1898). Reprinted as "W. L. S." with many stylistic revisions in Dreiser's *Twelve Men* (New York: Boni and Liveright, 1919), pp. 344–60.

2. Dreiser was editor of a music magazine, *Ev'ry Month*, in 1895–97.

3. Dreiser was genuinely interested in this subject since he had earlier written an article, "Where Battleships Are Built," *Ainslee's* 1 (June 1898): 433–39.

4. The Spanish American War of 1898.

5. See note 5 to Dreiser's article "C. C. Curran," included in this collection, p. 266.

6. William Louis Sonntag (1822–1900), American landscapist.

Index

Storey Farm, 165
Stroudsburg, Pa., 265, 266 n.4
Success, 10, 30–34, 50, 130, 158, 168
Sumner, Gilmore, 254
Supreme Court, New York, 157 n.6
Swanberg, W. A., 36 n.2; *Dreiser,* 36 n.2
Swinburne, Algernon Charles, 90

Talisman, 93
Tammany Hall, 35
Tammany Society, 156, 157 n.18
Tarrytown, N.Y., 24
Taylor, Bayard, 25, 43–49, 49 n.3, 84, 87–89; "Home Pastorals," 47; *Love at a Hotel,* 46; *Masque of the Gods, The,* 48; *Poet's Journal, The,* 46; *Views Afoot,* 45
Texas, 78
Theocritus, 89
Thomas, George H., 254
Thomas, Theodore, 10
Thoreau, Henry David, 20, 36, 63
Tolstoi, Lev Nikolaevich, 27, 68–69, 72, 106
Trinity Church, Boston, 241 n.2
Twain, Mark, 34; *Adventures of Huckleberry Finn,* 37 n.33; *Roughing It,* 37 n.33
Tweed, William M., 149, 157 n.5
Tweed Ring, 157 n.11
Twentieth Century Club, 88

Uncle Tom's Cabin, 37 n.33
Union Iron Mills, 166
Union League Club, 147
United States Government, 245
United States House of Representatives, 228 n.4
United States Supreme Court, 143
U.S. Treasury Department, 54
University of California, 144 n.2
University of Pennsylvania Library, 37 n.9
Upper Union Rolling Mills, 166
Urbana, Ohio, 256, 258, 262 n.6

Van Brunt, Charles H., 150, 157 n.6
Vanderbilt, William, 18
Vandyke beard, 267
Verlaine, Paul, 72
Victoria (queen of England), 226

Villon, François, 72, 76 n.5; "Ballad of Hanged Men," 76 n.5
Volk, Douglas, 220–21

Wall Street, 25, 84, 90, 116, 153
Ward, John Quincy Adams, 217 n.2, 245, 254–62, 262 n.1; *Bust of Gilmore Sumner, A,* 254; *General Garfield,* 254; *Gen. George H. Thomas,* 254; *General Grant,* 254; *Henry Ward Beecher,* 254–55; *Indian and His Dog, The,* 254, 259–60; *Indian Hunter, The,* 256, 262 n.6; *Israel Putnam,* 254; *Lafayette,* 254; *New England Pilgrim, A,* 254; *Seventh Regiment, The,* 254; *Statue of Commodore Oliver H. Perry, The,* 254, 260; *Statue of Dr. Lincoln Goodale, The,* 254; *Statue of Engineer Halls, The,* 254; *Statue of Gen. Daniel Morgan, The,* 254; *Statue of Gen. John Reynolds, The,* 254; *Statue of Greeley, The,* 254; *Statue of Horace Roebling, The,* 254; *Statue of Shakespeare, The,* 254; *Statue of Washington, The,* 254; *Statue of William E. Dodge, The,* 254; *Statue of William H. Fogg, The,* 254
Washington, D.C., 54
Washington, George, 230, 254, 259
Watts, George Frederic, 19, 218–19, 222 n.2
Wayside House, of Hawthorne, 64–65
West Newton, Mass., 64
West Park, New York, 50
West Point, 215
Whipple, Edwin Percy, 65, 66 n.11
White, Arch Herndon, 181–91, 192 n.1
White, Henry, 37 n.33; *Quicksand,* 37 n.33
Whitlock, Brand, 37 n.33; *13th District, The,* 37 n.33
Whitman, Walt, 19, 181
Whittier, John Greenleaf, 65, 84
Wilde, Oscar, 72
Wiles, Irving R., 19
Williams College, 93
Willis, Nathaniel Parker, 45, 49 n5; *Convalescent, The,* 49 n.5; *Pencillings by the Way,* 49 n.5
Woman question, 83 n.3, 142–43
Woman-suffrage question, 142, 144
Woodlawn Cemetery, 246
Woodruff, T. T., 164
World's Race Congress, 156 n.4